TRUE STORIES & OTHER ESSAYS

TRUE STORIES

OTHER ESSAYS

FRANCIS SPUFFORD

YALE UNIVERSITY PRESS
NEW HAVEN AND LONDON

For information about this and other Yale University Press publications, please contact:
US Office: sales.press@yale.edu   yalebooks.com
Europe Office: sales@yaleup.co.uk   yalebooks.co.uk

Set in Minion Pro by IDSUK (DataConnection) Ltd
Printed in the United States of America

Library of Congress Cataloging-in-Publication Data

Names: Spufford, Francis, 1964– author.
Title: True stories : and other essays / Francis Spufford.
Description: New Haven, CT : Yale University Press, 2017. | Includes
    bibliographical references and index.
Identifiers: LCCN 2017021076 | ISBN 9780300230055 (hardback)
Subjects: | BISAC: LITERARY COLLECTIONS / Essays.
Classification: LCC PR6119.P84 A6 2017 | DDC 814/.6—dc23
LC record available at https://lccn.loc.gov/2017021076

A catalogue record for this book is available from the British Library.

10 9 8 7 6 5 4 3 2 1

CONTENTS

INTRODUCTION: 'TRUE STORIES'

'The imagination', said Coleridge, 'is the power to disimprison the soul of fact.'

Except he didn't. Say it, that is. I read this sentence a few years ago, and took to it immediately. It sounds so right, with that awkward word-coinage 'disimprison' in it – surely just the kind of thing the poet would pull out of the air as he scratched along in a notebook at the speed of thought. And it's such a tempting idea, especially if you yourself work by choice in the kinds of writing that cross backwards and forwards between what's factual and what's not.

Fact with something inside it that will *stay* factual, when you let it out; fact that *wants* to be let out, from its prison of literal dates and documents, to roam free and have non-literal adventures. As Tolkien said, who doesn't approve of escape? Jailers, that's who. If fact did have a soul – an essence, an inward spirit of faithful correspondence to reality – and this wisp of truthfulness could exist independently of particular data to be true to, you could export the ethics of fact into quite other projects. You could let imagination noodle out into wild paisley filigree, and still dot each nested curl of fancy with rigour, with puritan conviction. Conversely, you could award yourself fiction's freedom to invent in situations where, strictly speaking, it would only be possible to select from the menu of the real. You could be essentially true to the facts, rather than literally so.

It would be a manifesto for a non-literal fidelity to the world.

I thought I'd just pin down an exact source before I made it *my* manifesto. Not in the *Biographia Literaria*, the home for Coleridge's most organised thoughts about imagination. Not in the many ragbag volumes of his *Notebooks* either. Not anywhere in his collected works, or in any other single person's collected works, in fact. For the real (and rather boring) history of the sentence turned out to be an object-lesson in the flinty resistance of actuality to being organised into nice narrative.

Wordsworth (not Coleridge) referred to belief (not imagination) being 'the soul of fact' in a dull poem of 1837 about looking at Italian churches. Thomas Carlyle, grumping about the extension of the British franchise to working men in 1867 in *Shooting Niagara*, said that 'real "Art" is definable as . . . the disimprisoned "Soul of Fact"'. In other words, proper art lets back the fervour that nasty democracy locks out. Then, in 1949, the critic Basil Willey published an essay on Coleridge in which he quoted Carlyle from memory, unattributed, without internal quote marks, and in a context open to misremembering. Someone did misremember, and a chimaera of a thought was born, with three separate authors none of whom intended it to make the point it now seems to, and a fourth author's name on it. Mislabelled, anonymised, pseudonymised, it's not an elegant poet's paradox. It's an accidental assertion, clotted into existence from historical white noise.

And yet the thing it claims by accident must be true. Mustn't it?

There is a fidelity to the real that can be manifested in non-literal as well as literal ways, and it must be active in fictions, to prevent soul-loss, to keep us able to tell the difference between stories and lies. However complicated and necessary the lines may be between different kinds of representation, we still know instinctively that

Plato is wrong to ban the poets from the just city, as if all the truth we need we could get without imagination.

We see immediately – even if it pitches us straight into the paisley filigree to try to reason it out, afterwards – that there is more truth to be got to than we could reach just from the data. There is more of what binds us to the world of everything that is the case than you can arrive at through the metaphor-free glacier water of early Wittgenstein. Some truth inheres, and only inheres, in impure, compromised, unreliable, representative speech. It can't be distilled out. (That's why late Wittgenstein became an explorer of language.)

Even if facts have no souls, or souls themselves are only a metaphor, we still need the jailbreak that lets us revolve the facts in story; or lets us tamper with them, fix one fact as the variable of interest and alter all those surrounding it. Maybe that shouldn't be jailbreak in the singular but the plural. Multiple necessary liberations. I look at the contested line between the factual and the fictional, and I don't see smooth blending, a zone of blur where the qualities of each dilute into the other. I see mosaic, a particulate inheritance from fiction and non-fiction where any smooth combining of the two is an effect of distance or of successful trickery; where, at tiny scale, the necessary tensions and differences between what's selected and what's invented reproduce themselves in individual elements of the writing.

A non-fiction writer must have the freedom to imagine the facts they use, so that they stand partly in the relationship as creator even to materials that are fully attested and verified. A writer of fiction must have the freedom to treat (and the burden of treating) the things they make up *as if* they were facts, so that they may disclose what facts never have done, never having existed in that particular configuration or been seen from that particular angle. And a writer who happens also to be a believer – my own particular complication – must have the freedom to remember that the story they believe is truest is, as well as being true, a story. To be a Christian is to hold (among other important things) that the unverifiable

Word preceding all individual words, the creation underlying all specific creations, the vast polyvalent Yes on which we try to orient ourselves, makes one of its nearest approaches to us, narrative creatures that we are, through story, where the absolutes we cannot possibly comprehend gleam momentarily into sight on the moving surfaces of represented people and events. Gospel truth is story truth.

The non-fiction writer needs to imagine their facts because that is part of selecting them. There's reality, happily existing without your intervention: the manifold of innumerable objects, systems, histories, persons, languages, interpretations, ideologies, disciplines; knowledge of which is divided often inaccessibly between different knowers, partly available to you on easy terms, partly almost impossible to understand on any terms. But you can't just contemplate the real. A separate act is required to pick out from it: an act that turns a given thing into a chosen one. You have to imagine the real, just as you have to accept the inevitable, if you want to *do* anything with it. For, once you hold a fact in imagination, temporarily detached from its context by your attention, you can interrogate it. Or maybe that's too transitive, too impatient a word, for a process that so centrally requires *waiting*, patiently, for a fact to disclose its qualities.

This is something like the non-fiction version of Keats's negative capability, 'capable of being in uncertainties, mysteries, doubts, without any irritable reaching after fact and reason'. Even when 'fact and reason' are the very game you are playing, it turns out that you must deliberately hold off with your over-rapid, over-directive certainties about what kind of story your fact tells, or fits into.

You have to be prepared to sit with it in suspension for a while, till it tells you in its own good time – what? What its connections are, causal, historical, associative; what filaments bind it into different possible patterns. What human narratives must lie behind and around it, given the kind of thing it is, though you can see them only dimly. What its mood seems to be, or conceivably its little repertoire of different moods. What ironies may leap or flicker into being around it, depending on the different contexts of the reader's existing knowledge into which it may be put. What acceptable inventions of supporting detail or abstraction-turned-palpable-through-metaphor may help to bring these half-glimpsed potentials into full narrative visibility.

For example. When I was writing *Red Plenty*, my half-dramatised book about the planned economy in the Soviet Union, I discovered from reading the dusty volumes of the translated *Digest of the Soviet Press* that Soviet factories that didn't hit their plan target were written up in newspapers in the 1960s in tones of laborious sarcasm.

There were connections for a start to all the wider traditions and practices of hostile journalism, which in the USSR both corresponded to Western expectations and absolutely didn't. Also to other kinds of mockery, and other kinds of social policing through ridicule, from tar and feathers to the saucepan-banging 'rough music' with which early modern English villagers showed their disapproval of their neighbours. Already, there were two possible ends to the action: from the point of view of the mocking journalists, or from that of the mocked factory managers. And then in came the richly ironic truth that this kind of mockery was almost entirely a ritual action in the USSR. The reasons that a plant missed its quota were very often not at all in the power of its managers to affect – but the ritual mockery pretended that it was all their voluntary fault. The journalist dispatched to do the job was not following a lead, or acting on their own judgement; they were taking an order handed down to the press for execution – but they pretended to be concerned citizens spontaneously shocked by the wanton failures of their local steel mill.

This pretence of personal error and personal condemnation would have happened over and over again, so no-one involved could have been in any doubt about the impersonal character the event really possessed. Not the manager, not the journalist, not the reader. Yet real persons marched through these compulsory roles.

Which meant, fascinatingly, that there must in each case have been a story of real feeling present behind the fake one, an actual human interaction unofficially haunting the ritual interaction, depending on how the individuals concerned handled their parts, with resignation or with malice, winking co-operation or fury.

Having imagined my way to the dramatic pith of this apparently inert fact, I then knew what clues I might look for to betray the nature of the hidden drama, and could also begin to think about what I might need to do, narratively, to make all of this explicit within the moment for readers who didn't share with its actors a native understanding of this world. Not bad imaginative traction for a single, seemingly unproductive datapoint about Soviet manners, both in terms of opening further territory for discovery and of planning effects within the writing.

Meanwhile, a novelist must be allowed to treat the invention that yesterday was only an inkling, a stray particle of possibility, and today maybe only has as much wispy purchase on existence as you get from being tried out in a draft paragraph, as if it were as solid as an anvil. This is a form of testing. If its consequences are useful, if they interlock viably with the consequences of other inventions, it may stay. If not, its hypothetical solidity will sublime back into possibility-gas, and it will return into the vapour from which an alternative will solidify. This must happen because the parts of a story need a mutual dependence similar to, but not the same as, the mutual relationship of the parts of the actual world.

Story stylises and simplifies wildly, with a bias at all times towards a greater lucidity and coherence than un-narrated reality ever possesses. It offers a contractual reliability in the development of events which reassures a reader everything in this counterpart world works towards resolution. Story economises its efforts. Where reality (wastefully) is evenly detailed all over, story is organised along sightlines, so that only events and settings and people at the focus of its attention are fully filled in. The rest are ruthless portraits-in-passing, just real enough to pass hasty muster, and receding, the farther back you look, into dim outlines and cartoons. Yet the object of these economies, this blatant nipping and tucking that folds the invented world together along lines the real thing never bends at, is to allow truths of observation, as real and serious as the writer can make them, to meet in constellations that are themselves truthful.

True pieces of noticing which in experience come to the writer widely scattered, as intermittent signals across different human domains, relationships, eras of life, can be gathered into coherence in story so that it can be seen they form a pattern. What otherwise could maybe exist only as an observing mind's reflective conclusion, diffuse and tentative, can in story click into immediate and intuitive sense. Story's ruthlessly unreal stylisations can be the vehicle for, well, wisdom. There seems no other word.

Take a really famous example: the pair of contrasting young women at the centre of *Middlemarch*. There have never been any such people as Dorothea Brooke and Rosamond Vincy, but there have certainly been high-minded girls desperate to be taken seriously, and apparently fluffy girls who are actually monsters of selfish willpower. George Eliot gathers her observations of both (some of which were observations of herself) and solidifies them, making a few crowd-pleasing concessions to fictiveness in the area of personal beauty but imagining and re-imagining the two figures at every step as particular people, not as types or embodied ideas. Then she sets the pair of them into relationship, in the same country-town milieu but in different parts of it, and not too close: a social step-but-one apart from each other, so that the pattern they are going to make has the appearance of contingency.

It will seem to be something the reader does the work of noticing, as she or he notices patterns of human behaviour in the world, only now with the world origami'd into position to make salient the pattern that is to be noticed, like a conjurer forcing a card. Dorothea, determined to participate vicariously in a male world of scholarship and thinking which won't let her enter it in her own person, talks herself into a desiccated marriage to a man whose thinking she doesn't have the experience to see is second-rate. Rosamond, happy to exist in vampiric dependence, attracts a man of genuine talent, in which she is completely uninterested: all she cares about is that he is naively patriarchal in his tastes, and therefore mistakes her for a sweet, submissive helpmeet. Two catastrophically unhappy marriages follow, not in parallel but at an ironic angle to each other, remixing to different effect their common themes of inexperience and mistake – and creating, by delicate interference effects, one picture of the conventional stunting of women's power of action in the world, and its costs, which we can now see being borne both by women and by men.

See, not understand in the abstract. The truth that Eliot nips and folds her paper story-universe to show us comes in the concrete spectacle of Dorothea lonely and still shut out on her honeymoon, and Rosamond's husband Lydgate sacrificing his medical research to the upkeep of the pretty blonde monster in the parlour.

True, there are sometimes ways in which it is the deviation of the story-world from fictive artificiality that brings us the sense of being told truth. We are exquisitely sensitive, as readers, to relative changes in conventions: to there being less or more than we expected of some basic fictional thing. If a novel deliberately shows us boredom, as David Foster Wallace was wrestling with the task of doing in *The Pale King*'s tax-office scenes, we're likely to experience that as an iconoclastic truthfulness, since what's boring is one of the things that, usually, the stylised selectiveness of fiction expressly leaves out. Fictional worlds are tilted towards interestingness as they are tilted towards coherence, resolution, and better-than-average looks in the protagonists. Boredom taken on as story-material therefore strikes us as truthful because less fictional. It seems like a step into raw, unshaped experience.

And the same applies to other deliberate violations of convention. Fictions that refuse to resolve, fictions that withhold the casual interiority we're used to, fictions that attend to aspects of our biological life we agree to exclude – Leopold Bloom seated in your outhouse, I'm looking at you – all, also, ask us to find them truthful in proportion as they don't do what fictions normally do. Implicitly, they invoke the binary in which fiction is not-truth, and truth is not-fiction. Though we may not consciously equate stories with lies, a suspicion lingers in us, and can be awakened. A novel can suggest to us, for effect, that we ought to worry about all this contrivance.

But most of the time, the truth-telling a novel can do is enabled by its artifice. It is because fiction can fold the world that it can interpret it. It is because fiction can offer us a world more legible than the world that it can lead us to truthful recognitions that would elude us in the world. It is because fiction can select and concentrate aspects of our experience – can distil the 'booming, buzzing confusion' in which everything happens at once into one singular mood at a time – that it can return us to the confusion better able to distinguish what really tangles and mingles there. It is because fiction can swap out qualities from characters, persons from settings, cultures from histories and vice versa, that it can recognise true possibilities for our experience that the world has not, in fact, contained yet. It can put real toads in imaginary gardens, and imaginary toads in real gardens. It can be telescope, microscope, tool, consolation, distraction. Also, of course, it can be a box of nonsense: if not quite lying to us, then still purveying sweetened, pre-chewed, over-easy alternatives to truth. But that's the price of its power.

The narrative nature of the Christian gospels, and therefore the need to take them (in part) on the tricksy ground between truth and lies where story lives, is not their most-advertised quality. But there it is, implicit in their secondary status. While for Muslims the Quran is God's direct action in the world, His presence and voice textually realised, for Christians, Christ is: the man, not the books describing him. The gospels point to God's presence rather than being it. In serviceable but not literary Greek, the trade tongue of the eastern Mediterranean in which you might negotiate for a shipload of olive oil, they offer us narrative biographies which trace the same figure onto paper four times over, slightly different in outline each time.

Thanks to textual criticism, we have learned to see the layers in the writing, the uncertain readings, the evidence of patches and insertions from previous manuscripts, the elements that are left-overs from debates at the time of writing, or rhetorical common-places. Yet, through this darkened and imperfect glass, if you are a believer, you see. And what comes blinking and swimming, and then flicking into momentary clarity, and then blurring again in the optic of the prose, is truth in the form of story.

Not the form of sermon, or philosophy, or persuasive argument, but story, requiring as all stories do the active participation of the reader to bring it the rest of the way to life; and just to intensify things, to deepen the narrative abyss, to make it all a bit more meta, it's the story of a storyteller. The greater arc of the story is the bizarre tragedy-with-a-happy-ending of Christ's life and death and life – the only one I know that ends with an execution *and then* a wedding, featuring the same protagonist. Then, inset within it, and often forming the passages of the larger story about which the gospel writers feel most confident and unanimous, are all the stories *he* told. The famous ones that have spread out in the culture and gone proverbial; the radiantly clear ones; the harsh ones; the obscure ones; the paradoxical ones that make you dizzier the longer you look. As parables, they are necessarily in the business of offering non-literal truth; and they won't summarise, they can't be accurately reduced to abstract rules and principles. They show rather than tell because what they want us to know – what he wants us to know, reaching out to us through layers of text, and layers of translations, and the litter of olive-oil receipts – can be shown better than it can be told. Or maybe it can only be shown and not told to narrative-loving, finite creatures like us, as we bustle our way briefly through our loves and our sorrows and our tribal loyalties and our zero-sum games.

Christians take what the fictions of the Prodigal Son and the Talents and the Good Samaritan show us, as truth. But it's creed, not credulity. We know that the structure of our belief rests on a histor-ical assertion about the nature of Christ which could, in principle, be falsified, but which is unlikely ever to be verified; we also know that to believe in a story, especially one like the gospel that's hybridised between non-fiction and fiction, requires patience and receptiveness, the reader's counterpart to Keats's waiting and responding without too much pre-emptive shoving of things into order.

Christian devotion has often been readerly in this way. There's the whole tradition of *lectio divina*, which deliberately diverts analysis into attention. There's the 'application of the senses' in St Ignatius' *Exercises* where, for four separate hours in a day, you attempt to smell, touch, taste, see, hear a gospel passage. A tree that is only a bare noun in scripture becomes a particular wind-bent olive or hawthorn which you know; the spilt wine at the wedding feast becomes a distinct red-purple puddle of Australian Shiraz; fish scales are rubbed like shreds of tarnish into the grain of the wooden seat in Peter's fishing boat. And there's more: beyond attention, there's active embroidery, the response to scripture that generates para-scriptural narrative, producing names for the three wise men and Mary's mother, backstories for the thieves crucified to Jesus' left and right. Beyond that again, there's the presence in imagination of the story for a writer who holds to its story-truth when you're writing something – you think – quite different. Hard to describe but undeniable, it pulls on you from beneath the surface of your ostensible attention like a narrative attractor, drawing your hand more in some directions than others, until you find you, too, without consciously meaning to, have wanderingly traced on the surface of what you did intend a partial outline of it. As if the gospel were a pea making itself felt under many, many mattresses. No, wait, that's a completely different story.

Is it difficult to be truthful? That depends on how much truth there is available. Perhaps in the end it comes down to a perceptual choice, from which an aesthetic choice follows. Is the world full, or empty? Is it a bleak place in which every utterance tends towards silence, and the undoubted gravitation of our mortality tugs every something constantly towards nothing? Do representations of it, to be truthful, have to squeeze with immense difficulty and tenacity at this entropic landscape to produce rare droplets of meaning? Or, is the world self-replenishing, immensely rich in particulars, patterns of particulars, principles of patterns of particulars which we might be tempted to take as Theories of Everything till some other complicating truth sends us back humbled to the great variform living and dying mosaic? Do representations of it, to be truthful, have to be greedily, awe-inspiredly plural, ready to invent and select, to tell truths straight and slant, to tilt the fabric till it discloses enough different moiré markings almost to defeat us, to find usable riches in fact and story and scripture?

I vote for the second, always and every time. I vote for the second vision and the second plan of work. I would rather build in gopherwood and potato peelings and broken circuit boards and bicycle spokes than in pre-cast concrete. And I don't even know what gopherwood is, except that you can make arks out of it. I would rather babble than be silent. I would rather laugh, and weep, and praise.

Cold

The Arctic and the Antarctic are real places, with real histories: in the case of the Arctic, real human histories, both of the circumpolar native peoples and of settlers. But these exist in tension with the way that, for those who live elsewhere, polar places are created in imagination through story, are built up in culture upon a thick layer of tale-telling about heroic discovery, exploration, naming and claiming.

In Antarctica, indeed, where there was never a human presence until the twentieth century, the narratives of exploration actually provide the lowest stratum of the entire human experience of the continent, and the period in which they happened is known as 'the heroic age', like the archaic layer in the history of ancient Greece, only happening on the threshold of the twentieth century and terminating with the First World War, instead of having to be deduced from a layer of carbon in the ruins of Mycenae. It was the greatest of the books from heroic Antarctica, Apsley Cherry-Garrard's Worst Journey in the World, *that got me interested in the poles in the first place, and sparked the writing of my own first book. I took the two tatty maroon volumes of the 1930s Penguin edition down from the shelf in 1985, and was captivated. Nearly thirty years later, I got to write an introduction to it, included here.*

But over the decades, as well as the polar hero stories, I've found myself thinking about the strangely fictive qualities of polar landscape, so page-like in its whiteness; about the actual anthropology of real polar societies, and its ironic connections with the patterns outsiders see; about the roles that polar material has played in the 'grand narratives', both story and *history, by which cultures remember.*

WINTER NIGHT

Here comes the winter night. If we were our oldest ancestors, tucked into draughty recesses of caves with blue hands hugged around us as we slept, we'd be dreaming of summer: we'd be using our human freedom to step away from circumstances to wish that all mornings were June mornings, all noons burned yellow in the sky, all days ended in easy heat under green trees. But for us the night laps comfortably around warm houses. From within our walls the cold seems something to relish. The sharp air outdoors drives the blood from the surface of our fingers only so the soft air inside can return it, tingling. The darkness beyond the window glass gives us the black outer frame for winter comforts like a still-life. Red curtains, green leeks chopped for soup, oranges in a bowl. All glow more because they stand out from a border of shadow.

And, our bodies provided for, our imaginations travel – not away from winter, but farther into the elements we're safe from, towards the heart of them. Snowy days invite strange journeys. Outside our houses, flakes whirl in the cones of brightness hung from street-lamps. Look up the line of their descent, directly along the wind that flies them into your mouth and eyes, onto your skin with a soft sting, onto your collar as temporary stars. They come uncountably, a sweeping hypnotic bombardment. And it's there that we rise, in imagination, up the levels of the air through tumbling and weaving whiteness, streaking bodiless towards the symbolic source of winter. To the north, of course.

The shadows of the hedges lie violet on the white fields. Then the land ends beneath us, in a tussle of rocks and black water, and we arrow onwards, a gulf below and a gulf above, leaving home behind. No scheduled airline flies this route. This is the way the Snow Queen's sleigh carried little Kay in Hans Christian Andersen's story; this is a vector plotted across the geography of dream. The snow sinks into the black waves without a sound. Islands pass; Spitzbergen, Jan Mayen Land, spiky with mountains like coal pyramids dusted in icing sugar. But the sea's motion slows now, and as the water thickens, gathers, hardens to ice, the sky clears too, so that the monochrome scheme reverses. It's a world hard white below now, hard black above, lit by constellations quivering in their places. We have entered the Arctic of our minds: the silent domain of cold something in us demands as the proper form for the place from which the frost is distributed and the blizzards pour out. The six-months'-night that governs here seems the parent to the nights we know in December and January. They're shavings from this inky, original block. We glide above the tumbled plain of the frozen sea. The second hand sweeps through the last few divisions on the clock-face where the degrees of north latitude register. Eighty-eight degrees, eighty-nine; 90°N and we descend at the imaginary capital of the imaginary empire of cold. The whole Earth spins beneath us, but all the movement we see at the North Pole is in the sky. The aurora airbrushes the dark with stately lilacs and purples. And perhaps there's a polar bear. Its breath hoods its head in steam.

But that's only one winter journey. It's the one our imaginations have been taking for a while, encouraged by snowy works in every genre, from Raymond Briggs's *The Snowman* to *Miss Smilla's Feeling for Snow*, from *Snow Falling on Cedars* to the blizzard of interest in the polar explorer Ernest Shackleton. I thought I'd put all the familiar elements of winter's snowy journey together and use them up in one glorious burst – I'm fond of them, as you can hear – so that afterwards, some space would be cleared for all of winter's other journeys; which we need to hear about, because the real snow has been coming less and less often during the very time that imagination's snow has fallen most heavily. Winter need not be white. It's natural that we should want to assign one elemental identity to it. We're myth-making creatures. We need the ancient, slow, general meanings for time to persist behind the quick particular things that happen in our particular lives. That's how we make sense of the cycle of the seasons, which still overlays its rhythm on the linear time of our lives, even though in Britain now most of us have no working connection to seedtime and harvest. But without snow, winter is still the cold pause when nature slows; it's still the old year's death and the new year's birth, meanings combined in the Christmas feast of the baby born to die; it's still the ancient season of hospitality, when we put the still-life of winter food into sociable motion, and feed guests whose faces are also warmth in the cold to us. All of those are still there, and still open to all the colouring of circumstance, all the tragedy and comedy and anti-climax and indifference that events may bring. Look around; and take new journeys.

(1996)

ICE

Freezing is no mystery. At zero degrees centigrade the molecules of water interlock. They brace, then they expand, pushing a little farther apart from each other than they do in the sliding tangle of the liquid state. Each kinked trio of two hydrogen atoms, one oxygen, slots into place in a structure like a flanged, puckered hexagon. Water gains about 9 per cent extra volume, goes rigid, turns to glassy crystal: you've got ice, wherever it forms. In the chilled base of a cloud, though, ice grows in grains. The hexagons multiply on every rung of the ladder of size that leads up from the molecular to the visible world, till wafers of ice arranged in every possible permutation of the basic shape are mimicking, on a scale large enough to see, the molecule that first seeded the process. And snow begins the long tumble to earth – 'like feathered rain', said a Renaissance poet.

Mystery re-enters the science of ice in explanations of its bulk behaviour. The hard mathematics of complexity come in when you ask how the genesis of a billion individual flakes becomes the thrust of a blizzard, how the forces working on icebergs in Antarctica produce a particular candy-twisted specimen. Water's solid state can arrange itself in many forms, many textures, many colours even.

Ice glossaries and catalogues have been published by learned bodies to try to build at least an anecdotal vocabulary for the things you can observe ice doing at the macroscopic level. They'll tell you about *pancake ice* and *sastrugi, growlers* and *bergy bits*. These are only the counterparts in the wild landscapes ice dominates – the Arctic, the Antarctic – to the cold plethora of freezings that visits a winter garden. The fur of frost on a clothes-line; the hard white rim of leaves; puddles like windows or stirred to a cloudy porridge; snow (of course) crusted or sludgy or powdery. Or waxy and audibly squeaking beneath the first shoe to compress it. But the intent look at the differences of the ice (as hard to resist as the gaze upward into the numberless white-on-grey whirl of falling snow) involves you in a long history of fascination. You've been seduced by qualities of ice not reckoned by physics or chemistry. What happens to the billion molecules of ice is one thing: what happens in the onlooker is less calculable still.

In countries where snow defines the landscape half the year, or all of it, snow may be disenchanted. Where it is temporary, as in Britain, it is never wholly reduced to ordinariness, never quite aligned alongside mud and stubble as a constituent of the material economy of the real, from which no more can be expected than that it does what it does. It still promises transformation, a vague and magical erasure in accord with the dusting and muffling of familiar lines in whiteness. 'A miracle', said an Anglo-Saxon riddle for ice: 'water become bone'. When it snows, the ground is prepared. For strange departures: it's snowing outside the window just before Alice steps through the looking-glass. 'I wonder if the snow *loves* the trees and fields, that it kisses them so gently?' she asks her cat. Snow confounds ears, as well as eyes. Sound dwindles as snow wraps the surfaces of the world, abolishes echoes, takes the bounce out of the air. Yet the muting imposed by the snow registers as a positive hush rather than a simple absence of sound: a null signal broadcast by the cold, an unmistakeable white noise in the air that can be recognised on first waking without opening the curtains. The hush roared so loud it actually interrupted Coleridge's train of thought while he was writing 'Frost at Midnight':

> 'Tis calm indeed! so calm that it disturbs
> And vexes meditation with its strange
> And extreme silentness.

Meanwhile the 'secret ministry of frost' was hanging up icicles, 'quietly shining to the quiet moon'.

If ice seems unearthly, part of the reason must be that water is so intimate a substance for us. We drink, we spit, we cry. Blood is a solution of chemicals in water; human cells are a honeycomb largely filled with warm water. Below zero, the solvent of life has hardened into an altogether different material. And, left out naked in the cold, we would too. Even when it's artfully sheathed in clothing, the difference between the temperature of freezing air and human operating temperature imposes an exact sense of the body's boundaries. It makes the body a bubble of warmth rolling on a cold surface, life surrounded by something that would slow, immobilise, halt life if let in. The extra degree of conscious awareness of life that cold brings can be exhilarating. Existence fizzes in you while the faint retreat of your blood makes your fingers tingle. You're sole, sovereign, indivisible in a hostile world. A Victorian mountaineer said that climbers above the snow-line have 'the sensation that they do not actually press the ground, but that the blade of a knife could be inserted between the sole of the feet and the mountain-top'.

But this casts ice, in imagination, as deathly, almost as a kind of anti-flesh. The ramifications go down into the unconscious, deep and knotted. Dreams of ice signal – sometimes – wishes for a fixity, a hard calm, incompatible with the warm scurrying of being alive. St Francis of Assisi plumbed ice's possibilities one winter night in Italy when carnal thoughts were bothering him. He built a mound of snow, took off his robe, and (the story goes) leapt onto it, crying 'This is my wife! This is my wife!' He came back indoors, though, when he had achieved a state of indifference. To become ice would be a monstrous reversal, a metamorphosis of body into statue. The recoil is instinctive to the story of the seaman on a polar expedition in the 1820s who got his hand supercooled. Put into a bucket of cold water, it froze the water. It had ceased to behave like a part of a human.

Yet along with ice horrors go wonders, icy metamorphoses that enlarge human senses instead of curtailing them. The ice and snow of the Alps, wrote another Victorian, are substances so malleable to imagination 'that every human soul can fashion them according to its own needs'. Into the delicate and extraordinary shapes of ice, the mind projects meaning; moulds; plays. Shelley looked up at the glaciers of Mont Blanc, where to his vision

Frost and Sun in scorn of mortal power
Have piled: dome, pyramid and pinnacle . . .

People have seen cities in ice for centuries. The curious thing is that the style of the architecture changes faithfully with changing tastes. Towers and spires were perennial, while seventeenth-century sailors in the Arctic started glimpsing baroque fretwork, and Victorians added in Egyptian obelisks and Stone Age dolmens. Captain Scott's men saw a complete model of St Paul's Cathedral float by in the Antarctic – just like a Visit London poster on the Edwardian tube. But the impression of shape is always temporary, always fleeting. The illusion visits, forms, slips back into disorder. 'Yet not a city but a flood of ruin', Shelley's poem continues. Ice is a magic mirror to the imagination, but a mirror shattered, giving back fragments of reflection, to be enjoyed for the moment only.

There's a warning against lingering too long in Hans Christian Andersen's perfect winter's tale *The Snow Queen*, where the nuances of ice all meet. Little Kay has been seduced away from warmth: he thinks that the 'flowers' of snowflakes are far more beautiful than living flowers. He sits on the floor of the Queen's great ballroom where the polar bears dance, trying to make ice-fragments into legible words. If he can spell ETERNITY she has promised him the world, and a pair of silver skates. Every child who encounters the story knows he mustn't succeed. Complete the puzzle, and he'll be choosing eternity in the sense of rejecting time; choosing autonomy in the sense of forever losing connection; choosing the icy clarity of symbols over the messy, generative processes that give them meaning.

(2004)

WORST JOURNEY

The Worst Journey in the World is the single greatest book in the literature of polar exploration. There are others that are beautiful. There are others that are exciting. There are some that are more revealing about the whys and wherefores of expedition leadership, and some that make a better fist of explaining polar science for a non-scientific reader. There are many that deal with a wider sample of humanity in the polar landscape than Apsley Cherry-Garrard's band of all-male Edwardian sailors, scientists and gentlemen amateurs. But there are none that have anything like *The Worst Journey*'s power to evoke a time and a place, and to bring us intimately, almost eerily, inside the small world of an expedition: its sounds, its straining physical life as bodies in canvas harness pull sledges through smooth or granular snow, its chatter, its personalities, its moments of awe when the sweating humans in the foreground catch their breath and the picture opens out (and out, and out) upon the vastness of the Antarctic ice. It is written in an idiosyncratic homemade prose which somehow conveys the emotional pull of its age's grand talk about heroism without itself being captured by any of the heroic poses. It is not grand; it does not strut or mythologise. Instead it is fervent and melancholy, ironic and understated, absolutely individual and very English. It aims to make a private reckoning with the story it tells. And, since the expedition it chronicles is Captain Scott's disastrous return to the Antarctic in 1910–13 aboard the *Terra Nova*, the story deepens inexorably to tragedy.

For Apsley Cherry-Garrard, the tragedy was personal. When Scott's tent was discovered on the Ross Ice Shelf in November 1912, the spring after the group racing Amundsen to the Pole had failed to return, the two frozen bodies to left and right of Scott were those of Cherry-Garrard's best friends. He had joined the expedition as a diffident and rather aimless young man, unwilling to settle down to the management of the enormous fortune he had just inherited. On board ship heading south, and then in the equally frantic base camp on Ross Island, where the work of the expedition was got through on the principle of competitive self-sacrifice, and a volunteer could shine, he found his niche – and a mentor in the shape of the expedition doctor, Edward 'Bill' Wilson, and a quasi-brother in the ebullient, big-nosed stores officer 'Birdie' Bowers. 'Cherry', as he swiftly found himself nicknamed, had been the only boy in a large family of girls, with an admired but elderly father. In some ways, the expedition provided him with a thrilling overdose of testosterone. He, Wilson and Bowers had performed one of Antarctic history's great feats of endurance together, travelling for a month in the pitch-darkness and ferocious cold of midwinter to the breeding ground of the emperor penguin. And now they were dead, leaving him as the only custodian, the only rememberer, of the overwhelming suffering they had survived together. He was in the search party that found the bodies, and heard – a detail not in the book – the sharp crack as Scott's frozen arm was broken to pry loose the famous diary. He never quite got over it. For the rest of his life, and he lived until 1959, he revisited the expedition compulsively in memory.

So *The Worst Journey in the World* was intended as a memorial, but not of the official variety, with the dead explorers represented by statues and busts as frozen in their way as the corpses. Cherry-Garrard wanted, so far as he could, to create a shrine of words in which the experience of the expedition could be reanimated, from the practical jokes and the catchphrases to the hiss of the primus stove during a halt from the march and the passing effects of the light. He was more alert to the sensory detail of Antarctica than any of the other early writers except Scott – and Scott had tended to burnish up his detail into smooth tableaux for publication. Writing in 1919–21, with the First World War lying between him and the events he described, Cherry-Garrard was already reaching back, as he put it, 'to an age in geological time, so many hundreds of years ago' when the world had been different. He was dredging an Edwardian past that already felt remote. With his Hertfordshire neighbour George Bernard Shaw acting as literary adviser, he broke out of a relationship with the committee preparing the official history of the expedition, and was freed to write the book he needed to.

The eventual structure of *The Worst Journey* was both instinctive, because need drove it, and extremely artful. His own ordeal with Wilson and Bowers, the 'Winter Journey', became the book's emotional centre, placed at the midpoint of the narrative, and held up by implication as the experience that defines the nature of the whole. When the spring sledging season of 1911 opens, and Scott's complex caravan of motor tractors and dog sleds and manhaulers sets off for the Pole across the ice shelf, and up the Beardmore Glacier to the polar plateau, Cherry-Garrard gives it its full dramatic and historical weight: but he has already established the polar journey as being, in a sense, a tragic repetition of what had been (just barely) triumphant the first time around, in the winter, when 'three crystallised ragamuffins' had laboured through 107 degrees of frost (Fahrenheit) without ever speaking a harsh word to each other. He suspends the narrative of the journey to the Pole at the point when he, and the last supporting parties, turned for base. The diary entries that reveal the final dreadful death-bound homeward struggle of Scott's party must wait till the story has been told of finding the bodies. Again, emotional priority has quietly been given to the contours of his own, survivor's experience.

Since then the reputation of the expedition has passed through a complete circle. After decades in which the tragedy of the polar party seemed securely heroic, Scott's leadership was debunked in the 1970s by the historian Roland Huntford in a way which, again, appeared likely to be permanent. The world got used to a new default understanding in which the expedition stood for destructive incompetence. Yet the wheel continued to turn. Since then, with the re-examination of meteorological records that bear out Scott's claim of exceptionally low temperatures on the return from the Pole, and a renewed appreciation of the expedition's scientific agenda, and a friendlier revaluation of Scott's own style and character, it has become respectable once more to admire the story; though no longer as a fable of Empire, or as a showcase for the stiff upper lip. When we imagine ourselves onto the Terra Nova now, or into the bunks of the hut at Cape Evans, it is no longer in innocence of the possibility of gross blundering there. The accusations have been made, in the strongest possible terms. We know the case against.

One peculiar consequence of this is that it is now much harder for us to see that *The Worst Journey* was, for its time, a quietly heretical book, dissenting here and there from the heroic official myth. Scott's widow Kathleen was furious over the nuanced analysis of her husband's strengths and weaknesses in Chapter 6. 'He has criticised Con in the most appalling fashion', she wrote. Likewise, while holding to the official line that the organisation of the expedition had been superb, the book made it tacitly plain that almost everything had been improvised by exhausted people, with no margin for error. But the criticisms voiced since have been so much louder that, reading *The Worst Journey* as its centenary approaches, we are much more likely to notice its continuing discretion than the ways in which it was, actually, indiscreet. Cherry-Garrard says that Scott 'was a bad judge of men', but will not let us see any example of this bad judgement in action.

Yet the book never reads as if discretion has hobbled it or muffled it. On the contrary, it is as vivid as a dream. It is the dream of his past that Apsley Cherry-Garrard could not stop dreaming; and it is contagious, it infects us too, in passages of immersive, hypnotic recall. 'Come and stand outside the hut door ... You are facing north, with your back to the Great Ice Barrier and the Pole ...' Three times in the book Cherry-Garrard makes this deliberate break into the present tense, and gives us a set-piece description of what stands before his mind's eye. But even when the book is ostensibly running along in the past, or is tessellated together from Bowers' or Lashly's or Scott's journal entries, it still somehow possesses the quality of appearing to record something that is happening in front of us, in the very moment of reading. On the Winter Journey we shake to our bones in the ice-clogged sleeping bags along with the three travellers; we step with them across the uncanny hush of Windless Bight, holding a naked candle and steering by Jupiter; we despair of our lives with them when the tent blows away in the hurricane; we hear the calls of the emperor penguins with them at journey's end. It's this immersive power, along with the beauty and ironies of the prose, that has given *The Worst Journey* a stature independent of history's judgements on the expedition. Right through the trough of the debunking it was being read passionately and enthusiastically, and it is hard to imagine any further twist of events which could ever spoil its appeal.

George Orwell once wrote that when he read Dickens he saw a human face appearing behind the words: not so much a literal image of the author as a picture of the very strong personality the novels suggested. This book, too, has a human face and a human situation behind it. It is the work of a lonely man in bottle-thick spectacles, sitting alone at a table in the library of the grand house he has not managed to fill with a family. Laid out around him on the table he has documents in the handwriting of the friends he knew for two dreadful and wonderful years a decade ago, before the world was shattered. He writes; and while he writes he sees something altogether different from the empty house. He sees the rubberoid-insulated cabin under the icefall slopes of Mount Erebus, he sees the wind-scoured *sastrugi* of the Great Ice Barrier, he sees the Western Mountains showing purple above the gold mist of ice particles suspended over the freezing sea. In the frighteningly powerful magic lantern of memory, he sees the black specks of human beings on the white snow. As he writes, they begin to move, and become his friends, sledging towards him. There they are. The dream, or the haunting, enfolds him. He sees them, he hears them. And as we read, so do we.

(2012)

SHACKLETON

Pattern-minded species that we are, there's a particularly pure cognitive pleasure about the moments when we recognise order. It happens in history, when meaning's signal emerges from the noise of time. In science too: suddenly structure's apparent in the flow of an event. Last year I went to Antarctica, and most days there was an albatross swooping around in the wake of the ship. Then one evening I was standing on deck when the sun was low. Its gold light lay almost level across the big grey swells, and the shadows behind the waves brought the surface of the sea, which had seemed virtually featureless, into deep relief. It became legible, an intricately fluid landscape of hills and valleys, and suddenly it was clear that the albatross was following the updraughts of this miniature topography. It was gliding across the rising faces of the swells with a beautiful economy of motion. What had looked like another aimless bit of animal behaviour in the middle distance was actually expert navigation, deliberate grace. At 60° South the Antarctic Ocean goes right around the planet, a stormy immensity broken by just a few isolated islands. The albatross cruises through the ice and the storms, hardly flapping its wings.

It was there delivering its lesson of grace during one of the greatest dramas of human survival. In early May 1916, Frank

Worsley watched an albatross from the stern of the *James Caird*, the 22-foot ship's boat in which Sir Ernest Shackleton was trying desperately to reach the Antarctic island of South Georgia. Shackleton's plan to cross the Antarctic continent had foundered when the expedition ship froze in before ever reaching land. The ice crushed the ship: a process recorded in grotesque, astonishing photographs by the twenty-eight members of the expedition, left to fend for themselves on the ice sheet with three boats and the stores they had salvaged. After months of northerly drift on the slow-moving ice, six heart-stopping days of rowing through the violent backwash at the edge of the ice brought the expedition to Elephant Island. Here there were penguins and seals to eat. With seal blubber for fuel, the explorers could just about survive, living in the cramped, dark space underneath the upturned boats. But no-one back in civilisation had any reason to look for them on Elephant Island. While most of his crew dug in, Shackleton set off again in the *James Caird*. South Georgia's whaling stations lay 800 miles north-east across mountainous seas. Worsley, skipper of the sunk ship, was his navigator.

They readied the boat for the ocean by frantic improvisation. The seams were glued tight with a mixture of seals' blood and artists' oil paints, the 'deck' was a canvas lid sewn into place. The contrast with the albatross' adaptation to the environment seems very great. While every wave hurled the six men aboard up a summit of broken water, the albatross floated a couple of feet above the crest. While they baled for their lives, and lay in sodden sleeping bags, the albatross glided on, imperturbable. 'His poetic motion fascinated us', wrote Worsley in his diary of the voyage. 'The ease with which he swept the miles aside filled us with envy.'

But the truth is that of all the famous journeys by British explorers in the heroic era of Antarctic exploration, it's that one that has most in common with the grace of the albatross. It's crucial that the feat took place at sea. By land, the British at the poles were footsloggers. Unlike their competitors the Scandinavians, they refused to study the Inuit arts of survival. Even Shackleton, gifted though he was in so many of the disciplines of exploration, never learned to drive a dog sled. But on the water the British were in their element. They became tactful, expert, light of touch. Terrifying though Worsley's account is of running before the wind in the frail little boat, it is shot through with the unmistakeable pleasure-in-mastery of someone who knows exactly what they're doing. 'Half standing, half sitting on the coaming of the cockpit, I steered by watching the angle at which the pennant blew out; at times verifying the course by a glimpse of a star through a rift in the clouds. Dark hills of water reared sudden and startling ahead and astern, capped by pale gleams of breaking seas ...'

Worsley is not telling a story about helplessness in the face of nature, but one about deploying makeshift resources to give a nudge to the enormous forces surrounding them; about choosing the moment, and then flapping the butterfly's wings. One of the castaways' best resources was his own navigation, though Worsley is too modest to say so. To get the measurements of latitude on which their course depended, he had to kneel astride the prow of the *James Caird* with two men holding his legs. As the following wave lifted the boat he took out his sextant. Then in the instant when it was poised highest, and he had a view of the horizon, he snapped off a reading of the angle between the centre of the sun's disc and the line of the horizon; and the calculations he made under these circumstances, in roller-coaster motion through the roaring waters, drenched in spray that froze as ice, were as exact as if he had written them out in a quiet room to the sound of a ticking casement clock. The American science fiction writer Kim Stanley Robinson, an admirer, calls this 'British *feng shui*'. It's existing in space, done consummately well.

We live in snowy times at the moment. Perhaps the first flake that fell in the culture was David Attenborough's *Life in the Freezer* series, or maybe it was Peter Hoeg's *Miss Smilla*, and novels rather than natural history, that started the passion for cold places and gave us all a feeling for snow. At any rate, a full blizzard is now blowing, of novels, travel books, children's books, thrillers, science books, memoirs, picture books, drama and poetry, all set at the ends of the earth. 'Novels set in the Arctic and Antarctic will receive a development grant', ordained Julian Barnes mockingly in 1984 in *Flaubert's Parrot*. By now his grant (if it existed) would have been claimed over and over again. And the official bodies that govern access to Antarctica are helping the process along. Seeing the level of public enthusiasm, they have begun to give writers passage to places where only scientists were allowed before. The British Antarctic Survey welcomed Sara Wheeler to their bases and field camps when she was writing her bestselling *Terra Incognita*. The US National Science Foundation made Kim Stanley Robinson an Artist in Residence on Ross Island, so that he could write *Antarctica*, a kind of extra volume to his Mars trilogy, about the place on this planet that most resembles the cold deserts of Valles Marineris and Chryse Planitia.

Amid all this there's been renewed interest in the legendary figures of polar exploration from the beginning of the twentieth century. So it comes as no great surprise to hear that there may soon be a big-budget screen version of Shackleton's boat journey. The story is intensely dramatic, whether you read it in Worsley's journal, or Shackleton's own *South*, or Alfred Lansing's classic retelling *Endurance*. It's structured like early Spielberg: continuous action punctuated by very short pauses, for, once the *James Caird* reached South Georgia, the next little problem was to make the first ever crossing of the glaciers and precipices down the centre of the island, without a map or mountaineering equipment. So the men drove 2-inch carpentry screws through the soles of their boots, took 90 feet of ship's rope, and set off. Courage was rewarded with a happy ending: Shackleton reached Stromness whaling station and was able to rescue all of the stranded explorers on Elephant Island. He is the only expedition leader of the heroic age never to lose a single man. Film may be able to convey the grace of the boat journey better than words. Like the performance of a great athlete, it may be better seen than described.

But the choice of hero is telling. You couldn't imagine a Hollywood movie about Captain Scott, Shackleton's great rival. For many decades, Scott was the polar Brit most celebrated, famous for his heroic death on the way back from the South Pole in 1912; but Scott's virtues, and the whole idea of a nobility best displayed by *not* surviving the Antarctic, belong to a lost world of emotion now, which is harder and harder to enter on its original terms. Shackleton is much more our contemporary. Flamboyant where Scott was buttoned-up, phlegmatic where Scott was nervy, he had a charisma we recognise immediately. When Scott's leadership was challenged, he clung to the hierarchy of the Edwardian navy; Shackleton, bred in the less rigid Merchant Marine, knew how to make his will felt. There's a story about a merchant seaman who refused to accept an order on Scott's first expedition, when Shackleton was his subordinate. Scott was dumbfounded by the man's appeal to his contract of employment. Shackleton asked Scott to leave the room; then he hit the sailor repeatedly till he obeyed.

Ugly though that manifestation of it may have been, it was this same personal authority that on the boat journey made Shackleton endlessly comforting and solicitous towards his companions, doling out the driest socks in an almost motherly way, subtly bolstering up their pride in themselves. 'So great was his care of his people', remembered Worsley, 'that, to rough men, it seemed at times to have a touch of woman about it, even to the verge of fussiness.' Sure of himself, he could acknowledge his dependence on the skills of the others. At the beginning of the boat journey, as he and Worsley sat at the tiller during the night watch with their arms round each other for warmth, Shackleton said, 'Do you know I know nothing about boat sailing?' and laughed. 'All right, Boss, I do', replied Worsley. 'I'm telling you that I don't', repeated Shackleton, 'slightly ruffled'. He meant: I need you. It's a sure thing that if the movie is a hit, someone will swiftly publish a self-help paperback called *Management Secrets of Ernest Shackleton*. Emotionally fluent, sanely focused on survival, he speaks directly to the sensibilities of the present. He felt, of course, those codes of behaviour which are mysterious to us now, but the sense of his story does not depend on them as the story of Scott's death does. In a Hollywood in which a British accent is still usually shorthand for a cold heart, Shackleton is the one hero in the British pantheon who can embody the present-day urge to daydream ourselves into the titan-scaled land-scapes of the poles. And to daydream ourselves in the other sense, too: to imagine versions of us, clever as albatrosses or just heroically stubborn, who are titan-sized too.

(2001)

READ MY TOES

Seventeenth-century books of Arctic travels contained occasional reports of a kingdom in the far north of the Americas called Estoty: just out of reach over the icy horizon, of course, with its wealth, its monarch, its city of copper-roofed houses. Eventually the chimera-collecting eye of Vladimir Nabokov fell upon Estoty. The horribly spry cast of *Ada* live in a Russo-American arcadia of the same name, which maybe represents a suitable metamorphosis of one kind of impossibility into another. But the report also testifies to an aspect of European disappointment with the New World. Alongside the rapacious reasons for wanting to discover lost cities of gold, there ran a perpetual, self-defeating desire for encounters with a special sort of other, impossibly defined and therefore never met. These strangers had to be sufficiently like Europeans (in terms of monarchy, street plans, polite society) to command respect; and tough enough, too, to withstand the meeting, as the Incas and the Mexicans had not been; yet at the same time so completely different in their ordering of human experience that the European sense of wonder would be aroused by the mere report of the way they lifted a cup. It was a paradoxical appetite for similar difference, different sameness. With its *a priori* stipulations it did not make travellers especially good at noticing the real wonders to hand, at least until a couple of generations after they had vanished. Ufology probably inherits this sense of the insufficient wonderfulness of things as they are, though unexpected shreds of it linger even now in the Euro-American response to the world TV delivers. A touch of El Dorado clings to the discovery that modern Iranian diplomats, alone in all the globe, wear a *completely different kind of formal shirt*. And if so basic a thing as a shirt is different, then perhaps the houses of Tehran might be copper-roofed, and . . . no.

There was no Estoty. There was, however, Tikigaq, a 20-mile spit of gravel dunes extending into the Bering Strait from the north-west coast of Alaska. Continuously inhabited for 2,000 years, it served as the ritual metropolis for the westernmost Inuit. Little was visible above ground except a forest of whale-ivory stakes and tripods, rising, amid a clicking rubble of human and animal bones, from a cluster of hummocks. On a clear winter's night at the right vantage point you could see the lit skylights beneath which perhaps 800 people were living. (The same number again were distributed around the Tikigaq hinterland, and thought of themselves as *Tikigaqmiut*, Tikigaq people.) Complicated entrance tunnels lined with whale ribs joined the earth *iglus* of families related by blood or clan or ritual affiliation. Each part of the subterranean architecture had symbolic implications, from the passageway to the round entry hole to the skylight to the inevitable oil lamp, and besides the ordinary dwellings there were six *qalgi*, larger ritual lodges lined with benching where the men kept sacred puppets, masks and pictures. Tikigaq was the centre of the world, an exceptional zone that was neither quite sea nor quite land. When the sun reappeared in spring its disc was propped against Imnat cliffs 50 miles to the south. But Tikigaq knowledge extended much farther through trade contacts and hunters' memory. Tobacco reached Tikigaq in the eighteenth century, not from the lands to the south, but from European Russia, via the Cossacks and the Siberian tribes 'over there', 'on the far side' of the Strait. Tikigaqmiut could draw accurate freehand maps of the opposing coast. Tikigaq shamans flew over there sometimes to engage in aerial dogfights with their Siberian counterparts. (Indeed, Tikigaq's very last shaman claimed in 1953 that he had assassinated Stalin while hovering over the Kremlin.) Like practically every material aspect of the surroundings – a cold desert to outsiders, an overflowing plenitude to those who lived there – the Siberian shore was allotted a symbolic significance. 'Over there' counterbalanced 'over here' just as land and sea, male and female, sun and moon went together, in a series of tensed, productive couplings. So thickly inscribed with secondary meanings were the ordinary presences of the Tikigaq world that daily life amounted to an almost continuous ritual performance. 'Do you realise you are fingering the levers that control eternity?' asks Auden's *The Orators*. Tikigaq did. In addition its people took pride in playing faster and looser with taboo than other Inuit dared. Elsewhere in the Arctic land-foods and sea-foods were kept apart as strenuously as meat and milk in a kosher kitchen; Tikigaq kebabbed them together on set occasions for extra symbolic leverage, in accordance with the town's confident assessment of itself. *Inupiaq*, the term both for the regional language and the ethnic branch who spoke it, came from *Inuk*, 'person' (*Inuit* already meant 'the people'), and *piaq*, meaning 'true' or 'genuine'. They, the Tikigaqmiut would have you know, were the *real* people. The uncompromising demands their ecological niche placed on them had cemented a mixed corpus of knowledge, historical and practical, religious and technical. What it was necessary to know shaded over into what it was worth knowing. The anthropologist and poet Tom Lowenstein, who arrived in the 1970s, calls the Tikigaqmiut 'nationalistic'. Despite the absence in Tikigaq of every structure and institution that composed a nation in the European sense, it seems the right word for historic Tikigaq's intense approving awareness of itself.

Though intrusion from the West came later to the settlement than to almost any other point along the circumpolar band of Inuit cultures, collapse was assured from the 1850s when American ships began to work the lucrative waters of the Strait, destroying along with the whale stocks the vigour of the intricate Tikigaq whale hunt. The population slumped, and a vicious local strongman named Atannauraq used shamanism and a monopoly trading position to impose a reign of terror. After Atannauraq's murder, a Christian medical mission helped retrieve the situation, but at the cost of separating the modern Tikigaqmiut from their forebears. For two generations a barrier of retrospective shame lay athwart their history. The Tikigaq Lowenstein saw, a.k.a. 'Point Hope', was an underpopulated village of wooden houses, with a school and an incinerator. But, remarkably, he was in time to act as auditor to Asatchaq, a peremptory, formidable old man who had systematically memorised all he could glean of Tikigaq's traditional learning. He wanted his talk to be recorded, hoping rather sadly that some powerful outside agency could arrange for the lost pattern of things to return; seeing it also as a way of circumventing the ear-stopping fear he inspired, for as Lowenstein explains, 'to know the shamanistic order was partly to contain it'. Tikigaqmiut twenty and thirty and forty years younger than Asatchaq (b. 1891) felt mingled awe and alarm: the modern Inuit youth of Alaska, often monoglot English speakers, appreciated the pre-contact past as a legendary golden age, but were all the less connected to the specifics of the culture. Against this Lowenstein could offer an outsider's poetic and anthropological attentiveness. He also had an outsider's humility in the face of a history not his own. 'I got on well with Asatchaq – indeed, we grew to love each other – partly because it was in my interest that he should maintain his preeminence, and whether it involved recording his memories or emptying his wastepot, I did what he told me.'

The old man's stories, translated and edited by Lowenstein in the collection *The Things That Were Said of Them*,[1] reveal a people fascinated by blubber, shit and toes. Whale-fat, Tikigaq's constant fuel and food source, is an understandable obsession. At the beginning of the world the first grandmother made Raven Man from blubber-lamp sediment. Unctuous or crispy, raw or cooked, eaten

26

or ignited, blubber stuck to Tikigaq ever after: a primal material. Excrement's special place could be predicted too, as the body's outflow, food's final form, though Tikigaq's rules for dealing with it are definitely angled away from the familiar ones. Hunters took a ritual bath in urine once a year, and people could be called *Anaq* ('Shit') without it striking anyone as funny or insulting. A famous shaman passed a magical test by smearing a whalebone wedge with excrement before striking it. The comic tales of Kinnaq, mythic klutz and failed seducer, show woman after woman escaping from his kayak with the unanswerable cry of 'I want to have a shit!' It wasn't offensive in itself. On the other hand, Raven Man forced himself on an *uiluaqtaq* ('woman who won't get married') at the dawn of creation by slipping a defrosted turd into her sleeping bag, and threatening her with social exposure when she woke up sticky. This is Tikigaq's equivalent of Genesis; and in the other of the two paired origin stories a sister raped by her brother presents him with her breasts chopped up small in a grue of blood and shit, a potful of ultimate reproach. The role of toes in Tikigaq civilisation is harder to fathom. The wedge-smiting shaman drove off two ghosts by toe-menace. 'What do your toes eat?' ask the spirits, eyeing them nervously as they wiggle through the holes in Ukunniq's boots. 'People', he replies darkly; 'they eat people.' Perhaps toes' magic power has something to do with the 'joint-spirits', little supernumerary souls inhabiting human elbows and knees who might be expected to cluster in the delicate complexity of the metatarsal bones; but here no footnote wiggles helpfully.

Menace is commoner than solace in Asatchaq's myths and histories. Tikigaq's hunting economy depended on continuous kills: Tikigaq's culture accepted blood feuds, gang rapes and invasions into its weave. You would have to be very blindly attached to a Rousseau-esque vision of 'Eskimo' life to think of Tikigaq as a peaceable kingdom, serene amid the snows. Yet wonder is omnipresent in Asatchaq's narrations. They span the whole of Tikigaq's existence without breaking their tempo, from the ur-time 'when people were animals and animals were people' through to the events of his own life, and they are bewildering in their dense familiarity with the mysterious. You read them always conscious of the absent daily life in the *iglus* and *qalgis* that they are designed to reinforce. They are total; and they suppose the coherence of the overflowing world they deal with in passing, suns and moons and marmots, caribou and shamanic flights, snow buntings and blood and toes.

The Things That Were Said of Them is an academic work of record. Lowenstein's notes and commentaries tease out the stories ethnologically, and supplementary contributions from other inform-ants (and previous anthropologists) are slotted into the structure. But two projects, not one, were launched by Lowenstein's sessions with Asatchaq. Widely overlapping with the first book where mate-rials are concerned, *Ancient Land, Sacred Whale*[2] has a quite different intention and impact. It is a dazzling work of mimesis; it aims to enact the coherence of Tikigaq by tracing one annual cycle in the pre-contact life of the settlement. Seen beside the meticulously governed translations of the first book, the high risks of the strategy are obvious. The practical ones, for a start. Even with a surgical selec-tion of those myths and practices most directly concerned with the whale hunt, Lowenstein still has an enormous volume of material to marshal; to tamp into place in the reader's mind so that, as autumn succeeds summer and the drumming begins in the *qalgis*, what you need to know lies ready exactly when needed. Then the book is a vision, an interpretation of the irrecoverable, necessarily sacrificing anthropological caution, and the question of Lowenstein's poetic aptness to the Tikigaq-ish task arises. Asatchaq's opening narratives in *The Things That Were Said* are set by Lowenstein in 'lines which roughly follow units of meaning and rhythm' to distinguish them from the following ancestor stories; he warns there that though they 'look like poetry, they are poems only in the sense that their originals belong to the world of shamanistic imagination'. Much of *Ancient Land* is narrative poetry proper: does this make Lowenstein, the shaper of the year, a shaman himself? The book alternates explanations in exact, economic prose with short-lined 'storytelling' by two fictive Tikigaq narrators, musing at some distance, and with longer-paced cantos of direct action. It isn't clear that Western poetics provide the appropriate ground on which to reconcile this necessary diversity of voices. In particular there looms the danger of a modernist appropriation of a remote culture, of the kind which tells you far more about a literary programme than about the faraway object of scrutiny. Pound pounced on ideograms and Charles Olson seized Mayan glyphs as wished-for evidences of concrete, unalienated writing: language apparently conducted so that the sign itself for *flint* was rocky, and *comb* sprouted visual teeth. One up on onomatopoeia, any road. Both men can be counted as ancestral influences in Lowenstein's own poetry. There could be, so to speak, a contest of ancestors in *Ancient Land*: between modernist sages urging Lowenstein to choose Tikigaq for a distant mirror, and the shamanic ghosts for whom Tikigaq cannot be picked out as a mere potential subject, because it is/was the world. In fact the local imperatives have won hands down. Knowingly inter-mediate in the sensibility he brings to bear on Tikigaq, Lowenstein conducts his language with a wonderfully tenacious deference to Tikigaq's own rules.

Hummingly whole as it is in comparison to the town's tattered present, the past Lowenstein restores is no dream-time, no pristine origin. He returns health to an order of things which divided time, rather like Greek tragedy. Playing always against the chaotic, circumstantial happenings of the moment there stood the archaic example of Tikigaq's first people. The whale-hunter now strove to reproduce, imperfectly, the way that Raven Man had harpooned the first whale, which became the Tikigaq peninsula. Memory would preserve the names of present people in *uqaluktuaq* (ancestor stories, 'the things that were said of them') for a customary five generations before oblivion intervened; but the primordial stories would remain, would still be going on. And, since those oldest ancestors had spoken and behaved exactly in the same tenor as current Tikigaqmiut – slipping turds into sleeping bags without a whit of divine reserve – communion with them was continuous. Tikigaq ritual utterance was extremely practical. It had a directness of function which puts to shame the rhetorical or stylistic directness of Western verse. When the *umialiks*, the skin-boat captains, wanted to ensure a catch next spring, they assembled in the *qalgis* on the 'day of calling':

> They called Suluk, and he answered:
> 'I want to kill a whale! Right now!'
> They called
> Kunuyaq and he said:
> 'I want to kill a whale! Right now!'

The elaborateness of the hunt came of the universal symbolic relevance of the surroundings. Every material aspect of the hunt, and of quotidian Tikigaq life, required alignment. Lowenstein is metaphorically abstemious; his lines are poised, denotative, built on careful nouns. Even when the sense is densest, what may seem to be metaphors –

> Their words are soot.
> They tattoo the cosmos.

– turn out to figure accepted connections between things. Metaphor is hardly necessary when the busy parts of Tikigaq's world already have a far closer relation to each other than similarity. An identity is being revealed, not a comparison asserted. The soot that Raven Man's argument with Peregrine scatters here is the same as the darkness in the bag of aboriginal night that he stole earlier in the story; it recalls the soot (burnt blubber soot of course) which the raped sun-sister smeared on the face of her rapist moon-brother; it is visible every day in historic Tikigaq in the form of face tattoos on Tikigaq women, made by rubbing soot into cuts. Given this non-metaphoric webwork of affiliations – into which, Lowenstein explains, every newborn Tikigaqmiut was inducted, even down to membership in one of two symbolic football teams – he can deploy the terse, imagistic conjunctions of his own poetics without cultural rupture or opportunism. The reader travels further into mystery, rather than back westwards, when a shaman's body becomes a hollow vestment, and 'sky pours through the sutures and eyeholes'. There are lesser disciplines for Lowenstein to observe as well. He must avoid altogether the note of distancing doubt struck in the famously anxious passage of *The Golden Bough* where Frazer pointed out that none of the magic he describes actually worked. Only once does he seem to falter, and then it proves he is referring to other Inuit practices, regarded with scorn by Tikigaq itself.

From a Eucharist to a World Cup single, ritual depends on repeated action. Equally, it is a sign of living and rooted ritual that it can accommodate a degree of error and imperfect performance. Consensual ritual – unlike, say, a coronation service in Westminster Abbey – is implicitly fault-tolerant. It must be if it is to do its work as valuable praxis, reconciling ideal theory and inconvenient reality through a more or less set form. Lowenstein heard Asatchaq falter unworriedly when telling stories in 1975: forget a name, insert an irrelevant joke, suddenly demand his supper. None of this detracted from the authority of the telling. In *Ancient Land* he remembers to have his fictive speakers forget as often, patterning in small snatches of authenticating muddle. Moreover it is a principle that helps assure the dramatic success of the book's climax, the long-prepared whale hunt. He gives us one sample year's hunt; but sample in the sense that it incorporates an ordinary friction between plan and circumstances. The skin-boat's crew his poem follows keep their cosmos coherent from moment to moment, as inexperience strands them in an ice-locked pond, as a youngster who may only be an idle phoney claims shamanic exemption from the work, as a murder in another boat complicates the proper division of the kill. Despite and because of this, the grandeur of the hunt is complete and unforced. Sweat and metaphysics go together. To the hunters, what they do touches the whole structure of the world: *Moby Dick*, annually. To the reader, the hunt confirms Lowenstein's extraordinary achievement in focusing and recomposing the mysteries of his source material.

The kill achieved, everyone rejoices. Even the whale is pleased once its severed head has been dropped ceremoniously into the deep:

> The whale's soul escapes.
> It returns to its country ...
> It will find a new parka.

So ought we to be happy. Tom Lowenstein has harpooned Tikigaq from the edge of the feasible, using a composite weapon. Its sharp head is Inuit; the other braced pieces, which remain in his hand, he brought with him from afar. Two inflated floats named Ezra and Charles buoy up the catch on the water, turning slightly to show precepts etched in soot. He sends a runner to his publisher. She is happy. Soon the text will be distributed generously to bookshops. She is very happy. She has not stood on Bloomsbury's rooftop in vain, holding up her *qattaq* garnished with typewriter ribbons and royalty statements, crying '*Ui! Ui!* I want to publish a good book! About the Inuit! Right now!'

(1993)

BOREALISM

In the early 1980s, Dr Allen Counter, a neurophysiologist from Harvard, was on sabbatical in Sweden when he heard the rumour that the two American explorers who reached the North Pole in 1909 might have fathered Inuit children in Greenland. As an admirer of Matthew Henson, the African-American sledging veteran chosen by the expedition leader Robert Peary to accompany him on the final push to the Pole, only to be identified in polar history for decades as Peary's 'coloured valet', Dr Counter was excited. Equipping himself with a research project into hearing loss among Inuit users of high-powered rifles, he won permission to visit the military zone around the US air base at Thule in the far north-west of the island. And there, in the settlement of Moriussaq, with a miraculous ease suggesting that the 'secret' was largely so only because no-one else had bothered to unravel it, he met an aged dark-skinned hunter in a parka, who shook his hand and said, 'I am Anaukaq, son of Mahri-Pahluk' – the latter being the attested Inuit name for the legendary, laughing figure of Henson, the only foreigner of the time, Counter was later told, 'who could learn to talk our language without using his tongue like a baby'. The dates fitted, and, apart from a striking facial resemblance to Henson,

Anaukaq had also inherited a mass of confirming detail about the expedition from the Eskimo point of view. Nor was this all. The miracle redoubled. Not far away there lived the surviving son of the slightly less celebrated 'Peuree': named Kali, equally elderly, he was equally happy to talk about his family history, and his link to the *kahdonah* (white) explorer. For Dr Counter there was the flattering plus that Anaukaq Henson, never having seen another black man before, except an American airman in the distance, assumed at first that he must be speaking to a fellow descendant of the great Matthew.

It is a wonderful story.[3] Why so wonderful, though? What is involved in the attractiveness of Dr Counter's discovery of the two men? It seems magically appropriate, of course, that the great deepfreeze of the north should have preserved the traces and *faces* of Peary and Henson, bringing forth Kali and Anaukaq from the ice just as, in Siberia, it has disgorged mammoths, woolly as the day they died. But the same marvel happens in other places, without the suggestive apparatus of cold, simply as an accident of longevity. The daughter of Eliezer Ben-Yehuda, the man who began the revival of the Hebrew language in the 1890s, is still alive – and still using the obscure word for telephone (*sachrachok*) her father coined when his children were the only cradle speakers of the language in the world, instead of the *telefon* preferred by every other modern Israeli. It is, perhaps, the implied trick with time that appeals to us. Such accidents make the past seem, precariously, as present as the present is; retrieve from the grasp of history events that turn out to be still within the reach of memory; and open a private avenue into the past exactly as wide as one family. They seem to suspend the laws of time unexpectedly. Or rather they remind us that time has eddies and backwaters. It doesn't flow on at a constant rate, but moves to a number of different measures, overlaid on each other, one of which – proceeding without any reference to historical periods – is the slow tempo of generations. There are (not for very much longer) Victorians among us.

But in the case of Kali and Anaukaq, a polar expedition's half-Inuit revenants, a connection exists to an idea in Victorian theories of human development which were influential in the exploration of the Arctic. This is the thought that, because different races achieved lesser or greater advances in the Darwinian struggle, there were effectively tracts of past time geographically disposed here and there about the globe, which whites could visit with their superior travelling technology. Hence New Guinea was, more than metaphorically, 'in the Stone Age'. With its agriculture-preventing icecap, its treeless coastal margins and its total lack of metal, so was Greenland. According to theory, whalers and Danish churchmen and naval missions that went there were looking into their own tribal prehistory; a stage which the wretched inhabitants were stuck at, being heirs to the least desirable patrimony on earth. The idea was echoed in literature towards the end of the nineteenth century, though not with Arctic locations. Hardy's aptly titled *Return of the Native* has a moor which sustains ancienter modes of life than the surrounding farmland: a kind of human archaeology is possible. And Conrad draws on the same perceptions to produce a different irony in *Heart of Darkness*, when Marlow tells his listeners that Thames was once a river as dark as the Congo, for the Romans watching the tribe-infested woods along the banks. It is echoed as well by Dr Counter, though quite unconsciously, for his book is an ingenuously faithful account of his Greenland journey and its sequels, along with a valuable reshuffling of the Matthew Henson file, rather than (in any sense) a net set for the flying ironies he looses. What can he be doing except recapitulating the old paradigm, in novel fashion, when he voyages to 80° North to examine a bubble of black American history, left unpopped there for eighty years?

The corollary to this vision of the world divided into chronological reserves was the fascination with lost cities and lost civilisations; which was not confined to sensational fiction, for Southey had written an epic about Prince Madoc and Welsh America at the beginning of the nineteenth century, although it is the later, pulpier examples that tend to be remembered now: Shangri-La, the kingdom ruled by Rider Haggard's *She*, the endless succession of displaced Romans that Tarzan would stumble upon, brushing back the jungle creepers to see a tropically transplanted Temple of Jupiter where, after all these centuries, the sentries still cried 'Hail Caesar!' Many regions of the expanding, imperialised Victorian world had one of these myths of early European settlement attached to it. For the Americas there were Madoc and St Brendan, for Africa there was Prester John, and for the whole world there was the nomination of this people or that as the lost tribes of Israel. Such beliefs offered a satisfaction more literal and more direct than the somewhat abstracted idea that the Inuit were now what Europeans had once been. If they were true, it meant that a lucky traveller could find not just history alive in the present, but *our* history alive, the exact and veritable thing. And some evidence could be reckoned in support. Often there *had* been a historic settlement, or at least an early contact with Europe. One can then detect the mythic importance of the idea in the disproportionate attention paid by serious archaeologists to the meagre traces of such a settlement, while all around the indigenous culture of the region offered far fuller rewards. The fascination had a very definite racial subtext. But the purely fantastic component of the myth developed around the idea that the settlers might still be there, inaccessible, awaiting rescue and reunion.

And Greenland, of course, had one of these fantasies associated with it. Vikings from Iceland had colonised the south-east and south-west coasts, built houses and churches, had a bishop sent them by the Vatican – and disappeared from European ken two centuries before ships again began to call there. As soon as they did, the search began. Stone rings marking the base of Inuit winter dwellings were constantly mistaken for recent Viking ruins, on the principle that only Europeans build with masonry. The savages were (axiomatically) architects in snow alone. By the time of Peary's expeditions only the most hardened fantasists really expected that, breasting a difficult pass in the interior, an expedition might yet see smoke rising from a hotspring-heated crease of the icecap where, in a tiny enclave of skalds and sagas, a colony of brawny Olafs and plaited Gudruns still survived. On the other hand, there remained the chance that a pair of blue eyes in an 'Eskimo' face, or a head of blond hair, would announce a different kind of survival. If the colonies had gone under, the people at least might have assimilated, and in that sense still be there, disguised as natives. (Again Dr Counter, in a cloud of unknowing, recalls some very old obsessions.)

Considering Europeans' difficulty in confronting Inuit cultures, someone someday should write a modest northern counterpart to Said's *Orientalism*, and perhaps call it *Borealism*. Said describes the range of ways in which commentary on the Orient patterned away – defused – the challenge of cultural difference, reducing the East to a historyless annexe of the European imagination. The Greenland/ Viking fantasy was sometimes put to strikingly parallel use. It allowed European, and American, travellers to negotiate the contradictions thrown up in encounters with the Inuit. The particular difficulty was Inuit travelling technology: the low-friction sledges, the ergonomic tents, the heat-saving fur clothes and sleeping bags, the apparatus for handling dogs. It ought to have been that visiting whites, with their superior attainments and their supposed adaptability to all environments, could dispense with these savage solutions to the terrain. In fact, until the invention of reliable petrol motors, no expedition that did not adopt Inuit techniques succeeded. Franklin died, despite the steam-powered central heating on HMS *Erebus*. In Antarctica Captain Scott died, manhauling his sledges and wearing canvas clothing; while Amundsen, who had digested the lessons of the Arctic, rode to the Pole on a dog sleigh, dressed in furs. Peary and Henson reached the North Pole because they acted like Inuit, and drew on a fund of expert Inuit advice and labour. (The goal of the expedition, of course, was all their own, no Inuit being daft enough to think it was worth reaching an imaginary point hundreds of miles from land.) But this expedient adoption of Inuit methods did not necessarily imply any disruptive acknowledgement of the humans who'd perfected them. Just as the British in north India tended at first to attribute anything they admired to the distant influence of Alexander the Great and Hellenism, it was perfectly possible to credit Inuit material culture to the leavening influence of the vanished Vikings. Kayaks? Weeny longships. It was an identification that smoothed anxiety. And – a more general habit, familiar from Said – explorers separated people from objects imaginatively, put them in separate categories of consideration, so that Inuit stood in a more or less accidental relationship to their own creations. (The classic Saidian situation saw a European wondering over the draggled worshippers who inexplicably cluttered up the colonnades of a beautiful mosque. Here an Inuit substitutes for a Muslim, and a harpoon for a mosque. What cannot be admitted easily is that the one *made* the other.)

All this may seem to set the scene for the usual tragedy of misunderstandings, with those on the European side enforced by guns and commerce, and the Inuit parties in the encounter sinking under those traditional consequences of European contact, alcoholism and disease. But the patterns of prejudiced perception were also accompanied, it should be remembered, by varying degrees of practical co-operation, and individual recognition of features to be admired in Inuit life. The particular community of Polar Inuit that Peary and Henson were involved with seems to have survived rather well, on Dr Counter's evidence, perhaps because their home is not on the way to anywhere that Europeans have an interest in, except the Pole. And it is clear, too, that the births of Kali and Anaukaq did not signal quite the predictable rupture in Inuit society and mores. Their Inuit mothers' husbands were away on expedition errands when they were conceived, on board ship, by their American fathers; but the arrival of the babies appears to have been accommodated within the sanctioned Eskimo tradition of exogamy, which gives a newborn that many more relations to call on when times get hard.

(On this point Dr Counter unfortunately limits himself to a protest against the sexual stereotype of Inuit. He therefore only establishes that neither mother was Eskimo Nell.) Both boys were well-treated by their stepfathers. Though other children teased Anaukaq for his 'dirty face', his blackness was accepted as a personal peculiarity, and rather prized than not for its reminder of Henson. Neither of the two suffered the exclusion reserved for half-castes elsewhere, or the cultural uncertainty. 'I am Eskimo', Kali Peary told Counter. 'I was born and raised Eskimo. I think Eskimo. I was an Eskimo hunter ... All my children were raised as Inuit.'

But the heart-warming outcome cannot obscure the weight of phoney histories and racial expectations that bore down on the expedition. Again and again peculiarly charged incidents occurred. There was the discovery of a white man left behind in Greenland by Peary's rival Dr Frederick Cook, squalid and demoralised, the very image of the danger involved in 'reverting' to the primitive. Mister Kurtz, he alive. There was the adoption and 'uplifting' of a favoured Eskimo child by the ship's company. Henson wrote:

> After this boy was washed and scrubbed by me, his long hair cut short, and his greasy, dirty clothes of skins and furs burned, a new suit made of odds and ends collected from different wardrobes on the ship made him a presentable Young American. I was proud of him, and he of me. He learned to speak English and slept underneath my bunk.

Most of all, subtly disruptive of the vested interpretation of polar exploration, as later hostile commentary made clear, there was the suggestive presence of Henson himself. He was trusted implicitly by Peary, who had no time at least for the racial nostrum about black susceptibility to cold; he was liked by the other white team members, who never resented his selection for the final dash to the Pole ('he was a better man than any one of us', wrote Donald MacMillan); in dealings with the Inuit he spoke with full American authority, and acted as a patron to them in his own right. 'My boy Ootah', he calls one of the four hunters who accompanied him and Peary at the last, although Ootah was 'a married man, of about thirty-four years' – transferring a Southern mode of address to a different racial relationship. And yet, in some senses, Henson clearly occupied a position *between* whites and Inuit. His chief value to Peary, on whom he was the only expedition member to be personally dependent for money and encouragement, was as a mediator with the natives. Because of his rare mastery of the language, and his still rarer standing as an outsider equal to the demands of a hunter's life, he functioned as a bridge to the skills and support which the expedition required. Innovating equipment from the Inuit models, hiring and firing, he forged connections which Peary (a spikily obstreperous navy type, with a moustache slightly wider than his head) could not. This is why 'Mahri-Pahluk' is remembered with a greater warmth than 'Peuree'. By the single standard of Inuit life, he proved himself a thorough *mensch*.

Notice, though, Henson's careful choice of vocabulary, in case it should be thought his good relations with the Inuit were in any sense *natural*. He had made the same temporal trip as his colleagues, this passage from his *Negro Explorer at the North Pole* makes clear, and made the same automatic return to his twentieth-century identity afterwards:

> I was to live with a people who, the scientists stated, represented the earliest form of human life, living in what is known as the Stone Age, and I was to revert to that stage of life by leaps and bounds, and to emerge from it by the same sudden means. Many and many a time, for periods covering more than twelve months, I have been to all intents and purposes an Esquimo, with Esquimos for companions ... enjoying their pleasures, and frequently sharing their griefs. I have come to love these people.

Despite the mutual respect, and the love, Henson had his own reasons for insisting on the distinction between him and them.

Elsewhere he describes them as having 'all the characteristics of the dogs, including the dogs' fidelity' – making their loyalty to him their overriding virtue, much as Peary's praise for Henson himself stressed Henson's willingness to put his energies at Peary's service. The modern eye, like Dr Counter's, detects a cause for Henson's sympathy in his own experience of discrimination and racial injustice back in Jim Crow-racked Maryland and Virginia. While this must be true, it does not abolish the structural inequalities of the relationship, any more than Peary's observation that, at the conquest of the Pole, 'not individuals alone but *races* were represented', with its pleasing picture of human unity, means that the three contingents ('Caucasian, Ethiopian, and Mongolian') were of equal importance. To some extent, Henson reinscribed the tones and values of the white–black relationship on the black–Inuit one.

Dr Counter's new gleanings of information throw some parts of the story, previously bowdlerised by the conventions of 1909, into ironic relief. It now looks likely, for example, that Henson reached the Pole several hundred yards ahead of Peary, an act of *lèse-majesté* which Peary punished with a grim silence lasting the entire return journey across the sea ice to Cape Columbia – day after day. It seems certain, too, that the sole casualty of the expedition, Professor Marvin, was actually murdered by the Inuit responsible for getting him home when his supporting party turned back on the polar trek. They had resented his contemptuous attitude. We also discover that John Verhoeff, killed by a fall on an earlier Peary expedition and blandly described by Henson as 'a good friend of mine', was in truth a Kentucky yahoo who called Henson 'by the most vulgar of American racial epithets', and occasionally threatened to shoot him. And of course every characterisation of the Inuit is coloured in retrospect by the new knowledge that desire figured in the encounter. We know what Henson isn't saying: that the locals the explorers liked did not always sleep *beneath* the bunks. We read: 'never for an instant does the odor or appearance of an Esquimo's habitation suggest the rose or geranium. The aroma of an East Side lunch-room is more like it' (*Negro Explorer*), and must now reflect immediately that Anaukaq's mother Akatingwah lay beside Henson, skin to skin, mingling the human smells of Greenland and America. A lost intimacy hides beneath the lines. Did bed abolish hierarchy, as it can, or only prove how closely it clings in a close embrace?

There are hints that Henson was himself far more irascible and impetuous than the received accounts acknowledge. But Counter does not so much uncover the truth about Henson as illuminate the bind a black man of achievement faced at the beginning of the century. He could not ever afford to show anger, or any other ungoverned feeling that might disturb his standing with his patron Peary, on whom his access to achievement entirely depended. His ambitions had indeed to be expressed within the frame of loyalty; and he could cultivate self-respect only as an unvoiced certainty about himself, hoping all the while that the geographical victory over the Pole, when it came, would provide a marker of success too factual to be disputed. Whatever carping whites said, he would still have done it. Dr Counter prints as his epigraph a magazine verse that Henson copied into his journal: 'Only Remembered By What I Have Done'. The pressure must have been intense. Not responding to provocation was an art every black American with a sense of self-preservation had to learn; but Henson was extraordinarily isolated while he practised it, spending more than ten years in total on Peary's various Arctic ventures, without the relief of black company in which defences could be dropped. There were only whites and Inuit. It must have been a considerable compensation to be Mahri-Pahluk, admired for your jokes and prowess, as well as honest reliable Matthew.

The same pressure marks the writing of *Negro Explorer*, which Peary first tried to block because it further exposed him, in the controversy with Frederick Cook over polar precedence, to the charge of picking unreliable witnesses for his feat. The only people who had seen him hoist the Stars and Stripes at 90°N were four savages and a black man. This was the book by the black man, and it might make matters worse. Though *Negro Explorer* in fact sank without trace, Henson was thus compelled to reckon with reputations at every step, in a practical way that went beyond the usual codes of restraint when writing up an expedition. He wrote well, or his ghostwriter did. The book's style was fresh, vernacular and plain, with the high flights secured by humour. But the book was forced into the time's mould of approved feeling, a Teddy Roosevelt manly swagger. You can hear ecstatic cries of 'Bully!' from time to time in the background, and Henson presents himself as a diligent soul, proud to be allowed to be 100 per cent American. Here is the Polar Moment itself in his account, chequered with Peary's favourite phrases:

> Another world's accomplishment was done and finished, and as in the past, from the beginning of history, wherever the world's work was done by a white man, he had been accompanied by a colored man. From the building of the pyramids and the journey to the Cross, to the discovery of the new world and the discovery of the North Pole, the Negro had been the faithful and constant companion of the Caucasian, and I felt all that it was possible to feel, that it was I, a lowly member of my race, who had been chosen by fate to represent it, at this, almost the last of the world's great *work*.

Accompanied: such a politely passive word. Henson conceded humble terms for his participation. Only the fact of his participation was non-negotiable, a sideways claim to dignity. Elsewhere in snatches the book quietly declares an explorer's vocation for him. More than the accident of Peary's patronage was involved. 'Imagine gorgeous bleakness, beautiful blankness': paradoxical phrases that are the authentic signs of seduction by the snow.

Dr Counter's revaluation of Henson is not the first. The tide of opinion began to move in his favour, after long neglect, in 1947, with the publication of *Dark Companion*, a novelised biography based on the white author's long conversations with Henson shortly before the latter's death. Honourable, but lushly embarrassing to read now, *Dark Companion* instated Henson as a hero for the period of early civil rights activism that was then just beginning. A more racially integrated story could not be imagined. Despite the slurs and jeers of racists, Henson had been the embodiment of American virtues everyone could applaud; a black Huck Finn in his youth, prone to staring into the eyes of wise old sea captains, he had grown into an ebony Abe Lincoln. Dr Counter naturally writes with a far more assertive sense of black history, and of the separate strand of American culture to which Henson belonged. He wants Henson to have participated in the polar discovery, not as a 'lowly' brand of American patriot, nor as an imitation white, but as a representative of the African-American experience, his *active* presence at the Pole a marker for ambitions that need not exist on anybody else's terms.

Hence the last and largest unconscious irony of his book. Insofar as his primary intention is to vindicate Henson, Counter uses the Inuit, with the very best intentions, in a time-honoured manner: as human mirrors for American actions. Returned from Greenland, he sends Anaukaq an African-American flag of his own design that he uses to instil in black schoolchildren a pride in their history. Then, forming a committee and industriously raising funds, he sets about fulfilling Anaukaq and Kali's wish to visit the graves of their fathers. By the time it happens, the modest visit has become 'The North Pole Family Reunion', with a packed itinerary including a soul food breakfast with the American Hensons, and numerous presentations. (The Peary family were less willing to play, to Kali Peary's hurt.) Dr Counter shows America to them: he exhibits them to America. Though he has told the appalling story of the Inuit group brought to America in 1897 under Peary's auspices, who sickened and died and had their skeletons displayed in the Museum of Natural History, his revulsion does not alert him to similarities, nor lead him to question his self-appointed role as guardian of the

Henson heritage. Admittedly, Anaukaq, Kali and the family groups they brought with them were not boiled. Instead they were exposed to the gamut of American modes of public glorification, from the Ronald Reagan presidential missive ('truly proud of their legacy of heroism and accomplishment') to pulpit oratory in the Abyssinian Baptist Church ('Peacemaker, peacemaker. Learn how to be fair ... You don't need to have a PhD degree'). To all of which Kali and Anaukaq responded with polite thanks. Their principal function, among all these American reference points, is as testimony, living truth. Dr Counter, who narrates the whole journey in detail, seizes eagerly on signs that all the participants share the same celebratory purpose. 'We had all', he writes, 'become one big family.' And as the Greenlanders depart, he comments with amazing innocence, 'Ten-year-old Aviaq, who was already beyond her years in maturity, had grown tremendously. Entering the plane she sported new sunglasses, watches, and other gifts she had received ...'

This was not the end of the affair. It is everywhere apparent that Matthew Henson's scandalous public neglect after the Pole was won rankles with Dr Counter, and not just as a historic wrong. He feels the pang, as if it were happening today, of Peary's gold medals from the geographical societies – while Henson made do with a lacquered steel medal from the Colored Commercial Association of Chicago, and a silver loving-cup courtesy of the Bronx Chamber of Commerce. So he sets out to rectify the shame. No sooner have the Inuit flown away than he is designing a grand memorial for Henson and getting him reinterred in Arlington National Cemetery. Bands play. Speeches are made. Retrospective honours are conferred as if the past was revisable; Dr Counter wishes to heal it, and acts then as if it has been healed. But this very American grant of absolution has the unmistakeable effect, as he writes on, of dissolving the past as well, most notably in the eventual naming of the Henson–Peary relationship as a *friendship*, with every qualification dropped, and, one has to say, the reality of 1909 disappearing into a haze, lost as soon as found.

In 1912, Booker T. Washington contributed an introduction to *A Negro Explorer*. Henson was needed as a hero, he wrote, because 'a race which is doing all the fundamental things for the first time ... needs for its own encouragement, as well as to justify the hopes of its friends, the records of the members of the race who have been part of any great and historic achievement'. That style of black pride has gone, the idea of black Americans as trainees under tutelage replaced by an appreciation of the 'fundamental things' that they had done for centuries. But there remains – a testimony to the disappointments of the twentieth century – a need to welcome, as Washington put it, *any* achievement. The other histories entwined in the story give way to this need; and Dr Counter elevates Matthew Henson to a black hall of fame generously indifferent to the incompatability of different successes. And yet terribly susceptible to later disgrace. Henson's reputation is proudly placed alongside those of Mayor Marion Barry, Colonel Guion S. Bluford (an astronaut, prominent at Henson's new graveside) and Bill Cosby.[4]

(1992)

HUNTFORD'S NANSEN, HUNTFORD'S SCOTT[5]

Fridtjof Nansen could hardly have been more different from Robert Falcon Scott, knocked off his pedestal by Roland Huntford in 1979. Blond, athletic, a Viking in an aerated Jaeger suit, Nansen selected himself as a polar explorer because he actually possessed the requisite skill-set, rather than being nominated for heroism by a bureaucratic patron with polar fantasies. He grew up a junior ski champion in the Christiania (Oslo) of the 1880s with the wilderness of Nordmarka 'within view of his very own doorstep', so that mountain and glacier, snow slope and crevasse were the stuff of local geography and long experience, instead of sublime fairy tales. He drew on a social environment of immense mobility and applied intelligence, compared to the sticky hierarchies of Edwardian Britain. The personnel roster of the *Fram* reads like a daydream about the ideal, multi-skilled workforce: an electrician who was also a gymnast, a forester/mechanic/mental health nurse who had patented a potato-picking machine. Before Nansen did his exploring he made a foundational discovery about the structure of nerve tissue; afterwards he was a diplomat, an international negotiator, the father of the League of Nations' 'Nansen passport' for refugees. His was a career of verified achievements and consequential engagements with the world – vitiated only by an internal restlessness that emptied each achievement in turn of the possibility of happiness. He gave one of the bleakest definitions of polar endeavour: 'The struggle for nothing, in nothing, about nothing.' In private life he was an unhappy Don Juan.

Compared to the British version of the same period, this is polar heroism with a richly different hinterland, both geographical and personal. But while Roland Huntford is an extraordinary chronicler of early twentieth-century polar exploration, he is not necessarily a very illuminating judge of it. He is the most implacable sniffer-out of evidence: the Fates (or the Furies) seem to have appointed him to be the bloodhound on the trail of the 'heroic age' – the years of competition over the final geographic prizes of the Arctic and Antarctic which came to a ragged end with the First World War. He also has a great power of re-creation. Detail in his hands turns back into drama. The high points of his books are invariably the journeys themselves, expert syntheses of accounts by the different participants which move at an utterly convincing daily pace; so that dead expeditions become open-ended enterprises again, and you wonder what will happen even if you know perfectly well. *Nansen*, no exception, rises to its peak with its rendering of the explorer's sixteen-month ski run across the Arctic pack ice with Hjalmar Johansen, from the ice-locked ship *Fram* to the shores of Franz Josef Land. The two men scored a new record for north latitude; plastered layers-deep in seal grease by the end, constantly adapting their equipment as they went, they demonstrated that unsupported Norwegian know-how could master the chaotic environment which had thwarted huge naval forays for a century. It was the central event of Fridtjof Nansen's life, and it is hard to see how any better justice can be done to it as a feat than Huntford has here. This sort of integrated retelling, in the flexible third-person of biography, of events previously fissured by different memories, will surely be Huntford's lasting contribution to the literature of adventure.

But his immediate fame is as polar history's chief iconoclast. Some unambiguous respect is due to him here. Now that our picture of Captain Scott has been permanently altered by Huntford's work, it is growing difficult even to imagine the interlocked pieties which guarded Scott's reputation before *Scott and Amundsen* was published. Huntford had to move a mountain of mystification aside. In a way his own judgement of Scott's character was secondary to the process of opening the figure of Scott up to the possibility of truth. Whatever you think of the replacement Huntford proposed for the idol, for that artificially smoothed and unanimous set of voices from the past that characterise myth he had substituted the dissonant buzz of witnesses, which reminds us that the past was just a moment like this one.

Without Huntford's polemical drive, he might never have tuned in Oates's exasperated journal entries for us from out of the static and noise of time, or made the remorseless calculations required to show just how unready Scott was to face the polar environment. But *Scott and Amundsen* revealed a Huntford who slipped rather too easily from bloodhound to Rottweiler, who worked in what you might call the attack-dog mode of biography. Among the cries of pain as Huntford crunched cherished pieces of Establishment nonsense came protests as he bit down, with equal fervour, on things that were probably true; or at least were genuinely matters of interpretation. He did not know where to stop. Famously, the index listed twenty-three characteristics of Scott of which only 'literary gifts' and perhaps 'agnosticism' were positive. 'Command, unsuitability for' was followed by 'insight, lack of' and 'judgement, defective' in dire, and finally hilarious, sequence. Huntford made the gratuitous suggestion, completely unsupported by evidence, that at the last Scott had glared balefully at Oates 'in unspoken expectation of the supreme sacrifice' until he got the message, and then concocted Oates's heroic exit line. (Sue Limb and Patrick Cordingley point out in their biography of Oates that any quietus scripted by Scott would've been much lusher.) He insisted – a statement he repeats in this book – that because Kathleen Scott agreed to meet Nansen in a Berlin hotel while her husband was in the Antarctic, their romantic friendship must have been sexual. Until an attested piece of paper turns up written by either of them saying *Hot stuff with Fridtjof/ Kathleen on the sofa this afternoon,* this remains a speculation, and one at odds with her known preference for flirtation minus libido.

What these readings of circumstance had in common was a refusal or inability on Huntford's part to enter, except destructively, into the mental climate of Scott's England: its codes, its probabilities, its rituals and romances. Consequently he was not good at distinguishing between individual characteristics and collective or cultural ones. In my view he blamed Scott as a single man for the defects of a complex tradition shaping British behaviour at the Poles. To think this is not to let Scott off the hook: it is not necessarily a matter of diminishing culpability, but of assessing meaning. If Scott was Romantic in his perception of the polar landscape to the detriment of sensible plan-ning, he remains responsible for the specific errors which did for him and his companions; but if he inherited and enlarged that Romantic response rather than inventing it from scratch, the life in the world and the death in the snow make a rather different pattern. It might, for example, matter more that he was acquiescent (which he was) than that he was arrogant (perfectly true).

In history books the task of separating the individual and the cultural rests on the historian's sensitivity to convention. In biog-raphy, perversely, it is the biographer's skill at imagining personality that become the point at issue, as the means by which figure detaches from background. Huntford's imaginative, as opposed to forensic, record is not completely reassuring; and the effect is curious in a work like the present one, where the subject is somebody Huntford admires.

Nansen took his favourite self-image from Goethe's Faust, who promised to surrender his soul if he ever found himself content; and Huntford in turn takes up this sad wager on perpetual motion as the central motif of the book, and the main key to Nansen's identity. It is a good biographical move. Nansen's thoughts ran in Faustian channels, it seems, on most occasions as the possible rewards of his world were paraded before him one by one, from the favours of the Duchess of Sutherland to the presidency of a Norwegian republic. (He declined both.) His wife Eva, a successful mezzo-soprano, performed the Schubert setting of Gretchen's lament from Faust while he was away on the *Fram. Wo ich ihn nicht hab, / Ist mir das Grab*: 'Him gone, my room / Is like a tomb ...' But here the sense arrives of Huntford reaching the limit of his biographical skill. Faust is used as a catch-all explanation, a device that registers the presence of an inner life rather than a door through which it can be explored further. Huntford integrates narratives beautifully: not characters. Where contradictory impressions of Nansen are concerned that do not fit the single Faustian diagnosis, Huntford tends merely to amass the data, without weighting it by importance; without it being clear, even, to what extent he endorses this or that ripple in the flow.

In particular, there seems more to be said about the bad feeling that Nansen generated aboard the *Fram*. Every expedition produces the pressures that lead to evil-tempered journal entries; people stuck at close quarters get fed up. The bitterness comes, and then it goes again as pressures recede. Such is the normal pattern, the background to any one polar personality clash. To take the prime example from the 1910–13 British Antarctic Expedition, even Oates, up whose nose Scott had got so far that practically only his feet projected, warmed a little to his leader again once he no longer had to worry about the expedition's ponies. Huntford's way is to present the ebb and flow of the inevitably malign comment on Nansen as if it were, at each point in time, straightforwardly revealing. The result is a Nansen who just is by turns whatever his pissed-off shipmates call him: tyrannical, unthoughtful, conceited, rude, obnoxious. 'He thinks he knows everything and his word is law.' So much friendlier is Huntford to the *Fram*'s captain Otto Sverdrup – given the same rhetorical role as the quietly more effective man in relation to Nansen that Huntford gave Oates vis-à-vis

Scott – that it is sometimes necessary to remind yourself that Huntford approves of Nansen. It is as if the habit of dislike has grown on him as a biographer and now infiltrates even his complimentary portraits. The *Fram* insults cannot be simple truths. On the other hand, Huntford might have pursued what they do indicate about Nansen's persistently difficult relations with other men.

Nansen never relaxed into the affinities he had elected to have with men by choosing months and years isolated with them in the Arctic. A quick 'n' dirty psychoanalysis is possible. (It may be that a rather more authoritative one exists. Nansen's book *Farthest North*, with its sidelights on his thinking, reached Vienna, Huntford tells us. If you are writing a biography and it happens that Freud has analysed your subject's dreams, surely, surely you should do more than refer to the fact in passing?) Weak father, mother emotionally absent, then dead when Fridtjof was fifteen, leaving the Oedipal process of separation blatantly unconcluded. Women thereafter the object of a huge, hungry investment of feeling by Nansen, which was never satisfied because the lost maternal warmth remained the goal and could never be recaptured – while men kept their first, stereotypical significance to the Oedipal infant as intruders, threats to bliss, rivals just because they existed. Therefore the adult Nansen was forever trying to resolve the unease at these frontiers of himself by acts of embarrassing dominance, or over-interventionist bossiness: the 'endless preaching' his shipmates could testify to.

This is crass, but something of the sort needs to be ventured, since, from another angle, this same defect in Nansen, however it is defined, was perhaps the cause for his wish to be anything as flamboyant as a polar explorer. Many great achievements fall to those to whom it occurs to perform them, and a certain lack of balance, a certain literal-mindedness, obscured in Nansen's case by his great technical brilliance as an explorer, probably helps in the task of acting out what others are content to keep as fantasies.

(1998)

THE USES OF ANTARCTICA

Recently, the American novelist Douglas Coupland wrote this:

> I like to think of the subconscious as being very much like
> Antarctica. It was only really approached and explored in the
> late 19th century. It's very difficult and expensive to visit, and
> even then we're unsure of its long-term value or if it was worth
> the visit. It only seems to create worry and trouble: ozone holes;
> Oedipus complexes.

Needless to say I don't agree that Antarctica 'only creates worry and
trouble', and 'creates' doesn't seem quite the right word, either, for
the complicated relationship between perceived and perceiver,
when the perceived is an uninhabited continent 97 per cent covered
in ice up to a depth, in some places, of 3 miles; and the perceiver is
– what? We'll come to that. If we take Coupland's joke, though, in an
appropriately psychoanalytical spirit, we see that – of course – it
discloses more truth than the teller meant it to, and truth of a
different kind.

Because even though Antarctica, perhaps like the subconscious,
has been there for a very long time, it really did only come to

persistent human attention, with a similar uncertainty about whether it was being discovered or invented, at the end of the nineteenth century. What Ross and his crews first touched in the 1840s, and what the whalers and the sealers were seeing in the distance from the 1830s on, only came substantially into the domain of human awareness from the 1890s on. Geologically speaking, Antarctica is part of Gondwanaland, carried southwards by the drifting of the plates 160 million years ago. Imaginatively speaking, it is a product of the twentieth century, contemporary with jazz, or the internal combustion engine, or, yes, the Freudian unconscious. Twentieth-century science has defined it; twentieth-century cultural preoccupations have played out in the perception of it; twentieth-century social changes have worked through in the ways that human presence in it has been manifested. It may well be that what happens to Antarctica in the twenty-first century ends up determining its influence on human history far more definitively than anything that has already happened. It may be that the twentieth century ends up looking like nothing but a prelude, with ominous mood music and the grim interest of camcorder tsunami footage, where all the figures in the foreground are busily concentrating on their own concerns as the wave looms up behind them. But the ice sheets haven't melted yet, and eight years in, it's a little too soon to say what this century is doing to our Antarctic perceptions.

I want to think, today, about the twentieth-century-ness of Antarctica, and about the way that its particular perceptual properties have joined up with, have found a fit with, various of the twentieth century's changing human desires. These of course include twentieth-century senses of history; senses, made in the particular decades of the twentieth century, of what the near past and far past were saying. The Edwardian British explorers of Scott's *Terra Nova* expedition, for example, brought multiple histories to bear on their present-tense experiences in 1910–13: the deep-frozen and reheated microculture of naval exploration in the Arctic, the inheritance of the sublime and of Romanticism, the Victorian tendency to moralise the polar landscape – all of these things, not as they were constituted in their own originating historical moments, but as they were received, as they were delivered reflexively or fragmentarily or in passing, much later, as constituent parts of the self-consciousness of another time. It would be just as true to talk about the understandings of the past folded into the experience of all succeeding visitors to Antarctica up to the present day. Twentieth-century cultures, twentieth-century consciousnesses, were always, among other things, founded upon selections of a relevant past; were always constituted by their present possession of particular pieces of memory, myth, knowledge, feeling, idea, from the fading memories carried along by Soviet scientists on the expeditions of the International Geophysical Year of 1957–8 of their compulsory encounter with Engels' *Dialectics of Nature*, to the back-stories of Alpinism and American sports culture and hippy reverence for 'authenticity' coded into awareness of those, from the 1990s on, who paid to ski to the Pole from the private camp at Patriot Hills.

So we could, for instance, in the same spirit trace through the different phases of the twentieth-century encounter with Antarctica one of the very strongest imaginative themes in the response to it, the sense of the southern continent as a repository of lost time; and watch the response change and develop as different expanses of lost time become germane. As Louis Bernacchi describes it in 1901, coming ashore at Cape Adare with the Borchgrevink expedition, the just-encountered landscape oscillates between different types of mythological ancientness. The mountains appearing through cloud look 'like the tiers of an amphitheatre or the Great Pyramid of Cheops' – monuments from ancient human culture. Then the mixture of igneous rock and stranded bergs, of ice and fire, strikes him as they draw inshore as belonging to 'some unknown land of punishment' – to a Dantesque purgatory, located like Dante's in the antipodes, which would implicitly have existed since creation. And then, when they've landed the boat and smelled the penguins and climbed the ridgeline of the cape and looked around, he moves the antiquity of the scene back *before* the creation story, and his mythology gets all Miltonic. He's looking at dark materials. 'It was like a mental image of our globe in its primitive state – a spectacle of Chaos.' But Bernacchi was the *Southern Cross's* geologist, and so far he was only playing. He was letting imagination frolic about without science, which was going to be the twentieth century's most influential source of Antarctic perception. He was going to go to work now, replacing mythology with the chronology of vulcanism and stratification; replacing fanciful lost time with an era in geological history for Antarctica to contain, as geological history was understood before plate tectonics came along to shove the continents into motion. And indeed, the past that was found in Antarctica by the scientists of the heroic age was the far geological past, both displayed and hidden. Displayed, because the rocky bones of the planet were revealed here without the flesh of soil and the skin of vegetation; hidden, because only in coastal outcrops, in rare dry valleys, in the peaks of almost vanished mountains, were the rocks themselves visible beneath the continental sheath of ice, which did not yet itself seem to have a significant relationship to history. There was a kind of analogy to the early geological vision of Antarctica in the hope that ancient biology might be preserved there. If ontogeny *had* recapitulated phylogeny, then the emperor penguin egg collected from Cape Crozier in 1911 might have had a baby dinosaur inside it, miraculously contemporary with the fossilised leaves the Scott expedition dug out of the rock face beside the Beardmore.

The next kind of lost time to be perceived, though, was very recent. It was the human activity of the heroic age itself, once the First World War had ended the world in which it had been humanly and politically and financially and philosophically possible; made it as irretrievable as the Cambrian. The *temps perdu* we are *à la recherche* of, in *The Worst Journey in the World*, 1922, is 'an age in geological time, so many hundred years ago, when we were artistic Christians, doing our jobs as well as we were able ...'

Cherry-Garrard remembered his pre-war Antarctic time with a particular intensity, a particular desperate anxiety and appetite *not* shared by other veterans. Yet this almost hysterical sense that, because we cannot now reach it, because it is not being supplemented and overlaid by other experiences, our past might almost be thought of as *still going on* down there, at the end of the world – it is this sense which metamorphoses into a permanent element in the perception of time in Antarctica, once people are going back and encountering, not of course the heroics of the past, but the buildings of that past, the architectural containers of the heroic age. Primed perhaps by memories of Alpine folklore, of the stories about young men who die in glaciers and have their frozen bodies spat out decades later onto the terminal moraine, unchanged at the feet of the old woman who was once their sweetheart, people have been willing to see Antarctic huts as eerily unchanging, as domains where past fragments of the twentieth century still remain, iced into stasis, virtually ever since Byrd's return to Antarctica in the 1920s. When human presence in Antarctica stepped up by an order of magnitude in the 1950s, the huts of the heroic age became explicitly treasured as time capsules, as uncanny vaults of Edwardian existence persisting alongside contemporary endeavour as past time does not do in the warmer world. Tourism's arrival only strengthened the impression of the past being uncannily visitable, in Antarctica. I've made the pilgrimage myself to admire the continuing redness of the Edwardian ketchup at Cape Evans, and to feel the strange sensation of stepping into the frame of Herbert Ponting's photograph of the *Terra Nova*'s Midwinter Day party, and though I didn't feel the room was exempt from time exactly, it certainly seemed to have flowed there with a kind of withering slowness.

The desire to believe that the recent, human past persists frozen in Antarctica is very strong; strong enough to make people oblivious to the real conservation problems of the huts, a report has complained recently. And it isn't only the buildings of the heroic age this applies to. There is a thrill of anachronism, of small-scale time travel, to be had now in visits to the bases the Soviet Antarctic Programme had to mothball in the early 1990s. The tiny trickle of travellers to Leningradskaya Station, on its clifftop in Victoria Land, or to Molodyozhnaya, enter spaces where posters of Lenin still preside over the dining tables. They're going to the last, gelified outposts of the lost civilisation of twentieth-century communism. One happy camper compares Leningradskaya to 'a villain's HQ in James Bond' on his blog, which suggests he had a very satisfying encounter with historical evil there. Finally, and this is a bit more contentious, it's even possible to perceive an operating Russian base, with real live Russian scientists inside it, as somehow belonging to the past, if you're willing to interpret difference – non-American dentistry, non-American nutrition, budgets, décor – as signs of a different position on a unitary timeline of human progress. This is the essayist and travel writer Jason Anthony, visiting Vostok:

January 26, 2000: The impossible murmurs of bearded Russians followed me into the small empty dining room. Spare and plain, the room reeked so much of old culture and simple food that it seemed a survivor of ice ages and continental drift. Years of tobacco smoke and grease had browned the high pale-yellow ceiling. Much of the paint on the ceiling, and on the yellow walls, had long ago flaked off: above, dark rust bloomed, while below an older icyblue spread like frost, as if the snow outside the windows had seeped through. Small colourful paintings, mostly homemade rural and tropical scenes, gave a tilted hope to the hard-worn room. A mound of boiled eggs glistened in a large bowl like dabs of white paint. Withered window box plants stood silhouetted against the snow. In the dusty light, scuffed dark tables held slabs of black bread, a brick of yellow butter, and a plate of sliced pink salami. On the sideboard, a massive cutting board and heavy cleaver wore the deep scars of years:

the labor, hunger, anger, and celebrations of men living difficult, cloistered lives. I'd walked into a Russian still-life that seemed to breathe in its dark frame.[6]

Antarctica! Where even the butter is primeval!

Meanwhile, this domestic or personal sense of lost time in Antarctica abutted against, even seemed at times to merge with, proliferating scientific understandings of the way the continent stored the past. Indeed they had to jostle, these two quite different scales of time, there being (at least on the spot in Antarctica) no middle ground to separate them, no intermediate social time or landscape time. Look at the way that 'ice ages and continental drift' intrude into that Vostok dining room: the Antarctic past of the International Geophysical Year, when Vostok's first modules were hauled into place, opens straight out on Gondwanaland. Which, of course, the International Geophysical Year *did*. It was then, with remote sensing techniques that started to strip away the concealing ice, and continental drift brought in as a theory from the eccentric margins of geology, that the rock beneath the frozen sheath began to be, not a static lump repeating processes seen more accessibly else-where, but hidden evidence of a planet in motion, a piece carried south from Gondwana to crumple and shove and rift over and over again along the line now marking off East and West Antarctica. The rock was active, so long as you thought of it in rock-time; or, the same thought in reverse, if you thought of Antarctica as a kind of reservoir of slowness, a place where speedier processes were removed, leaving the great surges and pulsations of the crust to set the clock speed. Over the 1970s and 1980s, echo-sounding and radar measurements through the central cap started to reveal a whole preserved landscape down below, with plains and mountains and defiles all solidly packed with ice; and then, most recently and star-tlingly, it turned out, with liquid lake systems and running rivers at the interface between the rock and the incredible weight of the ice. A landscape not seen for maybe 35 million years.

But the ice, too, turned out to contain a history. It was not just an obstruction. Stephen Pyne puts it very well:

> The ice is not simply an opaque veil but substance with its own information content, however meager, and a matrix for embalming air, aerosols, microparticles, and meteorites. The air inclusions that ripple across white and blue ice are vials containing ancient atmospheres. The ice sheets are great archives of past climates. The polycrystalline fabric of the ice contains a history of stress fields. The meteorites that gather into blue ice placers, the debris of interplanetary space, and the cosmic ray interactions with the outer atmosphere that settle into the snow all testify to the power of Ice as a medium of information.[7]

A library, an archive, a mausoleum, a memory: all things which preserve a past by preventing its decay, and again, it proves, not because Antarctica is particularly hospitable to remembering, but because of the characteristic slowness of the continent, this time measured on ice scales rather than rock scales, a hundred times or so faster than the speed of the rocks, but still at such an infinitesimal crawl compared to the processes of the warmer world that it grants a long, long exemption from the normal scattering of time. Where the weather and the biology and the nice warm reactive temperatures up here keep molecules briskly cycling and recycling, down there in the dry cold desert, they stay where they are put. The borehole beneath Vostok passes through about 100,000 years of molecule deposition, and therefore 100,000 years of past climate, per vertical kilometre. Ice cores covering 400,000 years have been extracted now that the drillers are just about to break through into the lake water below.

So: *temps retrouvé*, time regained, from the twentieth-century encounter with Antarctica, on the scale of decades, and on the scale of hundreds of thousands, and millions, of years. But not on the scale of longer-term human historical memory. Over centuries, over millennia, Antarctica is blank; though you can line it up with history for the discordant, indifferent thrill of it, as the scientist Bill Green does, for instance, when he writes 'It was ... while the young Charlemagne was uniting Europe that an epochal event occurred in Wright Valley' – and the Lower Wright Glacier discharged fresh glacial water over the briny lower layer of Lake Vanda. The two scales do not mesh.

Now, I called this lecture 'The *Uses* of Antarctica', and all of this changing stuff about lost time does indeed constitute a *use* for the place, in a very direct and functional way, so long as we're willing to agree that accumulating the knowledge of climate history, and of the geological history of the planet, and gaining the chance of a reflective encounter with type specimens of our own recent past, are all functional. Whether the southern continent is preserving an ice record or a rock record or an architectural record, it is in effect doing something for us. It is offering us something we can completely assimilate. But perhaps we need to be thinking in terms of a wider, and more ironised, idea of *use* here, for after all the striking challenge of Antarctica, perceptually speaking, has been one of responding to a place which is overwhelmingly, blatantly *not* subordinate to our purposes, *not* assimilated into human systems of use and familiarity. Which we marry up, gingerly, to the word 'wilderness', as the best linguistic fit we have available, though Antarctica only has a distant family resemblance to the North American ecosystems that word got its denotation and first connotations from. The experience of Antarctica gives a particular force to the fundamental recognition behind any environmental philosophy, that a place must be respected as existing in and for itself, and not for us, not just for what we can make of it. In this case, the recognition has to go beyond respect for other life, into a kind of respect for the integrity of non-living systems too. Among the geopolitical motives and the climatic self-interest that helped to bring the Protocol on Environmental Protection to the Antarctic Treaty into effect, there was also the attempt to honour this recognition of our non-possession of the continent by, exactly, putting it beyond our use.

And this presents a kind of stumbling-block for metaphor. Thinking from scratch: what does it mean for us that we have, in our world, an uninhabited continent? What does it allow us to feel? First of all, I would argue, a sense of possibility, bare and abstract, like the sense of pre-specific possibility attached to money; except that unlike the generalised (or, significantly, 'frozen') desire embodied in money, this possibility is unconvertible, it can't be defrosted into the satisfaction of particular desires, except by destroying it. It's a deposit that can't be cashed. But it can be borrowed against. It can be used as surety for the issue of metaphors; for ways of writing which chiefly take the ice as a source of resemblances, analogies, comparisons to human experience. Starting with, say, the inescapable association between physical and emotional coldness, so that the frozen sea is always metamorphosing into Kafka's 'frozen sea within us', which a book is supposed to be the axe to break. And then going on, for example, since we're on the subject of books, to the equally inescapable association between white snow and white paper. In writing, Antarctica has constantly vanished *into* writing, into the act of representation itself, as if being there and describing being there had collapsed into each other, perhaps because of the lack of middle ground I talked about. To travel across the whiteness is to inscribe it, very frequently; footprints have often recalled the other kind of printing. Here, the possibility of Antarctica becomes the possibility of saying anything, anything at all, on an empty page. The presence in the snow of a representing consciousness nudges us towards descriptions in which the snow is doing the writing.

Here I think we hit the one grand exception to Stephen Pyne's observation that modernism never really claimed Antarctica, aesthetically, despite the apparently irresistible match of sensibilities which makes tabular bergs look as if they were designed by Le Corbusier. Modernist self-consciousness about the act of writing *did* claim Antarctica, in the small change of all those snow/paper metaphors; and now and again in bigger works, written at a distance from the place itself. Take W.S. Graham's very wonderful poem of 1970, 'Malcolm Mooney's Land', for example, one of a sequence about his alter ego Mooney, who in this one, thanks to the generous amplitude of polar nomenclature, gets both to have a Land named after him and to *be* that Land – on paper. 'Above the bergs the foolish / Voices' – of the blizzard – 'are lighting lamps / And all their sounds make / This diary of a place / Writing us both in.' As well as aligning footprints and print, white-outs and you-know-what, he even manages to make the lice in Mooney's furs literary, by lining them up with 'the grammarsow and the word-louse'. I can't deny that there are Arctic elements here – those lice, a guest appearance by a polar bear – but I'd argue for the Antarctic pedigree of the final scene in the tent. (What could be more Antarctic than a final scene in a tent?) 'I have made myself alone now. / Outside the tent endless / Drifting hummock crests. / Words drifting on words. / The real unabstract snow.' And there's the stumbling block. Metaphor is not identity; only borrowed semblance. And however anthropocentric our metaphorical uses of the continent may be, there remains the still-unassimilated thing itself, the millions of square kilometres of Antarctica existing but not for us; the real unabstract snow. The anthropocentric metaphors are always in tension, always under challenge. Our awareness of the continent's dimensions, physical and temporal, mean that even in imagination it is always in excess of metaphor, always mutely huger than the currency we want to give it. There is always an inhuman remainder, after our descriptions are over. Antarctica is never *only* its uses.

But this means, paradoxically, that one of the major twentieth-century uses of Antarctica is as a focus for just this awareness of how much the world isn't ours, and isn't us; an awareness that is impeded elsewhere by the depth and persistence of human familiarity with the planet's landscapes. I want to look now at one example of this kind of use which is particularly interesting because it is, in fact, so commercial, so carefully calculated in its desire to come up with a version of the awareness I'm talking about which people were willing to pay for, to find desirable in a very straightforward way.

Richard Byrd's *Alone* was an enormous bestseller in 1938. It's an account, very compellingly written, of the four months in 1934 he spent overwintering solo in a weather station on the Ross Ice Shelf, and of the dark night of the soul he endured along with the dark night outside, partly because of the isolation, partly because of carbon monoxide poisoning. But *Alone* was not exactly written by Richard Byrd. As Raimund Goerler demonstrated at the nineteenth Polar Libraries Colloquy in Copenhagen in 2002, it is overwhelmingly likely that it was worked up from Byrd's original notes and diary entries by his journalist friend Charles J.V. Murphy. Murphy was a participant in Byrd's second expedition, and responsible for Little America's radio communications, so he actually appears in his own text as a minor character, the voice on the radio of good old Charlie Murphy. When he was working on the book, apparently, he told Byrd that the materials he'd sent him had 'nearly everything necessary ... but ... in solution'. What the reader needed would have to be 'precipitate[d] out' of it. Clearly he had a beautifully developed sense of what several different Depression-era demographics would respond to, and a considerable command of voice too; later on, his other books would include ghostwritten autobiographies for the Duke and Duchess of Windsor. For many years he served as Washington bureau chief for *Fortune* magazine, and just as there he dedicated himself to finding the romance in American business, so in *Alone* he set himself to giving Byrd's experience a sumptuous, streamlined gloss, with a score of film-music strings. Rarely has Antarctica's orientation away from us been so elegantly commodified. Several times he calls the ice shelf 'as austere as platinum', a wonderful phrase which is both visually exact, and also the most deluxe description imaginable for austerity.

Very quickly, on only the second page of the book, Murphy is making a pitch for Byrd's experience as something universally recognisable, because typical of the age.

> I had no important purposes. There was nothing of that sort. Nothing whatsoever, except one man's desire to know that kind of experience to the full, to be by himself for a while and to taste peace and quiet and solitude long enough to find out how good they really are. It was all that simple. And it was something, I believe, that people beset by the complexities of modern life will understand immediately. We are caught up in the winds that blow every which way. And in the hullabaloo the thinking man is driven to ponder where he is being blown and to long desperately for some quiet place where he can reason undisturbed and take inventory.[8]

Antarctica as Shangri-La. (James Hilton's *Lost Horizon*, with its dream of soothing escape into the Himalayan snows, had come out in 1933, Frank Capra's movie of it in 1937.) Against that, Murphy had to maintain the powerful selling-point of the experience's uniqueness, its incomparable unlikeness to everyday life, just as he had to defend the passivity of Byrd's endurance against any suggestion that it made him less of a can-do kind of a guy. But all these things, it turned out, could be reconciled in his vision of the place. Byrd would struggle against the killing cold, and against the poisoning fumes from his stove and his generator, and he would keep himself stalwartly busy in a Robinson Crusoe-ish kind of way, but as the twilight fell over the ice shelf, and the aurora arose, and the winter wind started to move the loose snow crystals on the shelf's surface like 'an incoming tide which creams over the ankles then surges to the waist and is finally at the throat' – then he would experience the excess of Antarctica, its inhuman scale and indifference, not as something antipathetic (anti-pathetic, opposed to feeling) but as transcendence. I'm emphasising, probably overemphasising, the rhetorical calculation involved, because I want to bring out the particularity of the move being made here:

> Harmony, that was it! That was what came out of the silence – a gentle rhythm, the strain of a perfect chord, the music of the spheres, perhaps.
>
> It was enough to catch that rhythm, momentarily to be myself a part of it. In that instant I could feel no doubt of man's oneness with the universe.[9]

In other words, Antarctica *isn't* part of the order of things constituted by human needs and uses and usefulness, but it *is* part of cosmic order (strike up the string section again), and therefore it and humanity, which is also part of cosmic order, belong together in some ultimate sense; they harmonise.

And Byrd holds onto this thought right the way through *Alone*, we're told, even when he's lying in his bunk in the dark too weak to lift his arms to light a candle. It's his credo, his take-home idea; what cannot be used in wilderness may therefore be seen as spiritual, in a very twentieth-century way that can hover, undefined, between religious and post-religious. Again, the obvious winning schmaltziness of the way the idea is expressed shouldn't be taken as vitiating it, but as a sign of how potent it is, how reliably it touches on a possibility in the human encounter with Antarctic landscape. It's a perception that recurs in different forms right through the Antarctic twentieth century, from Frank Debenham saying that if chance rules the Antarctic 'there is Something behind the Chance', to Sara Wheeler in the 1990s saying 'it would be almost impossible, in this landscape, not to reflect on forces beyond the human plane'. Or, as an entrant to the competition Byrd's publisher ran in 1930 to promote Charlie Murphy's first ghosted book for him put it, 'The star that led the Magi across their deserts and the star that led Byrd to the nether pole are not so different one from another as one might at first suppose.'

Stephen Pyne, however, pointing correctly to Thoreau as the distant model for Byrd's retreat into wilderness, argued in *The Ice* that picking a floating plain of ice, antiseptic, iron-hard, as your Walden doesn't make sense. It was nonsense, he said, in thermodynamic terms. 'On The Ice the Thoreauvian gesture must be reversed: stimulation, complexity, information, must be constantly added to such an environment or else one will succumb to solipsism or a white-out of personality.' That is, where everything that means anything has to be brought along, there can be no meaning in withdrawal. But this seems to me to be based on a mistaken sense of what's being inherited from Thoreau here, what the piece of thinking is, about the unuseful wilderness, which has descended into the twentieth-century repertoire of Antarctic responses. Byrd – or should I say, the first-person narrator of *Alone* – is aware of the thermodynamic implications of his position, but not especially worried by them. *Alone* contains one elegant evocation of the heat death of the universe, going on locally just outside the weather station, when he talks about the 'indescribable evenness' into which the silence, the dark, the cold, and the ticking of his clocks all merge; and one moment of temptation, to give in to entropy. But the Thoreauvian nourishment he's getting from his wilderness experience clearly isn't supposed to be an infusion of 'stimulation, complexity, information' anyway, so he isn't very vulnerable to the discovery that the environment sucks instead of blowing.

The cultural point of departure here, I think – the thing that is passing down half-remembered to Byrd, or to good old Charlie Murphy – is Thoreau's famous moment of revelation, not by Walden Pond, but on top of Mt Ktaadn: when Thoreau poured out a kind of hymn to use-transcending nature at its bleakest, and after it, after an apparent radical separation of it from all human connection, an awestruck declaration of affinity, based not even on sharing life with living natural processes, but just on sharing a common status as matter. Imagine, please, as you listen to this, rather than a summit in Maine in 1846 a storm on the Ross Ice Shelf in the winter dark of 1934.

Nature was here something savage and awful, though beautiful. I looked with awe at the ground I trod on, to see what the Powers had made there, the form and fashion and material of their work. This was that Earth of which we have heard, made out of Chaos and Old Night. Here was no man's garden, but the unhandselled globe. It was not lawn, nor pasture, nor mead, nor woodland, nor lea, nor arable, nor waste-land ... Man was not to be associated with it. It was Matter, vast, terrific, – not his Mother Earth that we have heard of, not for him to tread on, or be buried in ... What it is to be admitted to a museum, to see a myriad of particular things, compared with being shown some star's surface, some hard matter in its home! I stand in awe of my body, this matter to which I am bound has become so strange to me ... What is this Titan that has possession of me? Talk of mysteries! – Think of our life in nature, – daily to be shown matter, to come in contact with it, – rocks, trees, wind on our cheeks! the *solid* earth! the *actual* world! the *common sense! Contact! Contact! Who* are we? *where* are we?[10]

I promised we'd come to the question of the self that does the perceiving of Antarctica, and so we have. This ecstatic piece of Thoreau, visible through the smooth varnish of *Alone*, is not only the prototype for a whole vein of twentieth-century environmental awe – for instance, for Aldo Leopold's injunction to 'think like a mountain' – and with even more drastic force in proportion to the even more drastic bleakness of the southern continent, a prototype for awe at what in Antarctica exceeds our uses. It's also a prototype for a reflexive move back from seen to seer.

Who are we? Where are we? Richard Byrd was not worried by thermodynamics, but he was exceedingly anxious about the uncontrollability of his own mind. He resolves to 'extirpat[e] all lugubrious ideas the instant they appeared'. 'Only by ruthlessly exorcising the disillusioning and unpleasant thoughts can I maintain any feeling of real detachment, any sense of being wholly apart from selfish concerns.' Not surprisingly: he appears to believe, unlike Thoreau, that only right, calm, undiscordant thoughts put you in harmony with the cosmos. Here the half-conservatism of the twentieth-century encounter with Antarctica comes in: the distance of many of its twentieth-century visitors, particularly its early visitors, from the urban mainstreams of ideas. Byrd would very much have preferred his emotions to abide by the rulings of his will. 'A gentleman never gives in to his feelings.' But *Alone* shows a man aware of the slippery ground beneath him. 'Even in my most exalted moods I never quite lost the feeling of being poised over an undermined footing, like a man negotiating a precipice who pauses to admire the sunset.' Once it is acknowledged that the world is not only what we want it or need it to be, it begins to follow that we are not only what we want to want or want to need. Wilderness without; wildness, of a certain kind, within. There really is a serious connection, just as Douglas Coupland jokingly promised, between Antarctica and the unconscious.

(2008)

Red

I was interested in plenty in general, first, and only later in the colour-coded Soviet version I wrote about in 2010 in Red Plenty. *The dot-com boom of the 1990s was where I began, with its promise of an apparently drop-dead-contemporary cornucopia. But the more I looked at Silicon Valley, and at the loud insistence just then that something absolutely unprecedented was happening, the more I saw a very ancient fantasy at work. Abundance has a mythology, and here it was again.*

And then when I started thinking about the unsuccessful Soviet cousin of the familiar twentieth-century abundance of the West, I found the explicit jostling in it between folktales and the hard problem of economic planning too beautiful to pass up. Beautiful, that is, for those who are gluttons for historical irony, and who like the shapes made when materialism doubles up with metaphor and with surreptitious magic, in communist history and, just as much, in the capitalist kind. The actual physical consequences of the Soviet experiment were often strikingly ugly, as I found when I took a research trip to Siberia. But I was also drawn to the hiddenness or buriedness of what I was investigating, in a picture of the Soviet past which, as the twenty-first century began, mostly eliminated altogether from memory the disconcerting time in the late 1950s and early 1960s when the USSR had looked like a confident technocracy, with a chance at achieving its authoritarian utopia.

It was a vivid demonstration of the way that, at any point in history, a dominant story ripples backwards through our understanding of the past, reorganising it in retrospect, and smoothing away even very recent events that no longer fit the narrative – consigning them to unvisited annexes or lumber rooms of history, stuffed with discarded paradigms, anomalous expectations, obsolete futures. There were lost worlds everywhere. Lost worlds were normal.

And this particular lost world was also the one that crystallised my discontent with my own practice, up to this point, of writing ever more novelistic non-fiction. It was in trying to reanimate – to demonstrate in motion – a pocket USSR, small enough to fit in a literary snow-globe, that I found myself moving into a dwelling of my own devising, right on the border between the documentary and fictional, with doors opening out one way into the verifiable, and the other, into the completely imagined.

SIBERIAN JOURNAL

On the flight from Moscow to Novosibirsk, two middle-aged men in the row in front of us are drinking surreptitiously from flasks, getting overemphatic and using the aisle for their conversation, but maintaining what Simmi (my translator) says is the ideal of Russian drunkenness, always a bit lit up but keeping your balance, breezing on, not wobbling, nowhere near (for example) throwing up. One's in neat dark clothes, pepper and salt hair, face like an elderly little boy, and that high colour which happens to some Russian men in middle age and looks a bit Irish; the other's bulkier, more bouffant, with assertive hands and an air of somehow stupid confidence, wearing cream clothes and cream slip-on shoes at the end of unexpectedly spindly legs. Makes me think of the actor who plays Grouty the prison kingpin in the 1970s British sitcom *Porridge*.

Somehow Mr Cream Shoes has managed to annoy a young man from farther up the plane, who as we're just coming in to land comes and stands in his face in the aisle and clearly threatens him; at which Mr Cream unhelpfully laughs. Altercation in aisle; steward separating them; sudden appearance from rear of plane of decisive moustached twenty-something bloke – flight marshal? soldier? somebody trained, anyway – who grips the young man's arms in the air over his head from behind, bends him backwards, and frog-marches him swiftly away. It's the same posture the Militsiya use when we see them hustling the boy off across the concrete after we land. Throughout, Mr Cream and Mr Naughty Boy continue to throw in provocative remarks, barracked in their turn by a remon-strating old lady one row farther forward. I suppose the whole thing is not much different from pissed English people disrupting a flight to Ibiza, only there's something unfamiliar-feeling in the unrowdy boozing, the matter-of-fact force of the response to the situation, the sense of things being ordinarily a little out of control.

We skirted Novosibirsk on a ring road. Wonderful moment early on, driving in dawn light across flat open land tilted slightly downward to a horizon spiked with metal radio towers rising straight out of the red glow of the rising sun. Industrial crown of thorns. Then lots of avenues with trams, factories, etc. – low-density sprawl going on and on, till we crossed the dam over the river Ob. Seagulls on the chain link fence. And then the industrial scatter continued – massive sluices, more factories, hillsides given to apart-ments – without stopping, to Akademgorodok, which clearly isn't a separate oasis now, if it ever was. The trees got denser, that was all. And arriving at the hotel – eight storeys of raw yellow-grey brick, retrofitted with varnished Russian-ranchero woodwork – I was primarily disappointed. I felt as if I'd hoodwinked myself into enthusiasm over crud.

But the eye adjusts. Went for a three-hour walk with Simmi, to stay awake in the face of jetlag, and saw a lot more low-grade messy architecture, but also first inklings of how this had been found a beautiful place, a much-loved place, more than just an extension of the Novosibirsk sprawl.

Trees have grown back in along the avenues, so the lines of apartment buildings on, for example, Morskoi Prospekt don't declare themselves, don't form a streetscape the way they did in the 1960s photographs of the new town. These blocks – I think at the top end of apartment quality in the housing caste system, and

therefore for scientists who didn't qualify for the rare cottages –
are maroon and yellow now, with balconies that have been pretty
much but not universally boxed-in with varnished wood planking
to give a kind of overhanging semi-Arab look. Each balcony is now
a little wooden greenhouse, or a storage space stuffed with cardboard boxes. They might glow very cosily in winter. Wide roads,
with far more traffic now than in the past: the hurtling, bashed,
spectacularly dirty little buses, underlying colour cream, but also a
caste system of cars, with Ladas and old Gaz'es at the bottom, and
then newer and more Western-looking models of Russian car, then
at the top Toyotas and the occasional VW. Not the BMWs Simmi
says crowd New-Russian Moscow. Footpaths, back from the roads,
often losing their asphalt into potholes or a mosaic of cracked grey;
but a resemblance, because of the proportions of the spaces, to
a leafy American suburb. Houses/apartments under trees; paths;
wide road; mirror image of the same on the other side. A version,
strangely, of the same kind of civilisation; a similar outline with
different content.

We walked up Ilich Street – hotel, shops, cinema, post office –
crossed Morskoi to the Dom Uchonykh [House of Scientists] – a
concrete-pillared modernist cultural centre, its bare foyer with
a wall of unused enamelled noticeboards for the French Club,
Spanish Club, Philately Club, etc., and clubby 'restaurant' clearly
intended more for occasions of toasting and dancing than for
walk-in-off-the-street eating (but was anywhere for that? this is all
'special distribution channels', after all) and galleried two-storey
space with greenery, fish tanks, internal woodwork, double-height
windows, with meeting rooms opening off. Ugly-comfy Soviet
sofas. Presumably here was the exhibition area that showed the
avant-garde paintings that got people into trouble in the 1960s.
Amateur park-railing pretty landscapes now, for sale. An oasis in
winter, a Siberian vivarium, with scientific fauna and ferns.

But I really started to be delighted when we walked up Zolotaya
Dolina Street, that is, into the renamed 'Golden Valley' itself, a

downward-sloping crease in this forested bluffland above the Ob; and the sun shone in a blue Siberian sky as we entered the privileged zone of the cottages, in their (usually) overgrown gardens. As buildings, they themselves were no better executed. In fact, when you looked closely, they were boxes made of the same concrete panels as the apartment buildings, with the same clumsy cement seams, only with wooden gables and roofs on top, and lean-to conservatories with French doors. But Siberian grasshoppers were whirring underfoot, and a very kindly version of Siberian nature enveloped you: a feathery knee-high or thigh-high mix of ferns and bracken and nettles and flowers down below, some like hollyhocks, some like foxgloves, some like long-stemmed dandelion bushes, some like dog roses, some as blue as cornflowers – and clover, and seeded grasses: a whole ungardened ground-level ecosystem, fresh and green and washed clean by the rain and warmed by the sun and with a mingled warm smell of earthy growth. And above, the other half of the invariable mix of Akademgorodok, trees always tall and slender, silver birches and pines with paper-white or ruddy-barked narrow trunks in dense groves of slender verticals, rising to a canopy of (sometimes) dark-green needles and (mostly) silver-green little leaves in profuse, delicate hanging tresses (think of the way willows hang). It was deeply peaceful walking up Voevodskii back around to the beginning of the line of Institutes on Tereshkova. Under the canopy you don't have the fen-like sense of the sky's enormity. It's a sky of leaves you get, full of dappled light and swishing movement in breezes. Only from my room on the seventh floor of the hotel do I see above the canopy. Here I'm on a level with the treetops, and the sky is 180 degrees of the world again, and I can see that an ocean of trees all roughly equal in height fills this whole wide, wide valley of the Ob; a floor of leaves only broken by the big lumps of industry here and there on the horizon.

This is the Russian wood, or a locally delicate and delightful Siberian version of it, which I saw nineteenth-century painters learning how to see and celebrate in place of pastiches of picturesque

Italy in that very good exhibition of Russian landscape art at the National Gallery in London a couple of years ago. It seems to me that this is also the archetypal Russian wood of fairy tales, *skazki*. You can see this most strongly in the extraordinarily beautiful tract of untouched woodland between Science Prospekt and University Prospekt, where the path along which workers at umpteen Institutes could commute to the 'living zone' leads through groves so quiet, so removed from concrete panelling, that it's hard to believe you're in any kind of a town. It's a kilometre or so of perfect beauty, lit slantingly by tender evening light when we walk along it with Professor F on Sunday. Not quite right, I think, to think of the woodland as making up for the roughness and clumsiness of the buildings. Necessary to think of them as forming a compound truth about the place, a compound experience: silver birches and glowing ferns, and the Presidium of the Siberian Division of the Academy of Sciences built from crumbly grey strata of flat little concrete rectangles, ridged for minimal decorative texture, somewhere between mud bricks and breeze blocks; the courses wandering appreciably, if you look at them close up. The path leading to work, and work happening (in the Computer Centre for instance) in bare prison-like corridors, dimly lit by walls of glass bricks at the ends, stone composite underfoot like polished flattened sandwiches of the bilious little chips of marble in graveyards, and phlegm-coloured paint up to head height, and bare wood office doors, and wiring looping along in bundles. Ad hoc ugliness: improvised click-together monumentally vast, humanly indifferent zero-craft termite-mound architecture. (Watch out, potentially a cheaply biological metaphor for collectivism there, but it isn't the collectivism I'm trying to catch, it's the sense of buildings generated without reference to human bodies.) And this, the combination of forest beauty and crap concrete, being the physical embodiment of Akademgorodok's intellectual freedom. Its freedom by Soviet standards anyway.

Morskoi Prospekt bends down in a convex curve over the bluff so there's no actual distant prospect to be seen of the toy ocean the

Ob dam has made, and there probably wasn't a view forty years ago either when there were fewer trees. Over the two-lane highway to Berdsk, where a man is slumped over a little plastic table next to the *kvass* [soft drink made from fermented bread] wagon he's staffing, and down a winding forest path to a wire-boxed footbridge over a railway which turns out to be the Turk–Sib line of 1930s agitprop fame, and down terraced and railed concrete steps with a bit of annunciatory seaside pizzazz to them. And out the pines at the foot of the stairs, there's the beach; sudden sand with stones not shells in it, not surprising since all the sand came here by railroad car from some sandpit somewhere. Plus many bottle caps. Signpost offering Police, Administration, Café and Toilets. Beach occupies the innermost bit of the deep bay, bite-shaped, on this side of the Ob Sea. Dam's out of sight beyond the point to the right, which is good for the illusion, and on the left the low green rim of the bluff stretches a few kilometres away to another point at about ten o'clock as you look out from the beach. With, inevitably, something heavy-industrial on the point sporting one of those very tall tapered chimneys coloured barber's-shop red and white. All this industrial metastasis makes me wonder how directly the equation of heavy industry with progress can have affected people's perceptions, whether it was really possible here in the 1960s to feel a satisfied sense that things were going well, going according to plan, going in the direction of happiness, because the green Siberian horizon was being broken in all quadrants by chimneys, because the pylons were on the march?

But between ten o'clock and say two o'clock, a pretty convincing sea horizon, with the remote far side out of sight, and a couple of sandbank islands where the trees stand like stiff haircuts. Battered white pleasure boats passing, and the odd fishing boat, and distant dinghy sails. Waves break on the shore leaving a line of shingle ejecta. They're windblown waves of course, translucent organic green-grey in this greyish Sunday morning light, like a weak algae jelly. Not salty, naturally, and not too cold. This is another of the places, like the top of the hotel, where you get free of trees and see the big Siberian sky. Puffball clouds and grey sheets of down, visibly moving this way. Hardly anybody on the beach yet – a burly round guy sunbathing while his skinny son runs about, and an older woman in a red hat taking a dip. There are red cylindrical buoys about 50 metres out to show the end of the permissible bathing area. The sun comes out and the water warms to bluey-green glassiness. There are little shelters on legs for changing in. This is beautifully expressive of the 'Promethean' strand in Marxism that Kolakowski talks about: Man seizing godlike powers over Nature. Also geared beautifully to Soviet possibilities: we can't offer any choice in the colour of your swimsuit, and it may not fit too well, but hey, we can run you up the ocean itself, no problem.

(2006)

THE SOVIET MOMENT

1962. At the airport, Len Deighton's spy Harry Palmer – not yet played by Michael Caine, not in fact even named in the original novel of *The Ipcress File* – stocks up on his reading. For the flight he buys the *New Statesman* and *History Today*. And then he adds a copy of the *Daily Worker*. Not just because our Harry is keeping up with the communist enemy, but also because Harry, unlike the uppercrust nitwits he works for in MI6, is classless and intelligent and up to the minute, and so in a menacing way at this moment in the twentieth century does communism seem to be, thanks to the public image of its homeland the USSR. For Harry, knowing about the Soviet Union is a way of keeping the sad old, creaky old, shabby-genteel world of England ironically in its place. He's fighting it, but its existence is an asset to a grammar-school oik on the rise, like him. Out beyond the bedsits and the stale crumpets and the golf-club ties, there's a giant waking, and it's proof positive that the old order of things is shiftable, that there can be novelty under the sun. Two years later in Deighton's sequel, an egg yolk-stained has-been explains pityingly to Harry that there's no way a low-rent place like England is ever going to induce a Soviet scientist to defect. 'Simitsa works with refrigerated ultra-centrifuges. They cost around £10,000 each. He has twelve of them.' That same year, 1964, the classless and up-to-the-minute Harold Wilson makes it part of his pitch to the electorate that the sad old, creaky old British economy should be supercharged with some Soviet-style scientific efficiency. And the voters buy it, white heat, 'National Plan' and all.

This was the Soviet moment. It lasted from the launch of Sputnik in 1957, through Yuri Gagarin's first spaceflight in 1961, and dissipated, along with the fear, in the couple of years following the Cuban Missile Crisis in 1962. (It was already going, in fact, at the time of the 1964 election; it was a piece of Wilson's appeal that was premised on a fading public perception, and was dropped from Labour rhetoric shortly thereafter, leaving not much behind but a paranoid suspicion of Wilson among egg-stained old-school-tie spooks.) But while it lasted the USSR had a reputation that is now almost impossible to recapture. It was not the revolutionary country people were thinking of, all red flags and fiery speech-making, pictured through the iconography of Eisenstein movies; not the Stalinesque Soviet Union of mass mobilisation and mass terror and austere totalitarian fervour. This was, all of a sudden, a frowning but managerial kind of a place, a civil and technological kind of a place, all labs and skyscrapers, which was doing the same kind of things as the West but threatened – while the moment lasted – to be doing them better. American colleges worried that they weren't turning out engineers in the USSR's amazing numbers. Bouts of anguished soul-searching filled the op-ed pages of European and American newspapers, as columnists asked how a free society could hope to match the steely strategic determination of the prospering, successful Soviet Union. President Kennedy's aide Arthur Schlesinger wrote a White House memo sounding the alarm over 'the all-out Soviet commitment to cybernetics'. While the Soviet moment lasted, it looked like somewhere which was incubating a rival version of modern life: one which had to be reckoned with, learned from, in case it really did outpace the West, and leave the lands of capitalism stumbling along behind.

Which didn't happen. Which didn't happen so thoroughly that the way the Soviet Union seemed to be between 1957 and 1964 or thereabouts has been more or less displaced from our collective memory. In the quick associative slideshow that assembles itself in our heads these days when the USSR (1917–91) is mentioned, the bits with the flags and with Stalin's moustache now lead on directly to the images of the country's dotage, when old men in ugly suits presided over an empire of antiquated tractor factories, before Gorbachev came along and accidentally put the whole thing out of its misery. The era when the place seemed to be in a state of confident, challenging, expansive maturity has fallen off our mental carousel. If in the 1970s the USSR turned out to be only 'Upper Volta with rockets' – in the words of an American diplomat unimpressed with the way that the metalled roads ran out only a few kilometres outside Moscow – then it must have always, and only, been Upper Volta with rockets. The idea of an enviable Soviet Union utterly fails to compute. We tend to assume, therefore, that the Soviet moment must have been pure illusion. Perhaps a projection of Western fears; perhaps a misunderstanding of what the headline feats like Sputnik implied about the rest of Soviet life. It had been a reasonable assumption, for nervous Western onlookers in the early 1960s, that a society which launched satellites must also have solved simple everyday problems like supplying lettuces and children's shoes. When it turned out that it wasn't so, that the Hemel Hempstead branch of Start-Rite would have represented unimaginable luxury in a Soviet city, the space rockets stopped signifying a general, enviable 'high technology'. They started looking like some pharaoh's pet project, a pyramid scraped together on the back of poverty, cruel and a bit ridiculous.

But the image of the USSR that the West briefly nurtured in the late 1950s and early 1960s was not a pure illusion. It was an exaggeration of something real; a report of a real confidence, a real feeling of success in Moscow which the West did a lot of the work of falsifying, by translating it into Western terms, and tricking it out with the West's expectations. Something really did go right or go well, then, for the Soviet Union, which we're in danger now of tidying away, like all episodes in history that point in a direction not taken, and which therefore refuse to fit into the hindsighted narrative we make out of the past for our convenience. The truths learned later about the Soviet economy were quite real, of course. It did indeed prove to be wasteful rather than efficient, cack-handed instead of strategic, alarmingly incoherent rather than terrifyingly rational. But if we tell ourselves only a case-closed story of communism as an inevitable disaster, we miss other parts of the past's reality, and foreclose on the other stories it can tell us.

Give your imagination permission to engage with some unlikely facts: in the 1950s, the USSR was one of the growth stars of the planetary economy, second only to Japan in the speed with which it was hauling itself up from the wreckage of the war years. And this is on the basis not of the official Soviet figures of the time, or even of the CIA's anxious recalculations of them, but of the figures arrived at after the Soviet Union's fall by sceptical historians with access to the archives. The Soviet economy grew through the second half of the 1950s at 5, 6, 7 per cent a year. As Paul Krugman has mischievously pointed out, the USSR's growth record in the 1950s elicited exactly the same awed commentary as Chinese and Indian growth does today. Admittedly, 'growth' did not mean exactly the same thing in the Soviet context that it did in, say, the American one (average for the period 3.3 per cent a year) or in the British one (average: 1.9 per cent; have a stale crumpet). Soviet growth was counted differently, was biased massively towards heavy industry, and did not necessarily imply a matching growth in living standards. Yet there *had* been a palpable transformation in the way Soviet citizens lived. In 1950, as in 1940 and 1930, they had been wearing hand-me-downs and living for the most part in squalid, crowded 'communal flats' carved out of antiquated pre-revolutionary buildings. In 1950, you could be director of a major Moscow hospital and live behind a curtain in one-seventeenth of a tsarist ballroom.

Ten years later, Soviet citizens were wearing new clothes and moving in ever-increasing numbers into new apartments with private bathrooms; they owned radios and pianos, and were beginning to own fridges and televisions too. In 1960, the hospital director would be sitting pretty in a sunny new-build out in the Sparrow Hills, and driving to work in a well-waxed sedan with the leaping stag logo of the Gaz company gleaming on its bonnet. Going by the measure of the capitalism of the 1930s, which is what the Soviet Union had first set out to beat in terms of living standards, Soviet life was now spectacularly prosperous. The USSR could now feed, dress, house and educate its people better than Depression America or Nazi Germany. If capitalism had remained unchanged, the Soviet Union would at this point have looked like a reasonable, if tyrannous and polluted, version of the earthly paradise. Mission accomplished, materially speaking. Instead, of course, capitalism had unfairly shifted the target by doing some growing of its own. Which was why, even on a generous estimate, the average Soviet income still only amounted to 25 per cent or so of the average American one; not bad at all, compared with the recent Soviet past, and positively inspiring from the point of view of (to pick two Soviet allies) India and China, yet not really economic victory. But the Soviet march to wealth was not finished. This was only the halfway stage on the road to a far greater abundance.

According to Marxist theory, the USSR had been on a long strange detour ever since the October Revolution. Marx had predicted that communism would come in the most advanced of the capitalist countries, not in backward, roadless, shoeless, illiterate Russia. He had supposed that the plenty of the socialist future would be built on top of all of the cruel-but-necessary development work of capitalism – that socialists would inherit a machine they only had to perfect, and to direct towards the satisfaction of everybody's needs, rather than the needs of a few top-hatted owners. The Russian situation was utterly different, and so the Bolsheviks had been obliged to operate a socialism which was doing capitalism's job for it. They'd bootstrapped an industrial base out of virtually nothing to produce the steel and cement and machine tools on which any further advance depended. They'd trained a workforce and disciplined it in the rhythms of industrial life. They'd educated a peasant society till it was bristling with science degrees. They'd also killed several million people, and massively out-brutalised the capitalist version of the Industrial Revolution, all in the name of humanity; but their information was limited, thanks to the paranoiacally limited bandwidth of the channel through which they viewed the outer world, and the vision of capitalism to which they compared their own record was Marx and Engels' portrait of Manchester a century earlier as a laissez-faire heart of darkness. They could point out to themselves that, while they had the smokestacks and the squalor and the cruelty and the black grime on every surface, they also had Palaces of Culture offering ballroom-dancing lessons and opera at low, low prices.

In any case, the job was now done, and history could resume its rightful course. Atop the steel and cement, now that they existed, could grow the pastel pagoda of utopia; Marx's utopia, that deliberately under-described idyll where wonderful machines purred away in the background, allowing the human beings in the foreground to 'hunt in the morning, fish in the afternoon, rear cattle in the evening, criticise after dinner, just as I have a mind ...' So rich and comprehensive would be the flow from the mechanical horns of plenty that it wouldn't even be necessary to measure out the goods in proportion to the work people did. Everyone could have anything, and be anything. If you've ever read one of Iain M. Banks's 'Culture' novels you'll recognise the setting, except that this postscarcity paradise was to be run on the advanced technology of the mid-twentieth century, rather than the science of a galaxy far, far away; spun up from artificial fibres, and pneumatic mail, and computers made of glowing radio-valves.

The Soviet state did engage in a certain amount of expectation-management. An eminent Academician published a paper explaining that the happy citizens of the future would have all the shoes and socks and underwear they *needed*, 'but this in no way presupposes superfluousness or extravagance'. And First Secretary Khrushchev himself reproved intellectuals who might think the future held limitless 'freedom' (which he clearly associated with sloppiness and disorder). 'Communism is an orderly, organized society', he said in March 1963. 'In that society, production will be organised on the basis of automation, cybernetics and assembly lines. If a single screw is not working properly, the entire mechanism will grind to a halt.'

Yet the reason for insisting on the caveats was that the Soviet Union had gone ahead and promised Marx's plenty anyhow. Not as a vague aspiration for the future, either – not as a conveniently floating goal designed to keep the present hopeful. Nope: as a timed, detailed schedule of events, with 1980 picked out as the date that the 'material-technical' basis for full communism would be complete, and the cornucopias would be switched on. The 1961 Party Congress adopted the imminent end of all scarcity as its official programme, thus making possibly the rashest and most falsifiable promise in the entire politics of the twentieth century. An act so foolish can only be explained through idealism: Khrushchev's own, for he was a man whose troubled relationship with his conscience required a happy ending to give him retrospective absolution, but also the idealism coded, despite everything, into the structure of the regime. It was the same heedless true-belief at work which would manifest itself a generation later in Gorbachev. The historian Stephen Kotkin describes the USSR as an edifice 'booby-trapped with idealism', and that seems about right. The great grey tyranny ran on, in some sense depended on, hopes big enough to counterbalance the country's defects. Khrushchev really meant the promises that were spelled out with such excruciating frankness in the programme. Dialectical materialism was to imply denial and self-sacrifice no longer. The philosophy was going to pay off in the most literal and direct way; it was going to do what it said on the tin, and bring the materialists their material reward. It was going to make first Russians, and then all their friends, the richest people in the world. Naturally this would involve zooming past the United States. 'Today you are richer than us', Khrushchev had told a bemused dinner party in the White House. 'But tomorrow we will be as rich as you. The day after? Even richer!' Now, in 1961, he laid it all out, hour after hour, to an auditorium stuffed with delegates from all over Moscow's half of the Cold War globe. Soon, he told the assembled Cubans and Egyptians and East Germans and Mongolians and Vietnamese, Soviet citizens would enjoy products 'considerably higher in quality than the best productions of capitalism'. Pause a moment, and consider the promise being made there. Not products that were adequate or sufficient or okay; not products a little bit better than capitalism's. Better than the best. *Considerably* better. Ladas quieter than any Rolls-Royce. Zhigulis so creamily powerful they put Porsche to shame. Volgas whose doors clunked shut with a heavy perfection that made Mercedes engineers munch their moustaches in envy.

So the confidence that allowed Khrushchev to quip and hector and shoe-bang his way across the world stage was founded partly on a truth about the present, partly on a profound mistake about the future. That the Soviet dream didn't work out, that in 1980 Soviet citizens were not going to be strolling in the pleasure garden of red plenty, we all know. (Khrushchev's own colleagues worked it out very quickly. They ousted him from the Politburo in the autumn of 1964 and consigned the 1961 programme to unmentionable oblivion.) What we've forgotten is that anyone ever took such a thing seriously; that it was ever anyone's sober expectation (or giddy expectation) that the grim, spartan one in the superpower duo was planning to win at hedonism.

Given that it was an error, a mirage, an astonishing mass delusion, what do we gain if we do remember it? Well, for a start, irony enough to glut even the greediest palate. Alongside our well-documented, well-founded knowledge that Soviet history was a tragedy ought to run a sense of it, too, as a comedy; a comedy of ideas and of things; a comedy in which material objects spin out of control, like the production line running awry in Chaplin's *Modern Times*, and refuse more and more catastrophically to play the roles assigned to them by bossy human intentions. Think of Laurel and Hardy pushing the piano up flight after flight of stairs until, right at the top, it gets away from them and slides right back down. That's the economic history of the Soviet Union in a nutshell: ascent, followed by pratfall. But this shouldn't be the kind of comedy in which we laugh from a position of comfy security at the fools over there; and not just because the ascent of the Soviet piano was achieved at a monstrous price in human suffering. It should be the comedy of recognition we register, at this point in the early twenty-first century when we're in mid-pratfall ourselves. Our own economic arrangements are currently generating not one but two complete sets of disastrous unintended consequences. Our failure to price the externalities of our energy use is baking the climate; our romantic indulgence of financiers has imploded our finances. We should be laughing at the Soviet disaster ruefully – with sympathy.

Don't get me wrong, here. The Soviet Union was a horrible society. Even once it had stopped purposely killing its citizens in large numbers, it oppressed them, it poisoned them with a toxic environment, it stuffed their ears continually with nonsense, it demanded their absolute passivity. It wasted their time. This last item sounds trivial. It wasn't. It had been one of the main points of the Marxist indictment of *capitalism* that it obliged people to bleed their labour-time into producing things they could feel no connection to, commodified things which had no real qualities except their price. Capitalism, Marx had argued, was a meaning-vampire, sucking away lives. Yet the Soviet attempt at an alternative came up with something worse: a form of work so divorced from usefulness that it condemned people to squander their finite store of weeks and months and years on churning out stuff you couldn't even be sure people were willing to pay for. By trying to concentrate directly on the use of things instead of their prices, the Soviet system lost hold of the one guarantee that anyone needed what was being manufactured. Result: futility, on the grand scale.

And when Soviet citizens went home from their pointless toil, with their rubles in hand, they were then systematically disadvantaged as consumers. Soviet planners had done this deliberately at first, as a matter of strategy, to maximise the resources available for future investment, but under Khrushchev they tried to stop, and found they couldn't. The logic of the whole system compelled it. In a world where you'd get into trouble if you inconvenienced a factory waiting for its supply of widgets (so long as the factory had good enough connections), you could inconvenience a shopper looking for cheese with impunity, with no bad consequences at all. So the cheese, and the shopper, were always last on the list – an afterthought in an economy that was supposed to run entirely for human benefit. Contemporary joke: the phone rings at Yuri Gagarin's apartment and his little daughter answers it. 'I'm sorry', she says, 'Mummy and Daddy are out. Daddy's orbiting the Earth, and he'll be back at 19:00 hours. But Mummy's gone shopping for groceries, so who knows when we'll see her again.'

In turn, the permanent state of shortage warped and deformed human relationships. The smooth impersonality of money-exchange in our society is so embedded that we take it absolutely for granted. If you've got the cash, you can have the thing. In the Soviet Union, having the cash was the mere beginning of the campaign to acquire the thing. Every transaction became personal, and not in a warm and fuzzy way. Since the scarce goods weren't rationed out by ability to pay, they were doled out in proportion to clout, influence, connections, ruthless calculations of mutual advantage. Soviet society was a tangled web of bullying, sycophancy, arm-twisting, back-scratching and emotional blackmail. Everyone made life as difficult as possible for those they dealt with, in order to be able to trade the easing of the difficulty for something else. You want a restaurant table, a dress, your phone repaired? Then find me some roofing felt, a Black Sea holiday, a private tutor for my son. Instead of post-capitalist freedom and sophistication, the Soviet Union offered pre-capitalist barter, with a large helping of robber baron-hood on the side.

The loudest and most important lesson of the Soviet experience should always be: don't ever do this again. Children, don't try this at home. Leave alone forever, please, this particular authoritarian recipe for bootstrapping a peasant society to wealth, because it only gets you halfway there, and leaves you surrounded by crumbling concrete and rusting machinery.

Yet we'd better remember to sympathise with the underlying vision that drove this disastrous history, because it is basically our own. As the ideological conflicts of the twentieth century recede, it becomes clearer that the Soviet project for red plenty was just one in the twentieth-century family of projects to hoik humanity out of its ancestral scarcity. The Soviet version is the cousin of ours; the loony cousin with blood 'up to the elbows' (as Khrushchev put it, when asked in his forced retirement what he regretted most), but still one of the family. Through luck rather than virtue, for the most part, we happen to live in a variant that has succeeded better, so far. Our version isn't costless either. The steel and concrete required to sustain it are created for us elsewhere, out of sight, leaving us free to stroll around our pastel pavilion, on the side of which glimmers the word 'Tesco'. Inside are piled, just as Khrushchev hoped, riches to humble the kings of antiquity. But terms and conditions apply.

More surprisingly, there is something specific to sympathise with in the intellectual ambition of the Soviet moment. I'm sorry, you may say, thinking of the well-censored dullness of official Soviet thought – the *what*? Yes, for much of the eighty years during which the USSR was the planet's unique experiment in running a non-market economy, the experiment was a stupid experiment, a brute-force experiment. But during the Soviet moment there was a serious attempt to apply the intellectual resources of the educated country the Bolsheviks had kicked and bludgeoned into being. All of the perversities in the Soviet economy that I've described above are the classic consequences of running a system without the flow of information provided by market exchange; and it was clear at the beginning of the 1960s that for the system to move on up to the plenty promised so insanely for 1980, there would have to be informational fixes for each deficiency. Hence the emphasis on cybernetics, which had gone in a handful of years from being condemned as a 'bourgeois pseudo-science' to being an official panacea. The USSR's pioneering computer scientists were heavily involved, and so was the authentic genius Leonid Kantorovich, nearest Soviet counterpart to John von Neumann and later to be the only ever Soviet winner of the Nobel Memorial Prize in Economics. Their thinking drew on the uncorrupted traditions of Soviet mathematics. While parts of it merely smuggled elements of rational pricing into the Soviet context, other parts were truly directed at outdoing market processes. The effort failed, of course, for reasons which are an irony-laminated comedy in themselves. The sumps of the command economy were dark and deep and not accessible to academics; Stalinist industrialisation had welded a set of incentives into place which clever software could not touch; the system was administered by rent-seeking gangsters; the mathematicians were relying (at two removes) on conventional neoclassical economics to characterise the market processes they were trying to simulate, and the neoclassicists may just be wrong about how capitalism works.

But if the horrible society of the Soviet Union left any legacy worth considering, if a pearl were ever secreted by the Soviet Union's very diseased oyster, this is it. And so follows the oddest implication of the Soviet moment. It may not be over. It may yet turn out to be unfinished business. For, from the point of view of 'economic cybernetics', the market is only an algorithm. It is only one possible means of sharing out and co-ordinating economic activity: a means with very considerable advantages, in terms of all the autonomous activity and exploration of economic possibilities it allows, but not the only one, and not necessarily the best either, even at allowing autonomy and decentralisation. In the twentieth century, devising the actual apparatus for a red plenty was an afterthought to the ideology. In the twenty-first century, it may be the algorithm that appears ahead of a politics to advocate it. In which case, the contest of plenties will be on again. And every year our processing power increases.

(2010)

PLENTY

For 6,000 years, from the dawn of agriculture to a gnat's blink back, historically speaking, all human beings lived in one, universal situation. If you want to see it, you have only to go to the airport and catch a plane to anywhere that isn't Europe, North America or East Asia: because most human beings live in the same situation still. It's this. People work very hard, and goods are scarce. In the span of the year between planting and harvest, people go hungry, because they're waiting for the crops. If the harvest fails, people stay hungry, and they start to consume the means of their own survival – the cow, the seed corn – in order to last out till next year. Locusts, diseases and marauders make random raids. Droughts and floods make their visitations. If you find a large diamond in your field, someone more powerful comes and nicks it from you. If you find two large diamonds, the powerful person nicks your field and turns it into a diamond mine. Most people, most of the time, manage to rear at least some of their children successfully, and the struggle continues into the next generation. But people don't expect that the passing of time will see a reliable gain in prosperity. Like the White Queen in *Alice*, it takes all the running they can do to stay in the same place. Good times, as they know them, are a matter of cycles. The good times come and then they go again: whether on the short cycle of the agricultural year, when a good crop makes the land yield a brief fatness, or on the longer cycles of climate and history, which can make some decades or centuries better than others. At the very best, there can be a lucky time when everything seems to go right for a while at once. The weather smiles, the ruler is benevolent and competent, the trade routes swell, your particular nation does well at war, there are marble facings on the buildings in the capital city. Such times are remembered as golden ages, recalled again and again in fireside talk as the time of the great Augustus, or of Haroun al-Raschid, or of King Arthur. But they pass. They always pass. 'Cities and thrones and powers / Stand in time's eye / Almost as long as flowers / That daily die' – wrote Kipling, who knew that the British imperial time he thought golden was also destined to go, to turn grey and to blow out like the dandelion. The universal experience of mankind has been that feasts are brief, and are always, always followed by fasts.

So after a day getting no further forward, another perpetual resource for the skinny people sitting at the fireside has been the shared dream of a feast that never ends. Of an abundance that is permanent not cyclical. Of a state of being that seizes the instant when the fat of the land runs down your chin, and lets you live there forever, freed from the plough, freed from toil, freed from scarcity. The sign of these fantasies, the symbol under which skinny dreamers have stowed them down the generations, is the cornucopia, the 'horn of plenty'. Sometimes the cornucopia turns up in mythology in disguise – 'the little porridge pot' that never runs out in English folklore is a squat pewter version dispensing an oozy grey bounty, and the Magic Pudding of Norman Lindsay's Australian fairy tale capers about on little legs offering steak 'n' kidney with jam roly-poly for afters, in the tropical heat – but the classical form, the form you see it in in temple carvings, is the curved cone strung with flowers and ribbons. Somewhere back here in the shape is a fusion of the biological bits and bobs that achieve human fertility, and somewhere here too in the function is a salute to the everyday marvel of ordinary agriculture, which blows a raspberry in the face of entropy by giving you back ten turnips when you only put one in the ground. But the cornucopia goes further; wishes further. It asks for reproduction set free from biology's limits. It asks for quantity run wild. From its curved trunk which isn't quite like a penis, from its open mouth which isn't quite like a vagina, roll forth fruits without regard to season, vegetables that never needed to be manured or weeded. Out of nowhere pours abundance. Into the world of incompleteness, of straining to make do, streams stuff to make good all deficiencies, in amounts beyond counting.

Not surprisingly, the dream of plenty often merges with the prospect of heaven, especially where heaven is seen as God's recompense for whatever was in short supply in life. In the Quranic heaven, for example, water flows as it hardly ever does in Arabia. But since the dream is (after all) the dream of a full mouth, of working your way along the butter-dripping kernels of an infinite corncob, it also has manifestations that are cheerfully low and entirely this-worldly, in which physical abundance doesn't merge into the plenitude of the divine, but exists down here somewhere, if you could only find it. Not dreams of paradise, in other words, but of the earthly paradise. Medieval Europe had the Land of Cockaigne, where the rivers run with cream and ready-roasted piglets run around squeaking 'Eat me! Eat me!' Depression America had the Big Rock Candy Mountains, where the cigarettes grow on trees and 'little streams of alcohol come a-trickling down the rocks'. There was a lake of stew, and of whiskey too, and (it was reported) you could paddle all around them in a big canoe. This dream leaps over the boundaries of times and places. It is transcultural, just as scarcity is transcultural. It does not expect to be fulfilled. Or to be believed. It's the just-material, just-for-pleasure, foolish version of the serious religious dream of redemption. All the while, beneath the fantasy, the reality it's giving the dreamer a break from remains visible. Cockaigne's true context is famine. The song of 'The Big Rock Candy Mountain' could have waved a wand and made all the pains of a hobo's life vanish, but instead it only modified them to the extent of giving wooden legs to the railroad cops who chased him, and rubber teeth to the dogs who bit him. Dogs and cops remained, too solid for a mere dream of plenty to abolish them.

Then something unexpected happened. We learned how to build a mechanical cornucopia. Early models were clumsy. They covered acres of ground, leaked choking black smoke, and ripped off the limbs of unwary children. Later designs, though, ran with a clean reassuring hum, and did any damage safely over the horizon – or in such small increments that it was easy to forget about it. And the world changed, for some of us. Instead of the feasts and the fasts, the good luck and the bad luck, we moved into a world where time promised improvement, where we could expect there to be mostly a little more every year: 3 per cent more, 5 per cent more, 2 per cent more. Compounded. The dream began to come true. The unlikely dream, the dream not intended to have load-bearing qualities. Over the last half-century about a billion people have moved into the dream, and hundreds of millions more are presently making the escape from our ancestral scarcity. In our time, for the first time ever in human history, plenty has become a fact. We may not recognise it, but the Big Rock Candy Mountain is where we live now; we have become citizens of Cockaigne. The success or failure of harvests no longer makes any difference to the food supply, which is gigantic and continuous. There's more to eat in a single supermarket than in any medieval painting of the garden of earthly delights. We have to pay for it, of course, but mostly we can. We aren't pressed up against the glass looking at a plenty we can't touch. Compared to what came before, the cornucopia flows for even the poorest of us in the rich countries.

And food was only the first commodity in which scarcity was abolished. It looms large and urgent in the dreams of those who don't have enough of it, but we've moved on to the other scarcities that were waiting in a row to be abolished once hunger was dealt with. From our cornucopias also pour houses that keep out the weather, clean water to bathe in daily, medicines to prolong life, clothes no-one wore before us – and then *stuff*, oh a torrent of stuff of unimaginable profusion and variety, stuff to tempt us, stuff to entertain us, stuff to decorate ourselves with, stuff to transport us from place to place, stuff to store other stuff in. So much stuff that the idea of any one individual being able to sample all of it seems laughable. It seems self-evident to us now that even the richest person couldn't taste the whole cornucopia – wouldn't even want to – though in the scarce times that've only just passed away, kings and magnates really did try to drag some of whatever was going to their mud palaces. Our plenty far outweighs the consuming power of each of us as we contemplate it. Welcome to the magic porridge pot, welcome to the lake of stew.

Now we have it, though, we aren't sure we do have it. It doesn't feel the way that we expected, before, it was going to feel. People who live in scarcity and dream of plenty have a very clear idea of what plenty would be. It's what would make up the deficiencies they presently feel, what would lift the constraints that presently grip them. It is self-evident to them what 'enough' would mean. The fact that they haven't got enough enforces the definition of it. Enough is what they lack. When they look at the rich world and see that everyone (or almost everyone) in it is washed, clothed, housed and fed, they know what they are seeing. They say to themselves, if I lived there, I would rejoice and be glad that the fasting was over and the feasting was permanent; that my children could be certain of what I was never certain of. That's why they're willing to pay their savings to human traffickers, and to suffocate in freight containers. Even in the rich world, during the earlier stages of the transition to plenty, what it would consist of seemed obvious. When Keynes wrote *Economic Possibilities for Our Grandchildren* in the 1930s, he looked forward to a time near at hand when, quote, 'the economic problem would be solved'. Not an economic problem, or some economic problem*s* – *the* economic problem, the one singular finite problem that has existed from the beginning of economics as an endeavour, and about which it was originally so gloomy. That is, the problem of allocating scarce resources so that everyone has enough. The founding fathers shook their heads. Malthus believed that population always grew faster than the food supply. Result: famine. Ricardo believed that workers' wages could never rise higher than the bare minimum cost of breeding up the next generation of baby workers. Result: penury. So it seemed quite clear to Keynes in the Depression, working on the tools he thought could prevent all future depressions, that if a society could just provide everyone in it with a secure job, a place to live and enough to eat, then the one big issue of economics would be dealt with. We'd have done it. We'd have solved the whole of the material part of the problem of being human. We'd have enough, so we'd be free to move on and solve other problems. And how we'd flourish.

Well, we are Keynes's grandchildren, and great-grandchildren, and great-great-grandchildren. But that isn't how it feels to us now, living in the plenty that the whole world dreamed of, and the majority of the world dreams of still. Indeed, it's far easier to recognise from the outside that plenty is what we do possess, because our everyday experience amid the cornucopia's spilling fruits is certainly not that the striving is over, that the 'economic problem' is solved, that the material issues of human life are dealt with. On the contrary: we are still running as hard as we can, with apparently undiminished urgency, and our desires still feel to us as if they are thwarted and fulfilled in the proportions you'd expect from a resistant universe. We are sceptical of our plenty; we focus on what we haven't got yet, we ask ourselves if this is really abundance or not. (I propose a rule: if you aren't sure whether you really live in plenty, *you do*.) We tell ourselves stories about how plenty will really arrive sometime in the future, when the price of bandwidth falls to zero, when nanotechnology makes atoms assemble themselves just like that into the objects of our choice – not realising that those new dreams are just retreads, speeded-up repetitions of what already happened when the Industrial Revolution kicked our cornucopia into gear and first showed us that plenty doesn't come from diamonds, but from the power to multiply a widget by a million. By historical standards, the times are already magically good. But then, we don't judge by historical standards. Now that we're in plenty we don't constantly measure it against the scarcity it replaced. You can't be grateful for avoiding something you've never experienced. You can only count your blessings for so long, and then the new world has to be engaged with on its own terms; the new world in which the material struggle does not lie behind us, and new wants present themselves unendingly to be fulfilled.

Somehow we'd believed that achieving plenty would mean getting wants and needs disentangled. The whole idea of having enough depends on being able to tell the difference. Those in the past who took a utopian look forward to plenty tended to imagine, just like Keynes, that there was a common-sense contrast of feeling involved in the difference between wanting and needing; and so moving from one to the other, from the era of needing a bowl of soup to the era of wanting a Rolex, would be signalled by a change of mood, a kind of relaxation of urgency, or, to put it at its most positive, by the birth of a new kind of human freedom. Marx, for instance, who was as besotted by the runaway productivity of industrial technology as any enthusiast for the New Economy during the internet bubble, thought that, when the engines of plenty were running for everybody's benefit, we'd be free to start discovering what human beings were actually like, what our nature might be with the leg irons of need no longer hobbling us. No longer needing to scrabble for our daily bread, we'd gaze at the world of things with a playful, impartial curiosity; we'd gaze at other people and know for the first time with absolute clarity that they weren't things, since we didn't have to treat them as things any more to assure our own survival.

The trouble with this vision (and the others like it) is that it's incompatible with the recipe by which our plenty came. We don't know how many recipes for a cornucopia there are; we only know which have worked and which have failed among those that we have tried. Our local one is made harder to state because of some people's insistence that markets are its only ingredient, when laws and institutions are just as important. But at the heart of it is a decision to produce what people will pay for, and only what people will pay for, without enquiring further into why. Our cornucopia deliberately makes no distinction between things we want and things we need: it can't, without beginning to ration the tumbling flow of goods and to make unplentiful decisions about our best interests. Where need becomes want is left to our private judgement, at least in theory. All we can consult is the blurred continuum in our heads with soup at one end and the diamond-studded Rolex at the other. But the other peculiarity of our plenty is that, driven by desire without distinction, it doesn't include a way of stably stopping when an elegant sufficiency has been achieved for everyone. It's an economy of insatiability. It has to grow to function. It cannot aim at any particular level of prosperity. It can only achieve any particular tideline of plenty by overshooting it, and keeping on going. And if we all did decide, one at a time or all together, on some mark that represented adequate plenty, and stopped buying at it, our plenty wouldn't glide calmly to a halt. It would collapse, because the system depends on competition, and whatever ceases to compete in our system doesn't just stop rising, it immediately and inexorably sinks.

That's why in our age of plenty everyone who can is still working frantically hard. That's why our age of plenty does not resemble the age of leisure that was being predicted just as plenty's threshold was being crossed, back in the 1950s and 1960s. It's comical now to remember the promise that people in 'the year 2000' would only work two or three hours a day, and would need to fill the remaining hours with a glorious efflorescence of golf-playing, symphony-composing, helicopter-piloting and basket-weaving. It isn't that the wealthy future turned out less wealthy than the futurologists of 1960 imagined. On the contrary, a range of self-indulgences now exists that they never even dreamed of. Parascending, anyone? Karaoke? Broadband online wargaming? It's that the structure of our wealth forbids us to run any slower. And, to keep us consuming at the rate we need to in order to expand our plenty (which is to say, to maintain it) the persuaders labour night and day to keep us dissatisfied. We are more advertised at than anyone in history, because it is so vital that we shouldn't fall into happy, non-buying repletion. 'Maslow's hierarchy' is cited a lot as the basis for our continuing hunger. It says that, in order, we satisfy the needs for food, for shelter and for clothing, and then move on to our need for esteem, as manifested in a handily large number of ways, such as the need for a rewritable DVD player, the need for a sports car, or the need for an aromatherapy massage at an exclusive spa resort. But Maslow's hierarchy is a codification of what the economy of plenty *needs* to be true. The classical economists, the dismal scientists who said that scarcity would last forever, believed in 'diminishing marginal utility', the traditional view that as your appetite for something is satisfied, you want each extra helping of it a bit less. A hungry person really, really wants a slice of toast. The second slice is nice but not quite so nice; they can take or leave the third slice, and they probably do leave the fourth one. This, our age of plenty has supplemented. Okay, we say reluctantly. You've probably had enough toast for now – enough *multigrain granary toast with unsalted organic Normandy farmhouse butter* – but that doesn't mean there's nothing else you want, does it? Just alternate your hungers, and you can keep craving all the time. Go on, turn away from toast for now, turn with undiminished urgency to that wish for polka-dotted silk handkerchiefs, for tango lessons, for Art Deco ornaments. You know you want to.

Of course, the problems of having too much are far better than the problems of having too little, but no wonder we feel bilious. No wonder we feel confused. No wonder that some of us balloon into obesity on the cornucopian diet, and some of us starve ourselves, and some find artificial ways of bringing scarcity back. The little roasted pigs rush by, squeaking 'Eat me!' I'm sorry, we say: maybe later. I feel a bit . . . full. I feel a bit . . . sick.

(2005)

RESPONSIBLE FICTION,
IRRESPONSIBLE FACT

I can tell two completely different stories about how I got to the peculiar blend of the fictional and the documentary in my book *Red Plenty*, and both of them are true.

The first is pragmatic. My familiar tools stopped working on me. I had been a practitioner of a kind of non-fiction that used the language of experience to warm history, to make it intimate, to make it humanly satisfying in the way that biography and fiction are satisfying. My motto, if I had had such a thing, would have been Viktor Shklovsky's famous claim (in his 1917 essay 'Art as Technique') that 'The purpose of art is to impart the sensation of things as they are perceived and not as they are known.' This seemed to me to be as applicable to ambitious non-fiction as to fiction. Writing should vivify knowledge, I thought, until it wasn't knowledge any more but sensation. And I knew how to bring exposition to life, in this sense, starting with a process of interview, and building back towards narrative. That's what I'd done in *Backroom Boys*, a book about engineering as an imaginative, almost narrative act. I and my dictaphone – this is before smartphones swallowed the function of voice recording – went to see a series of British rocket engineers, radio engineers, software engineers, genome decoders and video game designers, and they talked. They were happy to talk; in many cases I was the first person outside the profession who'd shown an interest in their technical achievements. So, when I was commissioned to write what was then a reasonably conventional piece of non-fiction about mathematical economics in the Soviet Union in the 1950s and 1960s, I set off to apply my practised method. I emailed surviving mathematical economists, of whom there were still a reasonable number, this being 2004–5. A surprising number didn't reply, but some did; I didn't speak Russian, but I was confident that with the help of an interpreter I could get around the language issue; I booked a trip. And found that while people were willing to be very hospitable, and to feed me pickled mushrooms and homemade jam, and to get me agreeably drunk, they had no desire at all to spill their guts to a stranger with a tape machine. They had all grown up in the Soviet Union, after all, and Soviet experience, as I really should have realised earlier, had provided them with powerful incentives not to confide their private judgements of anything, least of all erstwhile policy initiatives that tangled ideology, science and the Soviet economic record together – not to strangers; not to anyone who had not demonstrated trustworthiness over years, rather than over the minutes of an interview. What they were signalling, with the copious vodka and plates of little gherkins, was that, if I cared to spend say half a decade proving myself, they might then be willing to creep up allusively, indirectly, to the subject in which I was interested. But I didn't have the time or the budget. My method worked for the history of the British twentieth century; it absolutely did not for the Russian twentieth century. Flying home from St Petersburg with my plans in disarray, I thought to myself, *I wish I could just make it up!* And then, *Could I make it up? Or at least find out how much of the job of exposition* could *be handled in fiction?* That's the pragmatic story.

But I have a literary one too. Arriving at (a strange sort of) fiction was also a matter of following out a logic within my existing model of writing. I was already dissatisfied, and therefore ready for the change.

It's not that I was disenchanted with non-fiction as such. I was, and am, a firm advocate of non-fiction's dignity, and its flexibility. I believed and still believe that, when written well, it has the scope to offer as rich and subtle an encounter with the world as fiction does. In part, because of its vast choice of techniques, its extraordinary array of different ways of knowing, which could be combined even *more* variedly, in firework displays of ad hoc consilience. Biographical knowing, biological knowing, mathematical knowing, art-historical knowing, psychological knowing, statistical knowing, poetic knowing: all of them available, all of them seeming to me to be divided by much more porous disciplinary walls than people imagine; all of them therefore open to combination and synthesis. Hybrids, built on the interesting boundary zones where things could mix, were what I was most drawn to. My first book, *I May Be Some Time*, was a combination cultural history and travel book; my second, *The Child that Books Built*, was a memoir mixed up with literary criticism and child psychology; *Backroom Boys*, as well as being about the minds of engineers, and therefore a piece of science writing, was also a stealth industrial history of Britain since 1945.

My motive in all of these was always to explain. But to explain by showing, by isolating a process or pattern, and giving it a visible body of narrative. You could say that my interest in anything was structured by the story I found to tell about it. I was especially attracted to cases where that was challengingly difficult to do, because the process was very abstract (or very dull), or because the story-like sense I could detect was distributed across much material, and only lightly or faintly present in each bit of it. But to bring out a story in those circumstances required a correspondingly intense commitment to selecting relevant detail, and then to separating it out from its background. Even if I aimed at the greatest possible documentary fidelity – and I did, because the point of the exercise was always to unfold something that was really there, to know more of the world as it actually is – I was still, I came to see, engaged in a kind of exaggeration. I was exaggerating things into visibility. I was altering the proportions of historical scenes to allow my chosen story to dominate their foreground; at least, the foreground of those scenes as they existed in my narrative. And narrative *isn't* experience. It's made out of experience, but of course it isn't the thing itself, and certainly it isn't the flowing, multitudinous, incommensurable sum of human experiences that constitutes the real past. Narrative, as well as ordering the real, imposes its own demands for the qualities that harmonise narrative. Narrative, to resolve, requires a shape that experience may not obligingly provide. Narrative, to be unified, requires an intelligible development of mood. It is a structure of feeling, unfolding in time. And therefore I was selecting for feeling.

As I did so, what I wrote worked less and less clearly as argument. This became particularly apparent when I came to revise my work. You can swap out the parts of an argument, but the pieces of a structure of a feeling aren't straightforwardly replaceable. Take one out, and you don't have a different contention; you have the same contention, sagging. Put in a piece of a different mood, and you don't (necessarily) have a differently mixed mosaic of data, pointing to a different conclusion; you may well have an aesthetic kludge, a mood-gridlock, a blend of colours summing to a murky brown.

Also, and pressingly, an issue was arising to do with the ownership of all this feeling. Back to Viktor Shklovsky. 'The purpose of art is to impart the sensation of things as they are perceived and not as they are known.' Fine: but, I was coming to think, irresponsible looked at one way, when it came to my kind of non-fiction. Because, perceived by whom, exactly? Known by whom? Experienced by whom? Serious history, history as an academic discipline, knows who is doing its knowing. It comes with its own epistemology built in. Ever since the nineteenth-century intellectual revolution that created it, it has proceeded by attribution, by labelling the source of every known item, and then adding it to the mass, to the general picture, of what *history* knows; what some ideal collective knower understands of the past. It can be continued through 10,000 or

100,000 separate efforts, and still be one enterprise. Fashion, new interpretations, new ideas change the picture and keep changing it, but every time the interpretations themselves are labelled, and can be weighed and disagreed with and if necessary discounted; and the aim remains, through all the never-ending evolutionary tussling, to have one picture, which is what history knows.

I wasn't doing that. I was creating, as it were, synthetic subjects to do my knowing. I was knitting together structures of feeling the reader could see, and share, which would not have been visible or palpable, quite, to any of the participants at the time. I was constructing stories that only made sense by angling the historical scenery to face outward along exactly the right sight-lines, whether or not, in the actual past, there had happened to be anyone placed at the focal point where the lines crossed, to see my artful effect. In the chapter about the beginnings of mobile phones in the UK in *Backroom Boys*, for example, and the engineers of the infant Vodafone radio-planning the urban and rural landscapes of Thatcher's Britain, I had coaxed and tweaked the technical explanations of how radio planning worked to summon the vision of a wave-swept invisible ocean overhead with the familiar A-roads and Little Chefs as its sea floor; this in turn letting me bring in the magic island of *The Tempest*, and to support the mood when I introduced Caliban's line 'The isle is full of noises' as an enchanted image for mobile chatter; this in turn putting the mobile-phone chapter of the book into unifying conversation with the opening chapter, about British rocket engineers of the 1960s launching satellites called Ariel and Prospero. Technology was deliberately blurred into magic, Shakespeare deployed as connective emotional tissue for British technology, even though the radio planners, so far as I knew, never thought in Shakespearean terms at all. (The rocket engineers did. They called the extra-fat version of one of their missiles 'Falstaff'.)

I was still proud of how these effects worked as art, but increasingly discontented with how they worked as history.

And I began to see advantages in going from an implicitly fictive process to an explicit one. It struck me, suddenly, that the way a novel attributes knowledge is actually an analogy for the way that scholarly history does it. Unless the viewpoint is omniscient, which is rare, all knowledge in a novel is owned knowledge. It is explicitly someone's. A novel deals, as E.M. Forster put it, in 'intermittent knowledge'; it sums knowledge by creating an interference pattern in which different, limited points of view overlap, contrast, and in an aesthetic sense complete each other. In other words, there is still a means to create an emergent effect, a synthesis not limited to the perceptions of any individual actor – but all the perceptions *belong* to individual actors. True, I thought, the actors would be imaginary, but the trade-off seemed fair. What I lost in direct non-fictional purchase on the world I would gain in a more responsible, therefore truthful, epistemology, and in a more unblurred line between real and not-real.

So the form of *Red Plenty* was two things simultaneously, for me. It was a pragmatic solution to a research problem; and at the same time it was a move towards the honesty of making characters, explicitly, the knowers in my work. Writing it the way I did enabled me to do far more justice to what I wanted to be my theme, which was always ideas *in lives*, muddy, murky, ambiguous, this-worldly, anti-abstract. I could deal with mathematical economics, again, as it was perceived, but now with the perceptions, the emotions, grounded; given time and place and setting, and filtered through Soviet souls one by one.

(2011)

IDOLS OF THE MARKETPLACE

When Francis Bacon was sketching out the foundations for experimental science 400 years ago, he drew up a list of the kinds of mistakes and confusions that were going to get in the way. 'Idols', he called them, after the statues and images of strange gods that the Bible tells you you must not worship, because he thought that, like a golden effigy in a heathen temple, these were ideas that misled people about how the world worked, that encouraged people to see qualities in things that weren't really there. Probably, at the back of his mind, he had the famous denunciation of idols in the Book of Psalms. Psalm 115: 'Their idols are silver and gold, the work of men's hands. They have mouths, but they speak not: eyes have they, but they see not.' In other words, they may look impressive, they may look as if they have power, but everything they have we actually gave them ourselves. The mouths and eyes are only dents in the metal, made by our own hands. This seemed to Bacon to capture something important about the perennial human tendency to mix up our own characteristics and the world's. His list of modern idols (modern for 1600) included the Idols of the Tribe – things we believe because the whole human species is set up that way; the Idols of the Den – things we believe because our individual temperament leads us to; and the Idols of the Theatre, which are the things we believe because they're the flimflam that happens to be live on stage in our culture just now. But, he said, 'the Idols of the Marketplace are the most troublesome of all, namely those which have entwined themselves round our understanding from the association of words and names'. It was *language* that was the very biggest problem, with its seductive network of connections between things, and echoes, and metaphors, and even rhymes, all linking the world up obtrusively as you tried to see what was really there; all telling you loud stories about the world while you tried to listen to the quiet facts about objects as they were in themselves. There you were, trying to do some botany, trying to have a careful look at a sample of *Rosa damascena*, wondering how the ingenious Turks and Syrians extracted attar of roses from its petals – and suddenly, give or take a century or two, in came Mr Burns, pointing out that his love was like a red, red rose, and then Mr Blake, claiming that an invisible worm, that flies in the night, in the howling storm, had found out its bed of crimson joy. Sex, death, corruption, the texture of silk sheets: before you knew it, you were completely entwined with stuff that had nothing to do with the flower in front of you. Stuff that made thinking clearly about it difficult, since the words seemed to have a logic of their own, running at cross-purposes to real observation and deduction.

Francis Bacon called his most troublesome idol after the market-place simply because that was where so much talking got done; talking, and exchanging, or as he put it, 'the commerce and associa-tion of men with each other'. But he would have been amazed by the idea that anyone could treat a market itself as an idol – that anyone could feel the kind of worshipful confusion he was warning against, about the actual process of buying and selling. Ideas start to look important at different points in history, and in 1600 markets were not yet the focus for very much thinking. As far as Bacon was concerned, they would have been functional, rather obvious things, about which there wasn't much to say. When he talked about the idols of the marketplace, the picture that formed in his mind could have been of the once-a-week markets held in the market towns of his England, all spaced out around 15 miles from each other, so no-one with a cartload of turnips to sell ever had to drive more than 7 miles or so there and 7 or so back, a roughly two-hour journey. Or maybe it was a picture of the daily street markets in London, or of the giant trade fairs still going from the middle ages, where the meadowlands outside cities turned into temporary grids of tent-stalls and tent-warehouses. As an educated person, of course, he knew about the *agora* of ancient Athens, which had been a space for shopping and a space for politics at the same time: a starting-point for the whole European sense that commerce *and association* happened in marketplaces. But in none of these cases will it have struck him, or anyone else much, that there was anything remarkable going on in the actual transactions in which the turnips changed hands. Or, to put it another way, that there was any wider significance you could pick out of the relationship between the buyer and the seller of the turnips, *as* a buyer and a seller, as opposed to all the other relationships that they might be in with each other, as social inferiors and superiors, as neighbours, as members of a church congregation, as friendly individuals or hostile ones. Why would you choose to concentrate on the turnips? The market relationship wasn't prominent yet. It didn't stick out in people's minds. It didn't look as if it explained anything beyond itself.

But over the centuries since, markets have played a larger and larger role in the ways we explain the world to ourselves. Taking their cue from the first sophisticated financial markets, in seventeenth-century Amsterdam and eighteenth-century London, then working their way back with new curiosity to the humbler domains of turnip-swapping, people started to see how much of human behaviour hinged on the moments the coins were counted out – even if people were unconscious of it, even in areas of human life apparently far remote from the buying and selling. When the buyer and the seller arrived at a price, it was realised, that one number, that one quantity of shillings and pence, worked as a kind of instant, spot calculation of the relative value, to those people at that instant, of drastically different uses of human time and labour. The price of a pound of turnips sold to a tailor tells you how much turnip-farming is worth in terms of stitching and bias-cutting. Suddenly, the two activities have become convertible. And calculations like that are going on all the time, and forming the basis on which people plan for the future, so the price of turnips will help to determine how much turnip-farming goes on in the economy – and how much tailoring, too. Without anyone having to give explicit instructions, without the participants necessarily being aware of it, markets co-ordinated the busy, various world. This was a discovery that particularly appealed to those who were eager for there to be sources of order in human affairs which didn't depend on the powerful *giving* orders: or who took a sceptical view of how important our conscious intentions were in getting things done. If, through markets, the world ran itself, where was the need for kings? If, through markets, self-interest tied society adequately together, where was the need for the enforcement of virtue? Adam Smith famously pointed out that it wasn't the 'benevolence' of the butcher, the brewer and the baker that brought us our dinner – just the exchangeability of a certain amount of butchering, brewing and baking for a certain amount of whatever we did. He *didn't*, quite, call the force that co-ordinated human affairs through the market the 'invisible hand'. That was a semi-satirical phrase of his, used to describe the way that the greed of the rich has consequences they don't expect. But it was taken up later as a name for what he preferred to call 'the obvious and simple system of natural liberty'. The invisible hand became visible shorthand for the principle that markets, on their own, create order.

Politics ever since, you could say, has been an argument about how much power market relationships should be allowed to have, about how much of life should be handled through prices. There were always limits. The question was only where they lay.

113

Conservatives of all kinds tended to like markets because they seemed, in a rough-and-ready way, to reward individual deserving; and conservatives tended to dislike markets because they threatened traditional, unpriceable relationships, including the traditional obligations of the strong to defend the weak. No, said conservative politicians in Britain in the 1830s, you may *not* calculate a price for sending a seven-year-old boy up a soot-choked chimney. Radicals of all kinds tended to like markets because they undermined old, encrusted social structures; they menaced toffee-nosed gits the world over. 'All that is solid melts into air', wrote Marx ecstatically, in this mood. He saw every link between people being destroyed except 'callous cash payment', and he almost seemed to welcome it. It might be a colder world, where the market ruled, but at least it didn't decorate its hierarchies with pretty sentiments. On the other hand, radicals disliked markets because they seemed to produce spectacular injustices towards those who only had their labour to sell. No, said social democratic politicians at the end of the nineteenth century, you may *not* calculate the price of a week's work in industry by seeing what Amalgamated Gigantic Ltd can persuade an individual worker to accept. You will have to deal with your employees in an equally amalgamated, equally gigantic form, in labour unions. Market prices might co-ordinate the world, but they clashed repeatedly with other values, old and new.

Then, for most of the twentieth century, markets had a rival; another system, in a variety of flavours from murderous through to humane and scrupulous, which promised to do the job of markets and do it better, do it more purposefully, so that the slow, lackadaisical flow of information about how much turnip-farming there should be every time someone bought turnips was replaced by quick, decisive, explicit choices. It didn't work. Twentieth-century socialism killed millions of people in its murderous versions, and in its humane versions won dignified, civilised lives for millions of people who wouldn't have had them otherwise. But the murders were pointless, and the dignified lives were achieved by redirecting profits that had already been made in markets. Once the flow of information through an economy reached a certain fairly low level of richness and complication, it turned out, the institutions that were supposed to make the quick, decisive choices started to flounder – whereas markets seemed to be able to go on digesting any amount of information, one lackadaisical bit at a time. Socialism didn't, after all, have a working alternative for the basic thing that markets do.

And now it's now. The rival has disappeared, and, perhaps in reaction, markets rule in our minds. We praise markets, we applaud markets, we reflexively attribute good things to markets, with far less scepticism than ever before, far less attention to the limits of the power of price. Not only are markets universally acknowledged as the one, the only plausible way for the economic life of societies to be organised. In more and more ways we have started to see markets, or market-like patterns, in the non-economic behaviour of the universe. It's as if they have become our one and only model for anything decentralised, our one label we have available to apply to anything that doesn't run on orders, from tornadoes to the eating behaviour of chimpanzees. I'm not kidding about those two examples, by the way: there really have been studies comparing the turbulent air flow in tornadoes to the global currency markets, and the fruit-gathering of chimps to the strategies of shoppers. This is an important change. When people perceived something of universal significance in markets before, it tended to be because they had a theory that they believed was universally true about the world, and had spotted a resemblance between it and something that markets did. First the theory, then markets as an illustration of the theory. The world's like this, and, to help you understand, it's a bit like a market. For example, the ancient philosopher Heraclitus believed that the cosmos was made of fire, with every other element being just fire in a state of temporary metamorphosis, sure to change back into fire in due course. What was this like? Why, like the way that olive oil could turn into money and (if you wanted) back into olive oil again, down at the *agora*. Heraclitus said: 'Everything becomes fire, and from fire everything is born, as in the eternal exchange of money and merchandise.' Now, though, when we announce that in this way or that way the world is a market, we tend to mean that the organisation of the market really is written into nature all the way through, like the words in a stick of seaside rock. You can find people saying, now, that the structure of a vegetable market or a stock exchange is a just a manifestation on our familiar scale of things of a kind of order that's manifested on every scale, throughout the universe.

Most of us, of course, don't believe anything so drastic. But then we don't have to. To have a consensus, you don't need everyone to agree. You need everyone to agree more or less about the bunch of beliefs in the middle of a subject, while its edges can be handily defined by propositions that seem bold, extreme or plain nutty, according to taste. You can also find people today, for instance, who think that markets are never-ending elections, more perfect and more powerful than the dreary old democratic kind, because they take ballots continually on every aspect of our shared existence, from our preferences in soap to – well, to our preferences in shampoo, really; that's one of the problems with that theory. You can find people who think that markets are artificial intelligences, giant reasoning machines whose synapses are the billions of decisions we make to sell or buy. You can find people, especially in America, who think that markets are God's providence at work, His way of taking care of His creation. And again, in these strong forms, most of us don't go along: we *don't* think that markets are universal ballot boxes, or that they're brains, or that the invisible hand is God's hand, any more than we believe that nature is a market. But that doesn't mean we aren't influenced. That doesn't mean that our sensible, commonsensical views here in the middle of the consensus aren't shaped by the wilder views that define its outside edges. Most of us *do* believe, in some vague, not-quite-defined way, that markets have something to do with us expressing ourselves: a weak form of the super-election idea. And that markets somehow incorporate everybody's combined knowledge, even if they don't exactly cogitate. And that they're kind of, sort of, *natural*, though we'll probably give the tornadoes a miss. And that – leaving God out of it, at least by name – markets *are* somehow wise; that they do produce the most benign possible outcomes that there can be, for the largest possible number of people.

Which brings us back to Francis Bacon. Because those are modern idolatries in just the sense he was talking about when he tried to clear the ground for the birth of experimental science. He thought that it might be possible to disenchant the world: to get the idol-worship, the magical thinking, out of it, and to see only the clear, factual, cause-and-effect connections between things. But it turned out that that could only happen by a special effort of self-discipline within a special type of thinking, reserved for science, and not perfect even there. The rest of the time, the world could not be disenchanted. It could not have the anti-wand waved over it which would kill the idols and make the magic die, for exactly the reason Bacon himself identified when he said that the most troublesome obstacle of all was going to be language. We think, for the most part, in language and through language, guided by its images, entwined with its network of connections. In the case of our present-day beliefs about markets, we don't necessarily feel that *we* know that our beliefs are true: just that it *is* known, that someone else somewhere else has worked these things out in detail. We also have a problem of perception where markets are concerned. We can't tell ourselves what markets *feel* like, directly, except in terms of atmosphere, in terms of the frenzy of an open-outcry trading floor or the tones of voice of a bloke on a stall trying to shift the last two boxes of slightly bruised bananas at four o'clock. The trouble is that markets as such are not really visible from any single vantage point, only the separate transactions that make them up; from them, the market emerges, a grand swirl of prices formed by all the interactions of all the buyers and sellers. We're in it, but we can't see it, any more than individual ants can see the logic of the whole anthill.

Unless, that is, we exploit language's power to fix it in our mind's eye, to give us (as it were) the impossible top-down view of it. So what kind of comparisons are we likely to make, given a culture presently besotted with markets, and a middle ground of opinion slung between *outré* valuations of them as embodiments of freedom, reason, God and nature? Remember: we make markets, but they don't do what any of us, individually, choose. Even the biggest individual actor in the most thinly traded market must usually deal with outcomes that are not under their control. This thing we make together acts back upon each of us as an independent force. We have a choice, in theory: we *could* carefully describe it to ourselves as a complicated phenomenon, partially of this nature and partially of that nature, different in different cases, sensitively dependent on the particular rules we institute to run it. We could, but on the whole we don't. We prefer, on the whole, to say that the market is like a red, red rose. We call on the gloriously simplifying powers of the images in our heads, which assert, in bright strong colours, that the market resembles this one vivid thing – or this one, or this one, from out of the permanent stock of images we keep for this job: the job of representing the powerful, complicated forces of our world on a scale we can handle intuitively. And so we use the imagery we used to use for good kings, for wish-granting spirits, for the God in heaven who follows the movement of every atom: for powers who are also persons, and who can therefore possess a person's intentions, a person's benevolence.

Meanwhile, here are some of the dull, detailed things that people actually do know about markets. Markets are never perfectly efficient, except in conditions of tightly defined mathematical utopia, where everyone knows everything. Markets do not handle the majority of the world's economic activity, because it's only a limited category of goods that can be traded as impersonally as turnips; for everything else, you need relationships of trust, in which price no longer does the decisive work. Markets do not run stably on their own, without regulation or supervision. Markets can be madder than any of those who participate in them, as well as wiser. Markets do not look after people. A nice severe depression is usually enough to kill that idea for a generation, but we haven't had one for a while.[11]

You can go further. Markets do not hope, dream, plan, help, show mercy, have compassion, do justice. They are silver and gold, the work of men's hands. They have mouths, but they speak not; eyes have they, but they see not.

(2007)

UNICORN HUSBANDRY

1. Unicorn husbandry

Red Plenty is wilfully devoted to the deadest of dead issues: the planning problems of a no longer existent system which has no prospect of ever becoming existent again. Unicorn husbandry, biplane manufacture, sermon publishing – take your pick of impractical comparisons. This seems like a good place to start. Because though the imp of the perverse played a major part in my decision to write the book; and I was positively attracted to the whole business of being the first person in thirteen years to consult Cambridge University Library's volumes of *The Current Digest of the Soviet Press*; and in general to the challenge of taking on the most outrageously boring subject-matter I could find, and wrestling it to the floor, and forcing it to disgorge its hidden jewel of interestingness; despite all this, I did also have some sensible motives for going where I did, and they have a lot to do with the generation I belong to.

I was twenty-seven when the Soviet Union fell, ceased to be, shuffled off this mortal coil. I was too young to have experienced the sense of it as a place which, barbarous and dictatorial though it was, nevertheless was essentially on the reasonable side of the economic argument; somewhere that, by opting for planning, had chosen the better economic model. On the other hand, I was too old to view it as a historical will-o'-the-wisp, vanishing as I studied it, and leaving nothing behind but tedium and stale air. For me, as a teenager in the early 1980s, having the traditional nuclear annihilation dream at regular intervals – my friends would usually drive past me in a bus while the asphalt melted just behind my fleeing heels – the USSR was not a possible object of admiration, but it was an object of solidity. Its defining feature was its permanence. It was an inevitable part of the planet's architecture: obsolete but immovable. And then it did move, and when it went its going suddenly disclosed a set of hidden linkages that pulled various aspects of my familiar, home experience away after it. It seemed that my Western socialism – the unbarbarous kind – had had an unsuspected dependence on the existence of the Soviet model. And not just because the USSR was definitionally useful to social democrats, letting us point and say 'Not that!' It had also served, it turned out when it was gone, as a sort of massive concrete tent-peg, keeping the Overton window (not that it was called that, yet) tethered at its left-hand edge in a way that maintained the legitimacy, in Western discussion, of all kinds of non-market thinking. When the USSR vanished, so with amazing speed in the 1990s did the entire discourse in which there were any alternatives to capitalism that had to be taken seriously. This was the biggest intellectual change of my lifetime – the replacement of one order of things, which I had just had time to learn and to regard as permanent, with a wholly different one, in radical discontinuity with it. The before/after photographs of my time might as well be pictures of different people, it seemed to me. And once we were in After, Before receded faster in the culture than it did in actual chronology, until the previous edition of the world came to seem not just remote but improbable, an unlikely past for the present to have had.

This seemed a subject worth my while to take as seriously as I could. From this point of view *Red Plenty* is not a perverse project. It was supposed to be a way of registering the scale of the change narratively, imaginatively, by restoring at least some of the weight of what had vanished. By immersing people in Before, I wanted to remind us of the strangeness of After; to point out that our present looks at least as odd from the vantage point of the past as vice versa.

Perversity did then immediately re-enter with the decision to take the voyage to the heart of dullness. I play on purpose in the book with a kind of deliberate inversion of the familiar stereotype of Russian novels. I have relocated the intense drama, the anguishes, the thwarted hopes, from the private lives of the characters to the fate of the system itself – though I hope I've left space for the characters to be plausibly happy and unhappy too. It has meant, in a curious way, reading Soviet life with a sort of deliberate naivety: taking the system at its official valuation in order then to keep crashing it into the obstructions of the actual.

It's had one other consequence too. I have certainly done my best to take my female characters seriously, and to make them something other than the orbital appurtenances of the men: but the book's commitment to following out the public business and the public claims of Khrushchev's Soviet Union has also meant that I'm echoing, albeit satirically, the priorities of an intensely patriarchal society. This was a place that required the economic participation of women, but removed none of the traditional family burdens from them; didn't promote them, didn't give them positions of power, didn't bother to save their labour with domestic technology, and celebrated International Women's Day as an occasion for the gallant presentation, by men, of little bouquets. Any profession women dominated, like medicine, was by definition a low-status profession, and even the rare woman with a senior and prestigious job was expected to function as her colleagues' skivvy too. For example: I thought about bringing in as a character the pioneer Akademgorodok sociologist Tatiana Zaslavskaya, who was an early and significant adviser to Gorbachev. I didn't in the end – it would have been too diffusing to bring in another discipline, on top of economics and computer science and so on – but I got a nice email recently from a retired American academic who had dined at her flat in Akademgorodok in the mid-1980s. She was the only woman present, as well as the grandest person in the room: and after the meal, the men chatted while she went to the kitchen and washed up. That's the world *Red Plenty* reproduces.

2. Mirrorball

One of the things I have been entertained by over the last couple of years has been the steady trickle of reviews by Trotskyists which explain that, despite my hostility to socialism, I accidentally offer a portrait of it which makes the reader feel a bit sceptical about capitalism too. Through mighty feats of self-denial I have managed not to write in and say: yes, and isn't it lucky the way that major rivers so often run right through the middle of cities?

For the record, I absolutely did intend *Red Plenty*'s USSR to function as a distorting mirror in which the reader would be able to recognise realities much closer to home in time and place. The backing for the mirror, as it were, is the historical USSR's strange and genuine Americophilia: the angrily unrequited love of Khrushchev's generation for the USA as they distantly understood and misunderstood it, the continent apart from the zero-sum rivalries of the Old World, where the ketchup came from, and the burgers, and the ice cream, and the roller coasters, and the Buick plants, and the Taylorist management techniques. (All of which the Soviet Union imported.) And I have strengthened the similarity as much as I can with small decisions of vocabulary and emphasis. This USSR, written in English, is deliberately as American in nomenclature as I can make it, with a layer of distractingly explicit ideological speech stripped out of Soviet reality to reveal what apparatchiks calling each other 'comrade' can hide: that Khrushchev and co. are, above all, *managers*. Bloodstained ones, yes, but still recognisable mid-twentieth-century organisation men, working for a bureaucratised conglomerate so vast it stretches to the edge of their world (and denies them any guidance from an exterior world of prices). I wanted it to be possible to read Soviet life as a kind of Dilbert cartoon printed all the way to the margins, a saga of corporate idiocy from which the citizens of the USSR never got to go home, because, with the firm and the country being coterminous, the management could pursue them twenty-four hours a day with bullshit about productivity and lean inventory management. For that matter, it makes perfect sense to think of the gridlocked planned economy as following a parodically over-achieving version of the Toyota Way, where you go one better on just-in-time and arrive at always-too-late.

But I wanted something more disquieting than just a funhouse glass in which the Other was displayed as a dysfunctional exaggeration of Self. That would be much too comfortable. Instead I had in my mind as an ideal a kind of impossible mirrored surface in which, whatever you brought to the book, you'd see *something* to recognise, and something you hadn't bargained for as well, which the recognition would entail. I wanted anyone, with any variety of politics, to be able to see their own face looming dimly in the metalled surface of events. So for a start I tried to eliminate as many markers of my own views as possible; and then, as a matter of literary ambition as well as of satiric reach, to try and make the human sympathy of the book for the characters as impersonally near-universal as I could, so you couldn't as a reader track liking or warmth as a surrogate for authorial endorsement; and then, as an exercise in critical self-discipline, to try to see an irony for every conceivable assertion, an exception for every truth, a complication for every simplicity. The Marxian utopia had to be genuinely attractive. The Hayekian objection to it had to be allowed its full disruptive force. Kantorovich's work-around of the price mechanism had to have its beauty demonstrated. I was trying to stitch together a sort of story that paid more attention than usual to the economic motives for human behaviour, but, even there, I wanted my account of causes to be as broad and open as possible, and not to collapse without residue into any single one of the rival diagrams of economic behaviour. Basically, I wanted to be awkward. I could take advantage of fiction's built-in tolerance of overdetermination, in which multiple possible causes for an outcome can be allowed to exist alongside each other without being resolved, or even given definitive weights. Storytelling lets you bring negative capability into economics. And this effort to stay plural in my understanding of the story, though it was a conscious discipline, didn't feel as I was doing it like some willed suspension of a more naturally argumentative or analytical state. My interest in the things I write about seems to be a narrative one, deep down. Far more than as paraphrasable ideas, I tend to perceive material that excites me in terms of possible patterns of story; often ironic ones. It would not be possible to overstate my incompetence at dealing with any of the science in *Red Plenty* in a quantitative or even genuinely abstract way. Person after person who was kind enough to talk to me for the book encountered a mumbling, stumbling individual who, not being able to talk in the language of maths, had no way to convey the scribbled cloud of nouns joined by arrows in his head.

But of course the book is not opinionless, and the ironic reflections of the present it offers back are not universal, or anything like it. It clearly channels its ironies within very definite bounds, and the non-fictional sections are blatantly partial in their shaping of Soviet history. You can tell the limits of my capacity for negative capability by who the book doesn't work for, politically. Conservatives can find their faces glimmering in the mirrorball, and so can social democrats and independently minded Marxists; but Trotskyists can't, probably because, of all the critiques of Soviet history, the one that doesn't interest me at all is Trotsky's. I'm with Keynes, where Trotsky is concerned: 'He assumes that the moral and intellectual problems of the transformation of Society have already been solved – that a plan exists, and nothing remains except to put it into operation.' If you can't even see that there's a deep and rich unanswered technical question in the Soviet record, then all that's left to talk about are the tedious differences between Stalin's and Trotsky's

cults of will. I think, myself, that the Bolsheviks in both their varie-
ties were a bunch of murdering scumbags, who turned Marx's bad
habit of rhetorical contempt, via Lenin, into a warrant for ending
arguments with a bullet to the skull, and who diverted what should
have been the civilised history of twentieth-century socialism
towards atrocity and disaster. But I do them the justice of taking
them seriously, as conductors of humanity's longest, largest-scale
experiment in the non-market operation of an industrial economy:
and *that's* where there's still something worth talking about.

What I meant the book to indict by reflection, to satirise by
reflection, was the whole family of schemes of dangerous perfection. The quality that capitalist idylls share with communist ones is
the illusion of control, whether the control is to be exercised through
Gosplan's card indexes or through the Black–Scholes formula for
option pricing. In each case the mistake is to take the map for the
territory, to proceed as if the system – either system – were fully
specified, and could be reliably manipulated through its formalisa-
tions. A genuinely doctrineless conservatism, some kind of really
thoroughgoing little-platoons preference for the small and local and
unsystematisable, would escape the mocking reflection, I suppose,
as would the socialism without doctrines which is my politics too.

Oops. Oh come on, though; *of course* the book is written from
the left. Why would anyone who wasn't on the left have enough at
stake, feel enough of a sense of unfinished business, to go picking
through the rubble that was left when the twentieth-century wind
stopped blowing out of paradise, to see if there was anything there
that was worth salvaging? Despite the occasional suggestion[12] that
I might have written the whole 450 pages to put young Occupy
activists off socialism – we bourgeois liberals are fiendish, and
patient – I have to report that the Soviet model was already sufficiently dead not to need assassinating again. If the book has an
ideological objective, it is simply that I would like the issue of
economic alternatives to become a little more prominent again. I
am almost entirely a nice, demand-managing, taxes 'n' labour unions

European parliamentary social democrat. But the other little piece of me wants to know if we can't, some day, do better than that.

3. Pretending to be Russian, pretending (not) to be a novelist

As anyone who has ever encountered the pink Englishness of me in the flesh will testify – aha, title for a future memoir: *Pink Englishness* – I am not even slightly Russian. I don't speak Russian or read Russian. I've visited the places I write about, but I haven't ever lived in them. I don't have close Russian friends. Nor do I have the alternative route in of intimacy with the science of the story. My only qualification is a kind of gift for pattern recognition, for seeing where, in the distributed mass of events and ideas and personalities, there is narrative sense to be made. Everything in the book had to be second-hand. Everything was obtained by reading, by staring as hard as I could through the narrow aperture available to me, and by using every last scrap of the pertinent experience I have had, to what has sometimes felt like a ridiculous degree. It wasn't just that I contrived to use the whole buffalo. I didn't even leave a smear of blood on the pavement where the buffalo had been. It was all turned into black pudding. There are things in *Red Plenty* that originate in remarks taxi drivers made to me. Yes, I am the Thomas Friedman of Khrushchev's USSR. So, while the book is, indeed, 'evidence-based' in the sense that the factual, the real, has been the fundamental stimulus to my imagination, the book's relationship to fact is a little complex; and the first complication that needs to be admitted is that it is *not* evidence-based in the sense of being a considered, selective response to some large, patient massing of data. The book does not represent a selection of detail drawn from a deep knowledge of the Soviet Union. It contains substantially everything I found out, with the directions in which I went looking for data often being dictated by my sense, in advance, that there was a piece of the narrative that needed to be supported. As the great Serbian writer Danilo Kiš said, when an interviewer praised the undetectability of the invented components in his Borgesian memorial to the Gulag, *A Tomb for Boris Davidovich*, 'Really? They seemed very visible to me.' *Red Plenty* is like the Ob Sea that the Akademgorodok scientists swim in: convincing as a pocket ocean in terms of width, but only a few feet deep at any point. It contains just enough facts, at any point, to make it hold together.

And how much 'just enough' is, was always a literary judgement. It was a world-building consideration, of a kind familiar to anyone writing SF or fantasy, and asking themselves what the minimum level of detail is that a reader can be fed to seed her or his imagination with a perception of solidity. The secret of even the thingiest SF, the most solid-walnut-to-the-knuckles fantasy, is that you don't need much to summon worlds out of air, so long as the details are the right ones. But – and I'm wary here of rushing too fast into the question of what kind of fiction the book is, which flattering genre claim to succumb to – there was also always the pressure on fact-selection, on imaginative shaping, exerted by the need to arrange the world of the USSR for comprehension. *Red Plenty* isn't just a book by an outsider. It's primarily for outsiders too. The explanatory load on the book kept pushing it towards trying to clarify the whole social function of some category of event we were just seeing one of. Most novels, I felt as I was writing, were not so foreign to the modes of human interchange they portrayed that they had to explain the basic definitions of things as they went along. It was as if I had to dip my steel-nibbed pen into the inkwell and say:

It is a truth universally acknowledged that a single man in possession of a fortune must be in want of a wife; a wife being the female partner in a pair-bonded relationship for life, sanctioned by religion and integrated into systems of inheritance, child-rearing and regulated sexuality; a fortune being a quantity of money at a high multiple of the society's average income, usually but not invariably available as a liquid resource; money being ...

Here was a large reason for the first sentence of the book. When I wrote, 'This is not a novel. It has too much to explain to be one of those', I was partly teasing. And partly I was negotiating a particular difficulty that had arisen during the original publication, which made it important to assert that, whatever it was, it wasn't a *failed* novel. But I meant it, too. I was – am – genuinely uncertain over whether, as a piece of writing in which individual experience ceaselessly takes second place to idea, and some kind of documentary purchase on the world is being asserted, it should really qualify. Heaven knows, I have been glad to be contradicted by my friend the Californian SF writer Kim Stanley Robinson, who says that sentence makes him laugh because there's *always* too much to explain; that it's the fate of the novel, every time, to digest down a load of heterogeneous stuff until it becomes a story. And if my having done my best to through-imagine it all as a kind of concrete (and viscose) poetry saves it in other people's eyes from occupying the place I feared it had in the uncanny valley, zombie-ishly half-alive itself – I'm certainly not going to argue. All right, it's a novel.

But – historical novel, or SF? I think the two genres are basically isomorphic. They share the increase in the story's explanatory load, and in the need to create familiarity from a standing start for the reader, and in the increased prominence of world-as-character. In terms of characteristic difficulties, they share the problem of how to make characters something other than just an expression of researched or invented perspectives. They both aim to transport. Where they differ is in whether they transport us to a combination of human possibilities which has already existed, or to one that only *might* exist, elsewhere or -when. Since the Soviet Union in 1960 existed all too solidly, it looks like an open and shut case for the historical. And yet ...

4. Otherwise

And yet it was a haunted solidity I was after. Solidity with a spectre in it, which nevertheless had power to promise, torment, console, frighten, cost, cause. Some people have read *Red Plenty* under the misapprehension that they are getting an alt-hist spectacular, in which cybernetics will come to save planning at the last possible moment, and the sky will fill with happy citizens in autogiros. This is an accidental artefact of *Red Plenty*'s marketing, and of the decision to lead the descriptions of it with what-iffery. But I'm not at all sorry. In some respects it's a kind of ideal reading for the book, allowing you to take literally and therefore at full expectant force what has to be metaphorical, a ghost you can be confident of seeing through, if you read it in the usual way, in the firm persuasion that the Cold War is going to be won by Ronald Reagan. (Joke.) By taking on the past's expectation as a real possibility (within the world of the text) you accidentally transport yourself to something approaching the subject-position, as I understand it, of actual mathematical-economical true believers in the Soviet Union, looking forward in hope from 1962. You put yourself into a state of the world which, like all states of the world, is partially composed of what it is and partially of what might be. Counterfactuals aren't just an implied presence in historical explanations. They're surely also the form, or one of them, in which we put our sense at any particular moment that a potential is present for things to change. They are the floating home of 'otherwise'.

The picture of the future world is also, almost always, a picture of an alternative present: a state of things in terms of which, from the standpoint of which, it is possible to critique daily reality, or to find it more bearable, or to justify it. Which are three very different psychological uses for the counterfactual, rolled together and made available together, even when, as in the Soviet case, the future in question is a compulsory one, an organising destination which everyone is supposed to apply to make narrative sense of present events. The Soviet Union in the 1950s and 1960s seems to me to have been a society haunted by its hopes in a peculiarly powerful, equivocal way. It was a place that, in its very recent past, had granted a hopeful goal an unlimited precedence over actual human lives, and then stepped back from mass murder without ever fully acknowledging what had happened, leaving hope tethered in private experience to a layer of sorrow and suffering; and it was a place that ceaselessly mobilised hope as self-deception, 'psycho-prophylaxis', compulsory pretending, applied to push you into ignoring all the defects of reality; and yet it was also a place that admitted louder and louder, the harder it lent on hope as anaes-thetic, the need for the present to be redeemed or transcended. Hope revealed *and* concealed the nature of the times. The USSR was haunted by horror *and* utopia at the same time. I wanted, by picking the most sympathetically geeky and cybernetic version of hope, to make us feel the force of the haunting. (Us now; us outside the experience chronologically, or geographically, or politically.)

Meanwhile the fairy-tale framing of events is supposed to bring the magical interpretation of the counterfactual to the surface. But not, I hope, to estranging effect: not by banishing a particularly Russian story into the realm of local folklore. The book's insistence that the dream of planned plenty *is* twentieth-century magic, a cultural script or spell (grammar, grimoire) with connections stretching back to the hunger-dreams of the ancestors, is intended to suggest the effect that enchantment of this kind is normal, universal. That the entwined sense of possibility/failure is threaded through times of change or choice in all sorts of societies at all sorts of times. Its presence is not to be taken as confirmation of the absurdity of any particular hope it gets attached to. History is made with refractory, recursively patterned material, always. There is always available, in the human repertoire, the move of laying the imaginary against the real, and taking it as the standard by which the real is judged, and found wanting.

And surely this is right, as well as dangerous. Surely we have to grant imagination the power to keep interrogating what happens to exist, and to keep asking if it couldn't be better. The 'otherwise' at the end of the book is supposed to be open enough to gather into it our general suspicion that some kind of less wasteful and destructive composition of the human pattern is possible, as well the specific longing of the socialist tradition for some kinder measure to dance to than the zombie-hop of the commodities. It isn't in there just as an all-purpose rhetorical dreamcatcher, or as an exercise in the novelist's impersonal sympathy. That's my yearning you hear in the Akademgorodok wind, too. But it seems to me that to keep faith with the power of the imaginary requires you also to keep the most honest tally you can of its costs. Which is notoriously hard to do, of course, without reliable prices.

5. History and comedy

Praise for the novelty or innovativeness of the book's form has been overplayed. The overall patterning of it is fiddly, but the pieces of which the pattern is made are as straightforward as I could make them, and not just because, as I get older, I increasingly think that simple is more interesting (and difficult to achieve) than complicated. It's also that I had lots of very well-established precedents to draw on. On the historical-novel side, the whole Tolstoy-does-Napoleon recipe for dramatising the viewpoints of the grand historical figures, and the equally available rule of thumb that tells you how to mix the documented and the imagined to create the illusion of comprehensiveness. And, drawing on SF, I had the scientist-fictions of Ursula Le Guin and Kim Stanley Robinson to follow. My Kantorovich very clearly has the DNA of Le Guin's Shevek and Robinson's Sax Russell in him. Not to mention – as I've carefully confessed in the notes – that the whole alternation of character-driven scenes with italicised authorial narration is lifted straight out of Robinson's *Red Mars*. And collections of linked short stories that fill in different vertebrae of a narrative spine are not exactly unheard-of, either, from Kipling to Alice Munro. I am proud of the two 'machine' sections, set in Lebedev's logic and Lebedev's lungs, one in which determinacy produces indeterminacy, the other in which the arrow goes the other way; but it's not like Don DeLillo doesn't already exist, and Pynchon, and for that matter Nicholson Baker. It's not as though there isn't a blazed trail for paying imaginative attention to system.

But Vasily Grossman's *Life and Fate* occupies a special place for me, as an object of admiration and source for borrowable techniques. For one thing, it is a masterclass in how the toolkit of socialist realism can be turned to heterodox purposes. For another, to be more frivolous, the novel is a monument of imaginative and moral witness – I can't read Sofya Levinton's journey to the gas chamber without weeping helplessly – but line by line the prose is not so fabulous that it forces you the way reading Tolstoy does into endless *Wayne's World*-ish cries of 'I'm not worthy!' Grossman seems to be a more assimilable master from whom to learn.

Life and Fate, however, is tragedy, while *Red Plenty* is comedy, albeit unhappy comedy. This might mean that the book is open-ended, leaving the characters (and leaving them is what it frequently does) with something more fluid than tragedy's inevitable arcs of descent. Or it might mean a kind of airless comic closure, a sealing shut of the possibilities of the fictional strand of the book because the story all takes place under the overhang of non-fictional certainties, which suck all genuine life out of words like 'hope' in the story, leaving only ironic slapstick behind. Needless to say, I'd rather the former were true. But I can't adjudicate. The way the book assembles itself in other minds, the patterns of effect that my intentions settle into there, aren't within my competence at all. I haven't got any interpretative authority over the thing.

What I can say is that the whole interrelation of the fictional and non-fictional elements in the book was set up as my improvised solution to the problem of allowing a story with a known end – failure – to take on some unpredictable life. I wanted to permit some space for hope, for expectancy, in a situation which would, I thought, be perceived by most people as self-evidently over, done with, a closed ledger, productive of neither interesting questions nor sympathetic human emotion. It seemed to me that if I stipulated the facts, and used them as a kind of authoritative backdrop or sounding board, I might then allow myself a cleared space next to them in which there was room for something else to expand, something looser, composed of moments of experience rather than of reasoning about outcomes. And experience isn't teleological, even if it's the experience of hope. Its truth as experience doesn't depend on what happens next. But to create this zone of not-fact, free as story because of what it wasn't, I had to create a 'historical' narrative which represented solidity, which was to be taken as the singular and dependable truth, even when I was being highly opinionated and questionable in my judgements, as in the italicised sections' dismissal of the Bolsheviks before 1914 as a tiny political cult. In a conjured-up tension with a certain truth, fiction could billow out into undetermined life. (I hoped.)

But that isn't what history is. History as practised by historians is not an invocation of unquestionable fact, at all. It's a vast collective text, implicitly discursive, in a state not only of continual revision but of continual argument over method. Even in its most narrative, singly-authored forms, it poses continual questions about representation, and in this respect is not so very far away from fiction at all. The reason why, in *Red Plenty*, the two genres remain distinct, with a historical apparatus (italicised intros + footnotes) of assertive statements, is that both strands of the book, both components, are in truth equally rhetorical. The 'history' does not contain anything that I know or believe to be untrue. But it is there to help fiction live, to pull open the space of not-certainty. If, instead, it has the effect of capping off and closing down the fiction, that will be – well, not the first time in my writing that I have managed to contrive the reverse of my intentions.

On the subject of comedy, though, and its not-necessarily-happy qualities, can I bring in Henri Bergson? He talks[13] about the internal equivalent of the 'mechanical inelasticity' of the pratfall being the state of adapting ourselves 'to a past and therefore imaginary situation, when we ought to be shaping our conduct with the reality which is present'. Hence the comedy of absent-mindedness. Bergson sticks to the past for his example: but it would work, too, as an explanation of what happens when a person (or a whole society) gives priority to the future. Comedy is one of the effects of cease-lessly pretending – or under compulsion, pretending to pretend – that the ideal society to come should shape conduct more than the disappointing present one. If you try to live in the palace that hasn't been built yet, you'll collide with the furniture of your actual tene-ment, over and over, and then be obliged to pretend not to notice. The USSR, on this account, could be seen as a society of compul-sory absent-mindedness, stepping through the slapstick of the plan under pain of worse. Or maybe you don't even need the future. The present would do, if you existed in a sufficiently imaginary rela-tionship to it. Then ideology *is* comedy. But again, as the person performs their compulsory mime of surprise at the discovery that the soup plate, for the umpteenth time, has glue or ink in it, I think – I hope – that a space opens for less predictable feeling. For the person alongside the tyrannical joke, as it does for the person alongside the closed history.

6. Feasibility studies

I take it as a vindication of my whole daft project that it has prompted such a beautiful piece of intellectual path-finding to exist as Cosma Shalizi's 'In Soviet Union, Optimization Problem Solves You'.[14] I wish the essay had existed before I wrote the book. It would have saved me months if not years of clumsy attempts to think through the underlying intellectual issue: whether, in any possible world, and not just under the hampering constraints of the Soviet environ-ment, anything resembling the Kantorovich scheme for optimisa-tion through prices could power a planned cornucopia. In science-fictional terms, whether Iain M. Banks's Culture Minds, and the nanoscale Babbage engines of the Solar Union in Ken MacLeod's *Cassini Division*, and the computers of the Mondragon Accord in Kim Stanley Robinson's *2312*, can plausibly be imagined to be running a programme for post-scarcity consisting of millions of linear equations. The Soviet case as such doesn't tell you this. In fact, it can't tell you much about the ultimate feasibility of optimal planning, because for a thick array of reasons to do with power and path-dependency and the lack of foothold for the reformers' ideas in the actual conduct of the economy, they never came close to being applied in anything but the most truncated form. (Perhaps luckily.) Instead the USSR provides only a kind of appallingly costly control study for the twentieth-century experiences of capitalist industrialisation, in which we get to see what happens when an industrial revolution is run again with some key institutions missing or different. The USSR from this point of view is something close to a real-world history experiment, a really nasty lab-test of an alternative time-stream: fascinating in an unethical way, but not directly addressed to the utopian proposition.

I'm not competent mathematically to challenge the conclusion Shalizi arrives at – which in any case squares with my own inchoate conclusion, gained from reading Stiglitz's *Whither Socialism?*, that optimised allocation of resources, even if possible, solves the wrong problem. I have a thought, though, about the desirability of the cybernetic cornucopia, independent of its feasibility. The power of the Kantorovich result, as I understand it, is that it proves that a set of prices exists for any plan which would allow it to be co-ordinated in a decentralised way, by having local actors simply maximise profits; which in turn, if the system worked, would allow a whole economy to be steered towards an agreed goal, rather than just passively following a trajectory determined piecemeal by all the aggregated decision-making going on in it. Result: emancipation, or at least greater human choice about our collective destiny. But, but, but. Not only are there the insurmountable problems of the Soviet context – for the system, to calculate the prices, would require the same impossibly complete information about capabilities which Gosplan had been failing to gather for decades – and the computational obstacles Cosma Shalizi lays out. There is then also the question of whether, by shifting from our captivity to the zombie dance of commodities to a captivity to the plan, we have really done any more than relocated our passivity, and gained any emancipating ground. If we don't like our unplanned subservience to the second-order consequences of our collective life (market, government, family), why would we like a planned, first-order subservience to the mathematical-economic masters of the glass bead game any better, even if they were acting as instruments of our collective choices? Even granted the perfect execution of a probably impossible computational task, wouldn't the quality we were trying to escape promptly re-enter the system under another name? The latter part of the commonwealth forgets its beginning, as a useful patsy of Shakespeare's said on another island, long ago.

Yet, if on the contrary we decide that like all panaceas, wildly overpraised at first and then shrinking to the size of their true usefulness, Kantorovich's insight has a future as something more modest, a tool of human emancipation good for some situations but not others – then we have a presentational problem. It's a lot easier to build a radical movement on a story of transformation, on the idea of the plan that makes another world possible, than it is on a story of finding out the partial good and building upon it. The legitimacy of the Soviet experiment, and of the ecosystem of less barbarous ideas that turned out to tacitly depend upon it, lay in the perception of a big, bright, adjacent, obtainable, obvious, morally compelling other way of doing things. Will people march if society inscribes upon its banners, 'Watch out for the convexity constraints'? Will we gather in crowds if a speaker offers us all the utopia that isn't NP-complete? Good luck with that. Good luck to all of us.

(2012)

Sacred

Religious apologetics, as I discovered both by writing some of my own and by reading other people's, is a mode of imaginative writing. It has to be. It's not just that it draws on memoir, on the virtues of essay construction, even on travel literature, as I say in the piece about C.S. Lewis here. It's also that it is essentially in the business of creating a bridge of experience from one mind to another, so that what the writer has felt can be recognised by the reader as something other than a distant abstraction, and conceivably even be shared.

Experience is the common ground; experience is the language that opens other languages; experience is the source for the only verification of an idea that is likely to be accepted, in a time when there is deep suspicion of (and misremembering of) the conceptual vocabulary of faith. To write towards a reader who has no reason to trust you or to be interested, and in whom the cultural inheritance of Christianity has mostly either decayed into the unrecognisable or been anonymised into the self-evident, requires you to make contact with the stories they are telling of their life, and to lay alongside them, with what self-understanding you can muster, the stories you tell of your own; and then to try to join both to the central story, told so it can be heard again, by which the immensely narrative religion of Christianity hopes to interpret all others.

I was doing this at the irritating cultural moment when the 'New Atheist' writers were busily dismantling a reasonably civilised détente between belief and unbelief, in favour of simple-minded oppositions between 'faith' and 'reason', with all religion on one side and all science on the other: inquisitors with thumbscrews versus freedom, logic and enlightenment. So some of what I found myself mounting was a defence of imagination as such, understood as the category of all that is luxuriant, provisional and unfalsifiable in culture – religion very much included – against a stupid positivism.

DEAR ATHEISTS

Allow me to annoy you with the prospect of mutual respect between believers and atheists. The basis for it would be simple: that on both sides, we hold to positions for which by definition there cannot be any evidence. We believe there is a God. You believe there isn't one. Meanwhile, nobody knows, nobody *can* know, whether He exists or not, it not being a matter susceptible to proof or disproof. The most science can do is to demonstrate that God is not necessary as a physical explanation for anything, which is very much not the same thing as demonstrating that He isn't there. So the natural, neutral, temperate position here would be agnosticism: a calm, indifferent not-knowing. Yet we and you – wild romantic creatures that we all are – rush instead to positions of faith on the subject. This shared (yet oppositely polarised) extravagance should surely make us soulmates. Or lack-of-soul mates. You say tom*ay*to, we say tom*ah*to, yet we agree in finding the big red salad vegetable important. Atheists and believers are, in opposite modes, the people drawn out by conviction from the dull centreground of empiricism. *Mes frères, mes soeurs, mes semblables!* Let us embrace one another as fellow refugees from the tediously pragmatic!

No? No. Because the idea of atheism as an extravagant faith-driven deviation from the null case goes against one of the most cherished elements in the self-image of polemical unbelief: that atheism is somehow scientific, that it is to be adopted as the counterpart in the realm of meaning to the caution and rigour of the scientific method. Flirting with a picture of yourselves as passionate enthusiasts of God-denial would obviously fuck this right up (as we like to say in the Church of England). The contemporary atheist shtick even has a meme prepared to cover this exact eventuality. Try saying that atheists have a faith position, because they believe in the absence of God, and seconds later, as sure as eggs is eggs, as sure as Richard Dawkins knows a great deal about evolutionary biology and fuck-all about religion, someone will pop up to say: no. Atheists do not believe in the absence of God. Atheists do not 'believe' in anything. Atheists merely lack a belief in the presence of God. The defining feature of atheism is its calm, principled non-participation in the whole crazy business of taking positions about entities you can't see. Phew. That's the flattering reflection in the mirror saved. (Though I'm sure your nose is longer than it was a moment ago, Pinocchio.) But it does indeed rule out the alternative possibility of seeing atheism as theism in negative; of atheists as a kind of glorious reverse-Trappists, devoted to noisily celebrating the non-existence of God, soaring free from the factual, just gone – solid gone, baby – on the poetics of absence. I guess the hugging will have to wait.

In any case, over here on the believers' side, we don't spend that much time fixated on the question of God's existence either. Religion isn't a philosophical argument, just as it isn't a dodgy cosmology, or any other kind of alternative to science. In fact, it isn't primarily a system of propositions about the world at all. Before it is anything else, it is a structure of feeling, a house built of emotions. You don't have the emotions because you've signed up to the proposition that God exists; you entertain the proposition that God exists because you've had the emotions. You entertain the proposition, and perhaps eventually sign up to it, because it makes a secondary kind of sense of something you're feeling anyway. The book I've written in defence of Christianity, *Unapologetic*, starts off with our current cultural bust-up over religion, but then swiftly goes somewhere else; and this is because, from our side, the address at which the argument usually seems to happen is not in fact the address at which belief happens. Belief, I want people to see, is made of real, human-normal experiences. It is not an extension ladder of supposition propped on the wobbly dowelling of conjecture. Christianity (which is the form of belief I can speak about from the inside, from within its pattern of experience) is a way of dealing with the territory of guilt and hope and sorrow and joy and change and tragedy and renewal and mortality on which we humans must live. And not necessarily an infantile, or contemptible, or craven way of dealing with those things: one with a certain emotional realism built in, we'd like to think, and a certain generosity of imagination, whether or not (which nobody can know) it happens to be true. So, we're busy too. Our belief is a concrete thing, grown from habit and memory and perception rather than from abstractions. It's a weight of experience which pushes us away from the indifferent middle of the scale on the God question.

And yet, of course, we don't know, and not knowing matters. The ultimate test of faith must still, and always, be its truth; whether we can prove it or not, the reality of the perspectives it brings us, and the changes it puts us through, must depend in the end on it corresponding to an actual state of the universe. Religion without God makes no sense (except possibly to Buddhists). So belief for most Christians who respect truth and logic and science – which is most of us, certainly in the UK – must entail a willing entry into uncertainty. It means a decision to sustain the risks and embarrassments of living a conditional, of choosing a maybe or a perhaps to live out, among the many maybes or perhapses of this place; where conclusive answers are not available, and we must all do our knowing on some subjects through a glass, darkly.

This is the basis on which it is, on the whole, rather easy for us to enter imaginatively into your position. For the most part, the attitude of contemporary British Christians to contemporary British atheism is one of sympathetic respect. Empathetic respect, even: I've never met a Christian who didn't recognise the experience of finding God absent. A lot of us have been atheists at some point. Most of us still are, from time to time, it being a recurrent feature of faith that you pass periodically back through doubt again. No, that does *not* mean that we secretly think you're right, deep down; that on some semi-conscious level we know we are only building pathetic sandcastles to be washed away by the surging, inevitable, in-bound flood tide of Reason(™). It means we recognise that you and we are both operating where we cannot know we're right. The appropriate response is humility, an adherence to a sense of ourselves as fallible, and yet possessed of the convictions we're possessed of, the experiences we're possessed of, the hearts we're possessed of.

Maybe too – all teasing apart – this might be the basis on which believers and atheists might manage to declare peace, and to talk to each other a little more productively. On both sides, we check our certainties at the cloakroom, and then settle down, fellows at decision-making under uncertainty, to compare the advantages and disadvantages of the houses of emotion our positions enable us to inhabit: both real, in the sense that both are built from experience, and both ultimately resting upon the unknowable. You bring out the dignity of materialism, and we put next to it the Christian acknowledgement of the tragic, the wasted, the unmendable. You bring out the decentring power of the discovery of humanity's smallness and contingency in the cosmos, and the recentring power of finding that human life nevertheless preserves meaning. We put next to it the egalitarianism of human failure, and the hope for a way out of humanity's endless game of Prisoner's Dilemma. We show you ours and you show us yours. And together we admire the patterned gambles that nourish us.

However – and now it's back to the teasing again – before we do that, I really think you lot need to be a bit clearer about what the emotional content of your atheism *is*. You are the ones who claim to be acting on a mere lack, on a non-belief, but, as absences go, contemporary atheism doesn't half seem to involve some strong feelings. It isn't all reading Lucretius, or thinking about the many forms most beautiful. For many of you, the point of atheism appears to be, not the non-relationship with God, but a live and hostile relationship with believers. It isn't enough that you yourselves don't believe: atheism permits a delicious self-righteous anger at those who do. The very existence of religion seems to be an affront, a liberty being taken, a scab you can't help picking. People who don't like stamp-collecting don't have a special magazine called *The Anti-Philatelist*. But you do. You do the equivalent of hanging about in front of Stanley Gibbons to orate about the detestability of phosphor bands and perforations. You wait for someone to have the temerity to express a religious sentiment, so you can spray them with scorn at fire-extinguisher pressure. It's as if there is some transgressive little ripple of satisfaction which can only be obtained by uttering the words 'sky fairy' or 'zombie rabbi' *where a real live Christian might hear them*. Now this, dear brothers and sisters, cannot be good for you. It is never a good idea to let yourself believe that the pleasures of aggression have virtue behind them. Take it from a religious person. This, we know.

(2012)

CONTRA DAWKINS

Speech at the Faclan Book Festival, Isle of Lewis, November 2012. Richard Dawkins was due to speak next, and was sitting near the front of the audience.

This is an unusual situation. I'm used to being one of the very few Christians in the room, and to be trying to build a careful bridge of words between what the world looks like to me, and the experience of people who are often a couple of generations away by now from any direct familiarity with belief from the inside; people who usually don't even have a Sunday School familiarity with Christianity's central ideas and stories and personalities. Now here I am suddenly part of a majority, a Christian among Christians. I am probably a more liberal Christian than a lot of you, with different views about a bunch of things including the authority of the Bible: but theological differences are not in the end as important as this truth, which makes us one. I am a sinner, whose hope lies in the love of God, and in the blood that Christ Jesus shed for me. I once was lost, but now am found; was blind, but now I see. My redeemer liveth. I hope you will hear the rest of what I have to say in the light of that.

Meanwhile, Professor Dawkins there, who is usually (when in Britain at least) part of what David Robertson yesterday correctly called a majority of 'functional atheists', and who in fact is at the agitating edge of that majority, the people who really hold to atheism as a positive virtue, not just a drifting accident of modern life, impatiently pressing for the last vestiges of religion to be removed from public life, trying to stamp into place a consensus that belief doesn't have any legitimate or respectworthy role in the serious business of our culture – suddenly, he's on his own. One solitary lion in a whole den of Daniels. Unfortunately that's not my joke. Oscar Wilde said it. For anyone who's listening to this on the radio on the mainland, or watching it as a YouTube clip later, Daniel was somebody *in the Bible.*

The book I've written about faith, *Unapologetic,* is aimed at that other order of things, where the lions outnumber Daniel, not this one. It is itself an attempt at bridge-building in words, so that people who have never believed can get from it, for a little while, a sense of what Christianity, or rather one man's Christianity, feels like from inside. Books are powerful things. They let you borrow experiences, they let you try out being other people: and the biggest gulf between belief and unbelief now, in my opinion, is a gulf of experience, not of ideas. For a lot of people now, the life of faith is literally unimaginable, except as a caricature. Usually a caricature of fanaticism, intolerance and bigotry. They do not know what it is *like* to believe. But you do – a lot of you. So I'm not sure how relevant my book can be to you. It isn't written to face towards you. The main thing it has to tell you is something you know already.

In honour of the occasion, then, I'm going to talk about the parts of my book which *are* a kind of response to *The God Delusion,* although that's pretty marginal as a preoccupation of mine. I certainly hope that *Unapologetic* isn't one of the fleas feeding parasitically off Richard Dawkins' fame, as he puts it so charmingly. Yes, it's billed as a 'riposte' to *The God Delusion,* because my publisher wants to shift copies, and so do I, because I am a working author with a living to make. But it is not really a reply to him. If anything it is an attempt to deal – a little bit – with the situation the success of *The God Delusion* has created. In my opinion, Richard Dawkins is *so* wrong about religion that there is scarcely any point of contact between his argument and actual Christian faith. They go straight past each other.

I do not agree that *The God Delusion* is a useful book because it makes God more prominent, more visible, and thus moves belief up the agenda. I'm not as generous as that. In fact, I'm not an especially nice person altogether – which is one reason why I need Christianity. I think *The God Delusion* has been profoundly destructive. It is one of the rare books with the power to make those who read it stupider. It leaves people thinking they understand what they do not, and that they are therefore justified in contempt for the thing that they do not understand. It has helped to make the public conversation about religion substantially cruder and nastier than it need have been. It has deliberately set out to undermine the state of mutual respect that largely existed between believers and atheists in Britain until the past decade, by suggesting that any – *any* – public acknowledgement, or sympathy, or civility, or curiosity towards religion represented an inherent betrayal of science, tolerance, enlightenment, human dignity. Worse, it succeeded. It worked on people not at the level of argument, but at the level of perception, of vague assumption about what is sensible and what is not, what is acceptable and what is not, what is dangerous and what is not. I do not think it could have done this if more people in Britain had been in a position to say, hold on, this is a description appropriate to Torquemada and the Spanish Inquisition; if I try to apply it to Mr Smith up the road who goes to the Baptist chapel, it looks ridiculous. But they weren't. And neither did the author bother to inform himself before he put pen to paper, apparently thinking that if you're sure God doesn't exist, you can treat all statements about him as equally nonsensical. He's on record as comparing theology to 'fairyology', saying that, since there aren't any fairies at the bottom of his garden, he doesn't see why he should waste his time on learned discussions of whether they have green wings or yellow ones. But whether or not you think that God exists, *religion* certainly does: and the idea of starting an argument without even bothering to find out what your opponents think is just astonishing. As one critic said, Dawkins on theology is rather like someone writing a book on evolutionary biology having once, long ago, seen a copy of *The Observer's Book of British Birds*. That isn't fearless, it's careless. And the content of the book is careless too. It's an assemblage of two centuries' worth of anti-religious old chestnuts, with one new idea in it, which is wrong. That idea being that God is improbable because he couldn't have evolved before the universe began in order to create it. If Professor Dawkins had bothered to check whether we think God is a creature like us, only more complicated – hint: no – he might have saved himself some embarrassment.

For all these reasons, *The God Delusion* in my opinion is a blot on its author's reputation: and all the blacker and inkier a blot because he is, otherwise, a wonderful writer, and someone I very much admire. I have learned a huge amount from him, both about biology and about how to communicate complex ideas. When he's writing about science, he has the most delicate, scrupulous aware-ness of language. He knows that biological processes can only be brought into view for the lay reader through comparisons, and that your comparisons have to be vigilantly managed to respect the complexity of what you're explaining. Somehow when it comes to religion he ceases to know this. Metaphor goes out the window, nuance goes up the chimney, imagination lies trampled on the mat. An account of religion without imagination is defective from the start. I'm coming back to imagination later.

The God Delusion gets a lot of mileage from a highly question-able assumption about religion and science being incompatible. I'm going to talk about this a bit, because I guess, going by the quotation from him in the programme, that Professor Dawkins is going to as well. I mean this one: 'I am against religion because it teaches us to be satisfied with not understanding the world.' He seems to think that religion is in the business of offering certainty at the price of ignorance; comfort, on condition that you look away from the richness of the world, and see instead only the deceptively painted inside of some theological container. We Christians don't want discovery, which is the essence of science, because we think we know everything that matters already. Well, no. If you're a Christian, you believe that God knows everything already, not that you do. You believe that the Bible contains essential knowledge, knowledge vital to human flourishing, vital to salvation: not that it contains all knowledge, or sets the bounds on what human beings are allowed to know. It does not tell you how to build a boat, how to bake bread, how to play the trumpet; it does not tell you whether a problem in computer science is NP-complete, how to calculate the relative velocity of galaxies, how to calculate the rate of propagation of a genetic trait through a given population. But finding these things out can be a form of reverence, and often has been. If you are a Christian, you believe that the breath of God – that's what the Holy Spirit, *pneuma*, means in Greek: breath, wind, life – blows continually through every detail of this glorious, wretched, intricate universe. Yes, Professor Dawkins: that is a statement with no verifiable factual content whatsoever. But it indicates an orientation towards the world, a way in which we can be facing: a way in which for us to be curious, to want to know all we can, to be hungry for all the truth in our reach, is to be appreciative of a gift. And, accordingly, a great many scientists who happen to be Christians have done just that, from Newton working out the laws of motion to Francis Collins of the Human Genome Project: people who treat the scientific method in all its rigour as a form of praise, a never-ending canticle to the physical world. I know that Richard Dawkins thinks there ought to be a contradiction here; that such scientists must be at best compartmentalising their minds, and at worst behaving as if they've got two heads – a sensible scientific head, interested in proof and evidence, for use from Monday to Saturday, and a silly spiritual head for the Sabbath, which is willing to countenance any old rubbish. But there is no necessary contradiction, if you believe that the human capacity to think – to hypothesise, to experiment, to deduce and to conclude – is a fitting response to the generosity that placed us here, among so many things to think about. *Laborare est orare*, to work is to pray, as the monks of the middle ages said. And the work of science, like the work of baking, can be an expression of faith. It doesn't have to be, of course. The scientific method works just fine whether you're religious or not, just as the bread will still rise. Conversely, there certainly are versions of religion – of all religions – which are hostile to free enquiry; that would rather you spent your time inside a painted cardboard carton three feet by three, when just beyond lies the million-mile strand of the great ocean of truth. But the two circles of faith and reason do overlap. There is a generous area of human understanding which is fully faithful and fully reasonable at the same time.

The God Delusion also assumes, like most of the New Atheist books, that religion makes you servile: inclined to truckle to authority. The reasoning here seems to be that the very act of worship is revoltingly submissive. I must say that this does not correspond to my experience at all. I feel humility, I hope, when I pray, but I do not feel humiliated by the greatness of God, any more than I tend to feel humiliated by the height of mountains or the depth of the Atlantic. Leave that aside, though, because it is true that the majesty of God has been assimilated into human hierarchies, has been used to legitimate the power of a variety of men (usually men) in golden hats. But Christianity carries inside it its own critique of this kind of easy confusion of God with kings, in the shape of the unsettling little voice which whispers that human power is an idol we're not supposed to worship. And Christianity, consequently, has always been available in morally egalitarian versions too. In this very place, it is a tough, undeferential, independent-minded religion; a religion for people living in a hard place that throws you on your own resources. The Free Presbyterian Church is not my church, and I differ from it

theologically in a number of important ways, but you really can't say
that they truckle to worldly power: that their understanding of the
sovereignty of God inclines them to obey any old order or suggestion that the world gives them. No. You can call that quality stubbornness if you like, or integrity, but really not servility. Instead, if
you're being honest, you should acknowledge that one of the powers
in Christianity, one of the possibilities coded deep in it, is that it can
underwrite self-sufficiency, by showing people that their relationship with God, when it comes to the crunch, is more important than
any duty to go along or get along. It can be maddening; but this
version of Christianity is one of the taproots of the English and
Scottish revolutions of the seventeenth century, and the American
Revolution of the eighteenth. It's the background to much of the
modern idea of a human being as a morally autonomous creature,
answerable to God, and therefore in this world primarily answerable
to him- or herself. This is why our puritan forefathers are worth
claiming as our own, even if we find ourselves elsewhere or nowhere
on the present-day religious map. Their stubbornness has a lot to do
with our freedom. I say in my book that if you're glad Darwin is on
the English £10 note, you should hug an Anglican, the Church of
England's acceptance of evolution having been one of the factors
sparing us an endless American-style culture war over the issue. In
the same spirit, if you're glad that it's King Conscience who really
rules in your head, and not some little onboard image of a man in a
gold hat – hug a Presbyterian. But you should probably ask first.

This brings us to a major problem, though. Here I am asserting
the absolute compatibility of science and religion – but what if this
admirable stubbornness manifests itself as a loyalty to creationism?
Shows itself as a commitment to Ussher's 6,000-year chronology
for the globe? Which it sometimes does, I understand, around here.

Let me make my own loyalties clear. [*Unbuttons top to reveal
'I ♥ Darwin' T-shirt underneath.*]

If it were up to me, I would say: Brothers and sisters in Christ,
your defence of a world in which promises are kept, and the world

possesses a human-sized meaning, and the Ark of Scripture carries us safe across a stormy sea, is admirable. But it makes its defence on the wrong ground. It is not trusting enough. It limits the sovereignty of the Lord by supposing that He can keep his promises, can hold to His Covenant, can carry us to safety, only in the terms of one human understanding of scripture. Whatever Richard Dawkins says, God and His promise and His love unto death for the human race *do not* vanish in a world in which the seven days of creation are not literal. The Lord our God is mightier than that. The sea is His, and He made it, and His hands prepared the dry land. We need not be doubting Him if we fearlessly ask *how*. He gave us the Book of Nature as well as the Book of Scripture, and as we look from one to the other, we can read fearlessly, knowing that no truth can contradict the God of truth.

But all of this is secondary, all of this dancing around the edges of science. Why do we think this is the stuff we should be talking about when we talk about faith? I myself do not think that it makes sense to talk about Christianity in terms of evidence, as if the inward experiences that promote faith were the same kind of thing as a collection of physical data. For me, the most we can prove is that God is not impossible – I'd quarrel with 'improbable' too, but that's a long argument for another time. I see faith and science as being non-competing but very different. Science is question, evidence, answer. Faith is – well, Hebrews 11:1: 'Faith is the substance of things hoped for, the evidence of things not seen.' That's a joke, of a kind. St Paul was as witty in his way as Oscar Wilde. No doubt it will strike Professor Dawkins as gobbledygook, paradox pointing nowhere. I prefer to think it points elsewhere, to the territories where feeling and imagination must be our guides.

Of course, God isn't imaginary – and I'm not saying He comes and goes depending on what you believe, either. I am not the kind of 'metaphorical Christian' Richard Dawkins refers to in the intro to the book. I don't think that God is a nice, grandiose way of talking about human aspirations; I don't think he's a fancy name for the warm feeling in your stomach when you do good. The Lord of Hosts is either there or He isn't: coldly, objectively, factually. Christians are people who take the risk of declaring that He is there. But we cannot prove it, so imagination must often be the tool by which we approach Him. Imagination is how we wake the printed words of scripture and discover how to join them to the stories of our own lives. Our whole lives.

The very worst thing *The God Delusion* does is to persuade people that religion is abstract; that it's a set of rather dud ideas, which, says Richard Dawkins, are in conflict with science, and which, says Richard Dawkins, can be proven to be scientifically unsound. Religion does not consist of a claim that God exists. He does – *I* think – but religion does not consist of going on and on and on about it. I do not rise in the morning and think to myself, 'Gosh, I wonder if God exists, as a religious person I am very interested in this question', any more than I wake up and subject my marriage to a cost–benefit analysis. 'Credit side: she's kind and lovely and cleverer than me. Debit side: we don't always get on, and neither of us are as young as we used to be. Yes, there's definitely a credit balance there – but I'll be revisiting this issue at dawn tomorrow.' I don't do that, and neither do I do the religious equivalent. Religion is as much about what you do and what you feel as what you think in the abstract. It's about the way we behave to each other. 'I was naked and you clothed me; I was sick and you visited me; I was in prison and you came to me' (Matthew 25:36). Religion exists in our relationships with each other and in our emotions. We have to feel it to know it. This is something the so-called New Atheists persistently get wrong. They talk as if you have the feelings because you've signed up to the ideas (or been brainwashed into the ideas by your evil parents). In my experience, it's the other way around: you're willing to sign up to the ideas, or to stay signed up to the ideas if you live in a Christian community, because you have the feelings already. You confirm in ideas what you already possess in experience. You hope, and so you credit 'the substance of things hoped for'; you see Christ, our God-with-us, our Emmanuel, in the faces of your fellows – your children, your husband, your sister, your enemy – and so you credit 'the evidence of things not seen'. I do *not* believe that any old thing can be true, just so long as you feel it. But I do believe that it is feeling that makes the truth *live* for us. It is feeling that binds our messy actual lives to the truth of our redemption. We are redeemed in practice, not in theory. We feel the grace that carries us when our own strength fails. 'See how these Christians love one another' – as Tertullian said the pagans used to say, back in the second century AD. Wars of religion, and bitternesses in Christian history which shame the hope we're supposed to stand for, have made that sentence seem ironic, but never completely. And that's where we have something which is beyond the reach of the atheist critique, outside its scope entirely.

In a little while, Professor Dawkins is going to be up here, and he's going to want to talk about science, because that's what he knows. But those are not the right terms for this conversation. Please, do not dance the literalist two-step with him. Do not agree with him that this is about dinosaur bones, or the age of the Earth, or about design versus natural selection. He will win that argument, and he deserves to, because he is right about those things. Do not agree with him that this is about measurable physical evidence. This is about the evidence of things not seen, the substance of things hoped for. This is about love, and sorrow, and suffering, and hope, and despair, and forgiveness. It is about love where logic would say: sorrow; and about hope where the rational expectation would be: despair. And Richard Dawkins has nothing to say to any of that, except: Look! There's a black hole! With luminous jets of interstellar gas! Isn't that amazing! And it is amazing. It is. But we need more than that. Man cannot live on awe, ladies and gentlemen, or by bread alone; but by every word that comes from God's mouth.

(2012)

PURITANS

When Thomas Paine was dying in Greenwich Village in June 1809, two Presbyterian ministers popped by to suggest that he would be damned if he didn't affirm his faith in Jesus Christ. 'Let me have none of your Popish stuff', he said firmly. 'Good morning.' Score one to Paine for exiting the world without compromising his convictions. But what he said had made, on the face of it, no sense. Faith in Christ as the path to salvation *isn't* 'Popish' in the sense of being particular to Roman Catholicism. He was speaking to a pair of impeccable Protestants. What he was doing, here, was to act as a very early adopter of a perception that would influence later atheist understandings of the world enormously. He was suggesting, in one charged and revealing insult, that the original Protestant critique of Catholicism should be extended to the whole of historic Christianity. All of it should be reformed away; all of it, absolutely *all* of it, deserved the contempt that zealous Puritans had once felt for indulgences and prayer beads and 'priestcraft'.

This post-Christian puritanism, largely oblivious now of its history, is highly visible in the 'New Atheism' of the 1990s and 2000s, and especially in *The God Delusion*. Strange indifference (except at the margins) to all religions except Christianity? Check. Sense of being locked in righteous combat with the powers of darkness? Check. Puritanism, it turns out, can float free of faith and still preserve a vehement worldview, a core of characteristic judgements. The world, it says, is afflicted by a layer of corrupting gunk, a gluey mass of lies and mistakes that purports to offer mediation between us and meaning but actually obscures it, actually hides the plain outlines of that truth we so urgently need. Moreover, this hiding, this obscuring, is wilful and culpable, maintained on purpose for the benefit of hierarchs, bullies, men in golden hats everywhere. It is our duty to take up the wire wool of reason and to scrub, scrub, scrub the lies away. For no mediation is necessary. We may have – we must have – a direct vision of the essential state of things. We must see the world as if through pure clear water, or empty air.

It's reassuring, in a way, to find this ancient continuity at work in the sensibility of Richard Dawkins, Sam Harris, Daniel Dennett, Jerry Coyne. It kind of makes up for their willed ignorance of all the actual emotional and intellectual structures of faith (as opposed to the will-o'-the-wisp 'Popery' in their heads). Richard Dawkins may be blithely indifferent to every word ever written about the differences between polytheism and monotheism, when he declares that Yahweh is the same as Odin, and all he wants 'is one god less' – but he is also keeping up a 400-year-old campaign against idolatry. That distant clapping sound you hear is Oliver Cromwell applauding.

However, the project is impossible – as impossible for the New Atheists as for every previous builder of a purified New Jerusalem. Direct, unmediated apprehension of truth is not available, except in the effortful special case of science. That gunk they scrub at so assiduously is the inevitable matter of human culture, of imagination. People secrete it, necessarily, faster than it can be removed. Metaphors solidify into stories wherever the reformers' backs are turned. We'll never arrive at the Year Zero where everything has its single right name and means only what science says it should. Religion being a thing that humans as a species do continuously, it seems unlikely that we'll stop, any more than we'll stop making music, laws, poetry or non-utilitarian clothes to wear. Imagination grows as fast as bamboo in the rain. The world cannot be disenchanted. Even advocacy for disenchantment becomes, inexorably, comically, an enchantment of its own, with prophets, with heresies, with its own pious mythography.

I think our recent, tentative turn away from the burning simplicities of *The God Delusion* (and the like) represents a recognition of this. The discovery by Alain de Botton and others of virtues and beauties that an atheist might want, in religion, is an anti-puritan move, a reconciliation of unbelief with the sprouting, curling, twining fecundity of culture. I don't expect the puritan call will lose its appeal to the young and the zealous, but maybe we're entering a phase of greater tolerance.

(2013)

WHO IS GOD? AN ANSWER FOR CHILDREN

First of all, here's who God isn't: He isn't a superhero. He isn't somebody like us, only stronger and faster and cleverer, using His special powers to zip around the world. In fact, He isn't part of the world at all. He's the reason there *is* a world. If you believe in Him, then all the things you see, from the faces of your friends to the stars a million light-years off, and all of the species of living things on Earth busily evolving away, are here because He made them. And He hasn't finished. He's still making them, pouring in love every moment to keep them all going. He never began and He's never going to end, and He never gets tired.

You can't prove He exists. (And you can't prove He doesn't, either.) But people who believe in Him – Christians and Jews and Muslims – tend to think we can feel Him being there. For us, He's there in the peaceful stillness of our minds, He's there in the sound of prayers, He's there when we don't feel lonely on a lonely road. Christians tend to feel He comes closest when we're being loving, and Jews and Muslims tend to feel it's when we're behaving fairly, but we all agree He cares about us, and He cares what we do.

We make mistakes and get things wrong, but He never gives up on us. He's the person who loves us no matter what. If that sounds like an ideal Mum or Dad, then it's not surprising, because to people who believe in Him, he is the Mum *and* Dad of the whole universe. Maybe we invented Him by thinking of mums and dads and then imagining a very big one: but it doesn't feel like that. It feels more as if the good things about families are a kind of little glimpse of what the universe we live in is really like in the end, despite everything.

When we do cruel things or destructive ones, we get further away from Him, and when we do kind things or sympathetic ones, we get closer to what He is like. Compared to Him, we're very temporary little people, looking at the world through the tiny windows of our two eyes. But, oddly enough, thinking of Him doesn't make us feel small – at least not in a gloomy or discouraging way. It's more like what you feel if you climb to the top of a very tall mountain, where the sun glitters like a diamond in a dark blue sky, and you can see for hundreds of miles in all directions. You discover that the world is much bigger than you knew it was, and that maybe, just maybe, you can be bigger than you thought you were, too.

(2012)

C.S. LEWIS AS APOLOGIST

It was writing apologetics that made C.S. Lewis famous. Not the
Narnia books, which followed after; not his Renaissance scholarship;
not the science fiction; not the autobiography. Not even the allegorical fiction that, with *The Screwtape Letters* and *The Great Divorce*,
became so essential to his imaginative power as a Christian writer. It
was out-and-out advocacy that created his connection with a mass
audience, beginning with the commission from James Welch of the
BBC in 1941 for the radio talks that eventually formed *Mere
Christianity*. The wartime BBC could only record sound on a very
limited supply of steel discs coated in acetate, so they preferred to
broadcast everything live where possible. Lewis travelled into Blitz-
struck London for each talk, returning by train to Oxford in the
middle of the night. In this setting of sirens and rubble, Lewis's voice
– drawling, unexpected, one part Belfast to nine parts Oxford –
reached hundreds of thousands, and then millions, of listeners, who
soon became readers too. The success of *Mere Christianity* in book
form opened the way to the rest of his public influence. Apologetics
turned him from an Oxford literary figure to a global one.

But the apologetic books are now far more important to his
reputation in the United States than they are here, because Britain

has moved much further away than the US from the situation they were devised for. As Lewis's friend Austin Farrar wrote in an early and brilliant essay on this strand of his work, 'the day in which apologetic flourishes is the day of orthodoxy in discredit; an age full of people talked out of the faith in which they were reared'. (And therefore capable of being talked back in, by a refreshment of what they once knew.) This may describe the contemporary American scene, where the theological vocabulary remains available and familiar even to those who think themselves indifferent to it, or hostile; but it doesn't match the contemporary Britain where faith is two or three generations distant, and the Christian inheritance persists only dimly and cloudily, in faint assumptions scarcely solidified into words. As Farrar went on to say, 'There can be no question of offering defences for positions which are simply unoccupied or of justifying ideas of which the sense has never dawned on the mind.' Where defence and justification do matter in Britain, Lewis's apologetics retain a following. Otherwise, this part of him has gone dormant for us.

If you look at *Mere Christianity*, *Miracles* or *The Problem of Pain* in Britain now, you find a mismatch between their chosen tools and the present-day audience. In the first place, though argument of some kind is intrinsic to apologetics, *their* argument is intensely, well, argumentative: knotty, up-front, in-your-face dialectics, explicitly foregrounding the sequence of the ideas. Lewis's favourite connectives are a teacherly 'See it this way', or 'Think of it this way', or even 'Now look here', none of which play well in a society that has taken the 'expressive turn' and which consequently values the authenticity of emotion over the appearance of logic. (Some of Lewis's logic now looks distinctly unconvincing *as* logic, too: more verbal procedure than rigorous thinking.) Then there is the problem of voice, which 'Now look here' already suggests. Lewis's literal speaking voice from the era of the radio talks is preserved in only one archived sample, the BBC having recycled almost all their steel disc recordings during the war, but he is metaphorically audible in every paragraph, and to a modern ear he comes across as painfully clipped and posh, his RP eloquence having been recategorised in the meantime as something class-discredited and authority-stained. Again, it probably supports his greater apologetic reputation in America that there his voice seems to come from somewhere off the social map altogether, rather than from a privileged and disreputable spot on it.

The irony is that these alienating qualities of his manner turn out to represent Lewis's rather brilliant solution, for *his* historical moment, to a problem that remains uncannily fresh. They follow from a diagnosis of what apologetics must do which has not dated at all. When the BBC first approached him with a request for 'a positive restatement of Christian doctrine in lay language', he said he thought that would be to begin 'a stage too far on'. 'It seems to me that the New Testament, by preaching repentance and forgiveness, always *assumes* an audience who already believe in the law of nature, and know that they have disobeyed it.' Unless people saw that Christianity represented an escape from an intelligible trap, a comfort for an intelligible sorrow, forgiveness for an intelligible guilt, there would be no reason for them to pay any attention to 'doctrine'. Apologetics had to begin earlier, with a recognisable account of what was wrong. He could reckon on far more knowledge in the reader than a present-day apologist, but the emotional ground to be covered remained the same.

Hence the ruefully cheerful insistence in *Mere Christianity* that a fallible chap was speaking to other fallible chaps; hence the acuity of its passing portraits of fear, spite, self-deception and other everyday sins. Hence the decision – rather strange to encounter, now – to introduce the Devil before either God or Christ, and to offer his hearers the metaphor of a world under enemy occupation. As they listened to their radios in streets of ruined houses, hearing the nightly bombers overhead, knowing that half of humankind lay that moment in tyrannical darkness, it must have seemed a plausible cosmic picture too. You can quarrel with the theology, and yet applaud the appeal that is being made to experience.

And he understood that voice was crucial. As Theo Hobson wrote recently in the *TLS*, 'Effective defenders of Christianity must sound like ordinary citizens ... Is this so hard? Yes. For they must also convey the awkward seriousness and strangeness of faith, its otherness.' It's true now, and it was true then. An uncanny doubleness of register was required: ordinariness, with a possibility of transfiguration.

Lewis's bluff broadcast voice (and its textual equivalent) solved the ordinariness part of the problem, for in 1941 it was easy to tell that this was a senior-common-room voice *off-duty*, gone down the pub and talking to its friends from within a set of shared reference points that included military service (in the Great War), family life, the pleasures of a pint and a joke. Meanwhile the transfiguration was supplied by Lewis's extraordinarily sensuous late-Romantic prose, which could be slipped into his ordinary sentences unaffectedly because it was genuinely the natural expression of his sensibility. He had genuinely been led into faith through the beauty of word and story, and he understood it himself through intensely vivid word-pictures that worked for him as apertures opening onto the far country of which faith was the news. As Farrar said in his funeral sermon for Lewis, his mind was at least as *pictorial* as it was argumentative. Which was both a power and a danger. It was quite easy for Lewis to make some subordinate point of opinion, some secondary metaphor of his own devising, so vivid that it seemed for the reader to shine with as much importance as far more central points of the creed.

Apologetics, after all, is a literature of the imagination. Its cousins are the memoir, the literary essay, even the travel book. Like the memoir it turns the private tissue of life into convertible coin, like an essay it makes the line of an explanation as concretely felt as it can be, like travel writing it delivers the sensations and incidents of a journey: all to accomplish for a reader on the outside of belief what an insider does not, strictly, need. (Though it's always a pleasure for a believing reader to see our own half-lit, half-understood experience more perfectly articulated than we could manage ourselves.) The apologist is trying, above all, to convey the body of a truth. For a believer, of course, truth already has a body, in several ways, 'body' being the site of one of Christianity's profound puns. Our truth *is* a body, the body of the incarnated Lord, and it makes *us* a body, the body of Christ which is the Church, every time we eat the bread which is also the body of Christ. More routinely, truth also has a body for us as believers in the sense that it is carnally present to us all the time, in bodily habit and bodily movement; in the lived shapes of a life. But if you're on the outside, this kind of body is exactly what belief has not got. Apologetics is in the business of trying to create for the reader of goodwill a kind of temporary, virtual body for faith; one they can borrow and try out, so that they may have a concrete inkling of what it might be like to assent, long before they do.

Lewis was superlatively good at this, leaving decades' worth of readers with the sense of having dwelled, on terms of almost uncanny intimacy, within the sense-world of Lewis's own faith. But he did it at some cost to himself. To perform this truth, to successfully stage the appearance of truth's true body, required the apologetic equivalent of the chip of ice in the heart needed for other kinds of imaginative literature. Like Charles Dickens weeping over the death of Jo the crossing sweeper as he wrote *Bleak House*, and yet noting in the daybook for that day's work 'Jo: *kill him*', it calls for you to manipulate expertly what at the same time you genuinely feel. Lewis was much too spiritually self-aware not to grow uneasy. 'I have found', he told a group of priests in Wales in 1944,

> that nothing is more dangerous to one's own faith than the work of an apologist. No doctrine of the Faith seems to me so spectral, so unreal as the one that I have just defended in a public debate. For a moment, you see, it has seemed to rest on oneself; as a result, when you go away from that debate, it seems no stronger than that weak pillar . . .

It has been a truism about Lewis for a while now – probably since A.N. Wilson's biography came out – that the turn towards Narnia in his later life was driven by apologetics having, in some way or other, gone wrong for him. The public defeat of his argument in *Miracles* by Elizabeth Anscombe in 1947 usually figures in the story. But Alan Jacobs has recently argued[15] that he may have fled to fiction because apologetics had gone so right for him; because he was feeling, with troubling intensity, the dangerous weight apologetics laid on his imagination. In fiction, even allegorical fiction, the layer of story and the layer of the truth it stands for are further apart. In Narnia, he could let imagination more straightforwardly be the power that makes things up. In Narnia, a lion in a snowy wood could stand for truth, without truth in turn depending on his successful storytelling.

(2013)

WHAT CAN SCIENCE FICTION
TELL US ABOUT GOD?

Speaking as a reader of SF who also happens to be a church-going believer – not much, really.

Part of the reason for this is cultural. In theory, speculative fiction's power to reinvent the world is unlimited: every category can be reconfigured, every familiarity subverted, any conceivable strangeness brought within the household of story. In practice – though enough of that power gleams and lingers to keep us reading, and hoping, and periodically being gorgeously surprised – the genre is as shaped by a particular history as any other school of writing, and it's got, if not walls round the edges, then very definite centres of imaginative gravity. Its roots in Britain are in the 'scientific romance' as H.G. Wells invented it. Its roots in the US are in pulp magazine publishing for an audience of engineers and technicians. The two strands had different defaults in terms of mood, with the British branch doing catastrophe and visions of entropic futility, and the American one a lot more chipper and technology-friendly. But both of them come out of the late nineteenth/early twentieth-century cultural buzz around science; out of para-science, scientism, the zone of cultural meaning and implication and metaphor science always seems to be generating, and in which, from then until now, it tends to look a great deal more certain than it does from within the actual practice of science itself that the enterprise is inherently anti-religious. That the way to understand the world is as a contest between faith and science, with SF naturally serving as reason's excitable little friend. So SF was watermarked from the beginning by the assumption that its cherished values are anti-religious, or at least un-religious, ones. There's a hint of the South Place Ethical Society, a whisper of the Rationalist Press Association, in the genre's DNA from the start.

And recently, it's been reinforced by the polarising effects of America's culture wars, which have successfully scared many writers into seeing religion as something they *must* be hostile to, if they wish to be friends to scepticism, generosity, sexual freedom, tolerance, irony, individual autonomy, and even storytelling as such. The sense of needing to pick a side produces gyrations like this, as Ursula Le Guin reviews a Salman Rushdie novel in the *Guardian* in 2005:

> Science and literary fantasy would seem to be intellectually incompatible, yet both describe the world; the imagination functions actively in both modes, seeking meaning, and wins intellectual consent through strict attention to detail and coherence of thought, whether one is describing a beetle or an enchantress. Religion, which prescribes and proscribes, is irreconcilable with both of them, and since it demands belief, must shun their common ground, imagination.

I revere Le Guin, but this is silly. It cordons off religion as the one domain of the human imagination which is not allowed to be called 'imagination', or to resemble the rest of imagination: it may not have any content except authoritarian commanding and forbidding. (And, meanwhile, the legitimate rest of imagination is stuck with mimicking scientific rigour, as if imaginative rigour didn't work in rather different ways.)

It's silly; but Ursula Le Guin isn't, and neither are most of the writers who feel obliged to maintain it as a line beyond which their sympathy and their curiosity stop, either in aid of the original American culture-clash, or in support of the strange, pale, out-of-toner photocopy of it which now seems to be overlaid on things over here too. So the effect is not that their work never engages with religion as a deep human pattern of meaning-seeking. It's that it tends to engage with it only on condition that the religion be an invented one, or at any rate, that it not be recognisable as monotheism. Le Guin herself has written with profound anthropological and poetic understanding about how ritual works, how devotion works, how wonder gets channelled in custom, how brutal and hopeful versions of the same belief can co-exist. But only when looking at the adapted Taoism of Earthsea, the story-religion of *The Telling*, the slave cults and warrior cults of *Four Ways to Forgiveness*. Bring back the familiar signifiers of turbans, mitres and yarmulkes, and suddenly we're in the territory of Sheri S. Tepper's *Grass*, where worshipping one God necessarily implies a nasty, closed-minded, patriarchal sham. Or we're in Neal Stephenson's *Anathem*, which devotes hundreds of pages to how cool medieval monasteries are, and must therefore reassure us at frequent intervals that theism is shtoopid. She was cataloguing the clichés of fantasy, not of SF, but Diana Wynne Jones's *Tough Guide to Fantasyland* gets both genres bang to rights when she points out that priests of one male God are almost invariably power-crazed and malignant. If you want to give religion friendly coverage, you go for plural female deities, feisty and sex-positive, or for an attractively gender-balanced triad.

Which is not to say that SF has *never* had interesting or mind-expanding things to say about organised religion. Serious Catholics like Gene Wolfe or the late Walter M. Miller brought with them into their SF a believer's confident readiness to play with what they confidently possessed. *The Book of the New Sun* is a darkly defamiliarised game with the fundamental Christian story; Miller's *Saint Leibowitz and the Wild Horse Woman* is, even more than his more famous *A Canticle for Leibowitz*, a song of praise for prayer in a mangled world. Then there's Kim Stanley Robinson's intimate imagining of Islamic mysticism in *The Years of Rice and Salt* – a Buddhist feeling his way into someone else's nirvana. Or China Miéville demonstrating, in *Kraken* and *Embassytown*, that, to a good Marxist, 'the opium of the people' can be the beginning of intelligent sympathy, rather than a dismissal. Or, to be a bit provocative, Ken MacLeod, officially a red-hot atheist, whose *The Night Sessions*, about a Calvinist artificial intelligence, is full of theological wit, and even a delicate regret for the impossibility of belief. A fine and godly discourse, Elder MacLeod, in the post-Presbyterian mode.

But it's not much of a haul, as I say. And maybe this is a good thing, because from a believer's point of view, there's another reason, fundamental to SF's modus operandi, why there'd be more loss than gain if SF *did* try to explore 'God'. It's a genre which, famously, does story rather than metaphor. It's a genre which explores an idea by solidifying it; by running a thought-experiment in narrative. What we mean when we say that SF can (in theory) represent anything – that it's a kind of Turing Machine of storytelling – is that it can project any idea as an actuality on the story-plane, the screen of imagination. So, yes, it is perfectly possible to write SF in which (for instance) the objects of Christian belief become tangibly, unambiguously *there* in the story, exactly as present as the rest of the stuff it represents. And it has been done, in C.S. Lewis's Cosmic trilogy: angels, the Devil, a literal Eden relocated to Venus, even a fantasmagorical glimpse of God himself. But the result is a reduction, not an enhancement. It's a demotion of a God who (says faith) precedes and exceeds the universe into a being with the same status as an imaginary coffee table, or starship, or character. If you're a believer, God is not a thought experiment requiring a special sub-creation to be tried out in. He's an actual, er, actuality, already, embedded in a necessary and true story about guilt, hope and liberty.

I don't *want* C.S. Lewis doing his resourceful best to render Him as a fabulous special effect. Speaking as a Christian, I'd rather be reading about Charlie Stross's guy from the Laundry who's waiting for Cthulhu with his shotgun.

(2011)

UNEASY IN IRAN

Last year, visiting Iran to write an article for a travel magazine, I went to see the tomb of the late Ruhollah Musavi of Khomein, expert in the law of contract, practitioner of the *erfan* school of contemplative prayer, founder of the Islamic Republic. Khomeini's shrine is surrounded by the acres of parking spaces you find in the West around a Disney attraction. And there I met a giant pulling a small trolley. He was a conscript soldier about 7 feet tall, perhaps a little slow in the head, set to guard the car park. The trolley contained his bedroll. We took his picture, and in return he showed us a little album of colour photos he kept tucked away. Most of them were pictures of the shrine's gold domes from various angles, at various times of day, but the last one showed the ayatollah sitting on a sofa blessing a little girl in a party frock, his hand resting on her head. Both of them were smiling. I assumed that this must be a memento of a treasured encounter between Khomeini and a member of the soldier's family, but no: it was Khomeini with his own granddaughter, and the soldier was carrying it because for him it represented a connection with the sanctity of the man whose grave he was watching over. In short, it was a relic. I had found it hard to recognise it as one because it was a slightly dog-eared print on Kodachrome, rather than an object marked out as holy by its great age, or by a container of precious metal, or by its location in a more obvious sanctuary than the pocket of a khaki jacket.

Khomeini was not a saint to me. I am not a Shi'ite Muslim, but an Anglican. Between me and the soldier lay the perceptual gulf which follows from the difference between Islamic and Christian histories of the world. For Christians, the possibility of using the power of the state to enforce righteousness is a temptation, and one often succumbed to over 2,000 years, but is always held in tension with the antinomian message of forgiveness at the religion's core. The structures of law Christians have built have constantly been challenged by their own belief in an ultimate grace greater than law. For Muslims, on the other hand, God and the law fit together exactly. The second is the earthly representation of the first's perfection. Muslims would find it unimaginable for God to behave as Jesus described Him doing in the parable of the day labourers, capriciously and *inequitably* giving the same reward to people who have deserved different ones. It is not just a possibility, but a duty, for Muslims to build the community of laws that will be pleasing to God. And so, to the soldier at the shrine, Khomeini was a blessed leader of the struggle for righteousness; while I, on my side of the gulf, did not think that God's intentions in history were of the kind that could be mirrored by a government, and I certainly could not believe that a good God would have endorsed the revolutionary cruelties of Khomeini's theocracy, and its intolerance, and its brutally expedient persecution of a British citizen for writing a novel.

But I could feel something else in my response to the soldier's photograph: an uneasy sense that my liberal insistence that it was very hard to identify God's will was dry, and sad, compared to the soldier's vivid feeling that holiness was alive and available in the world, and could easily flow into a snap of an old man and a little girl on a sofa. His tenderness towards his relic demanded respect. This became one of the constant motifs of my visit: the discovery of familiar spiritual substance in a different spiritual form, followed by a disquieting reflection on the greater passion of Iranian Islam compared to my own half-in, half-out Christianity, and perhaps to too much of Christendom in general.

The place wouldn't have touched me in the same way if it had seemed wholly alien, but I kept finding strangeness and familiarity layered inside each other, like the skins of an onion. Khomeini's shrine, for example, is unbeautiful inside. The roof is held up by metal trusses like the roof of an airport or an industrial estate. The ring of stained-glass tulips around the dome – they are the martyrs' flower – was crudely executed. Everywhere, in fact, the construction shows signs of the zealous haste with which the volunteer builders had worked. This was the place where that terrifying film was shot showing the helicopter trying to deliver the ayatollah's body while a hysterical crowd surged to and fro. When I left my shoes at the men's entrance, passed through the security search, and stepped out onto the marble floor, I was at first mostly aware of a lingering sense of threat, and of a need to be very cautious. (It was not a place where anyone with a sense of self-preservation would have shouted 'Salman Rushdie *lives!*') Then, gradually, without my sense of caution, and even fear, entirely fading away, I began to recognise the atmosphere. Pilgrims who had travelled from far away were sleeping on the Persian carpets provided for them, under the flags and the streamers and the placards wishing 'our dear Ruhollah' a happy birthday. Young men were softly saying their prayers, together but not synchronised with one another, so that the act was both corporate (in the same sense in which Christians say that the Church is 'one body') and, for each, an individual approach to God. Over in the women's section, one supplicant was lying on the floor beside the tomb itself, not in an attitude of abasement or prostration but one of intense yearning, her hand pressed hard against the glass wall enclosing it as if she were completing a circuit. The shrine was quiet exactly as a cathedral is: a quietness without passivity, an intent and directed quietness. In fact, it seemed to me that it *was* a cathedral, functionally speaking, for I found myself completely and instinctually certain that I was in

174

a house of the God who exceeds all descriptions, but whom all three monotheisms know to be the merciful, the compassionate. It was transparently a place where prayer has been valid. If a Christian can be reverent in a shrine dedicated to a strong-arm medieval saint like Olaf, you can certainly be reverent in the shrine of Ruhollah Khomeini: and still more so, I discovered later, in the ancient mosques of Iran, where beauty supplements faith.

The theology of Shi'ite Islam, too, seemed to return somewhere very familiar, after starting from a point of alienating difference. The problem a Christian has with Khomeini as a model of sanctity is repeated with every one of the great figures of the Shi'ite tradition, because, believing in the necessity of the just state here on earth, they took up the sword to create it. Before I came to Iran I saw a nineteenth-century devotional painting showing the Imam Husayn, with halo, splitting an adversary's skull in battle. You could not have a more complete contrast with Jesus' decision in Gethsemane. And yet history's foundational event for Shi'ites, after the revelation of the Quran to Muhammad, is one of profound and tragic failure: Husayn, who should as the grandson of the Prophet have been the guide and guardian of Islam, came to his own, and his own received him not. Every year, Iranians re-enact the death of Husayn in passion plays. Husayn was a holy warrior, not an incarnate God taking on the suffering of the world. But the bowl of water brought to the dying man by his brother Abbas parallels the sponge and the reed, and the onlookers weep with a familiar sense of culpable helplessness, and the result is that Shi'ites, like Christians, have a theology with grief at its centre. When they ask God for comfort in sorrow, they let their individual sorrows flow into the great river of the original grief: only for Shi'ites it carries their grief to God through the battlefield at Karbala, not through Golgotha. Karbala is in modern Iraq, but Karbala soil is available in Iran in compressed tablets, which the devout rub on their foreheads when they pray.

Out of the corner of my eye, as I walked through Iranian bazaars, I kept glimpsing what looked like icons of the Madonna and Child.

When I turned round, of course, they never were. The haloed child was Husayn, sitting on the knee of Fatima, the Prophet's daughter. Just as an Orthodox Jew must think of Christianity as a rather bizarre and distorted cult version of Judaism, so any kind of Christian, looking at this Islamic version of one of our most utterly familiar images, has to feel that this is a picture of the wrong people, that an approach is being made to the right God by the wrong means. And yet it clearly is the right God, which puts you in the strange position of disagreeing with Shi'ism over who is holy, and even over what holiness is, but still, simultaneously, agreeing about holiness's object: what it points to, where it wants to take us. At the heart of Islam, where the individual soul travels towards the plenitude and absoluteness of God, there is a huge area of feeling and experience that Muslims and Christians possess in common. The journey is the same, its surprises and difficulties and moments of grace are the same. Here, whether or not the law was necessary to get you here, the law falls away. George Herbert's poems charting the travails of the soul with its divine lover parallel those of Hafez the Sufi, writing three centuries earlier in Shiraz. The woman I saw pressing the glass of Khomeini's tomb so eagerly would surely have recognised herself in the psalm: *Like as the hart desireth the waterbrooks, so hath my soul desired the living God.* First the thirst was Judaic, then it was Christian too, and now it is also Muslim; and always the same thirst.

Liberals and semi-detached believers like me tend to draw an easy distinction for all three of the monotheisms, between a closed and fanatical version of faith and one which we respect because it is properly open to doubt. Perhaps it is too easy a distinction. It's true that fundamentalist certainty runs away very easily into emotional idolatry, with subordinate points of faith, or reverence for religious leaders, or attachment to cherished customs, wishfully inheriting the surety that ought to be reserved for God alone. I certainly saw enough of that in Iran: the disquietingly sexual murals, fading now, of the martyrs of the war against Saddam, which show young men rapturously bleeding as they hold tulips in ones, in twos, in armfuls. Or take what the revolutionary guards were chanting to Ayatollah Khamenei last summer as they counter-demonstrated against the students – 'Supreme Leader! We donate to you the blood in our bodies!' But perhaps my tenacious uncertainty has an equally besetting flaw. Perhaps, I thought as I travelled in Iran, I use my intellectual doubt to limit the power that I let faith have in my life; to keep the thirst that is so signally alive in Khomeini's shrine mild, and manageable, and incapable of disturbing me.

I was often moved in Iran. After dark at a shrine in Shiraz, a boy on crutches, washing his hands in the courtyard pool, unselfconsciously joined in the lament for Husayn broadcast over the loudspeakers. Strings of fairy lights lit up the shrine's dome like a Fabergé egg. But I was most moved by a small blue tile inset in the wall of the Sheikh Lotfollah mosque in Isfahan. This building is everything that Khomeini's tomb is not: a masterpiece of religious architecture, an exquisite late-seventeenth-century space knitted together by ceramic traceries of vines, on a background of brown and lemon and turquoise. The blue tile said, 'Constructed by Mohammed Reza son of Master Hoseyn Isfahani the mason, a poor small man in need of the love of God.' Mohammed Reza must have known, as a craftsman, what he had accomplished, but it seemed only justice to him, and to his possession of a soul that (like everyone's) requires forgiveness, to hear in his words a sincere certainty that the most he could do fell short of the glory he had set out to celebrate.

After seeing the Sheikh Lotfollah, we had lunch at an Armenian restaurant, where our guide was amused to find that his two European charges couldn't pick out Judas in a reproduction of Leonardo's *Last Supper*. 'Never mind', he said reassuringly, 'we call you Europeans "Christians", but I know you aren't, really.' I came home obscurely ashamed.

(2000)

WILD THEISM

To say, as people do from time to time, that science is the only source of meaning available to human beings is to consign large swathes of everyday experience to insignificance. (And to offer an open goal to any quick-footed apologist for religion who may be passing.) The implication of the maximal claim for science is that anything that can't be brought within the reach of hypothesis–experiment–conclusion is to be ignored. I've heard Richard Dawkins, on a stage, respond to someone asking why people's conviction of the presence of God doesn't count as data: 'Oh, all sorts of funny things happen in people's heads. But you can't measure them, so they don't mean anything.' Yet atheists, like everybody else, fall in love, read novels, hum songs, and value the unrepeatable shadings of their sensory and cognitive experiences. The subjective makes its irrefutable demand for attention as soon you quit the lectern. 'Funny things in people's heads' is where we live.

So after periods of intense polemic there often comes a point when the polemicists double back to give subjectivity its due. It happened in the nineteenth century at the historical moment after utilitarianism had made its maximal claim that we are all self-interested calculators. John Stuart Mill's *Autobiography* (1873) records his younger self's discovery that, alongside the utilitarian reading list, he could allow himself the unrigorous beauties of Wordsworth. 'I never turned recreant to intellectual culture, or ceased to consider the power and practice of analysis as an essential condition both of individual and of social improvement. But I thought that it had consequences which required to be corrected, by joining other kinds of cultivation with it.' And now, with the maximal claim of New Atheism just behind us, it seems to be happening again: a similar spiritual stirring, defended by a similar insistence that 'analysis', or its contemporary equivalent, has not been betrayed.

Waking Up[16] is the recently published memoir by the least-nuanced member of the New Atheist 'four horsemen'. Sam Harris outs himself as a surreptitious long-time practitioner of meditation, which he tries to show to be compatible in every way with a comfortable contempt for faith. Then there is *Living with a Wild God*,[17] the altogether stranger, more wonderful and more stubbornly independent book by the activist and atheist Barbara Ehrenreich. This account of a lifelong unbeliever's buried history of religious experience is radically open and undefended: a true seeker's document, written with a pen rather than a rivet gun. These are the best examples of a recent spate of books, perhaps a new kind of literature, that trace in personal terms the intersection of belief and unbelief (another, lesser example is Richard Dawkins' *Appetite for Wonder*). Welcome to the world of atheist spiritual memoir.

Though Ehrenreich and Harris enter from very different directions, they agree on many things once they arrive. Both have visionary or mystical material to report that they insist is not merely a mental epiphenomenon, not just a subjective fizz in the cortex, not a delusion. What has happened to them, they say, is real. It reveals something about the nature of things. Then, too, both of them think their experiences need to be protected from the ways in which religion would describe them. Both write as if American Christianity waits hungrily by with the wrong vocabulary, the wrong frame of ideas, and must be fended off. As Harris says, 'It is decidedly inconvenient for the forces of reason and secularism that if someone wakes up tomorrow feeling boundless love for all sentient beings, the only people likely to acknowledge the legitimacy of his experience will be representatives of one or other Iron Age religion or New Age cult.'

They even describe their experiences in recognisably parallel terms, providing a quick and dirty empirical demonstration that it is the common ground of human perceptual life they're talking about, not anything too bizarrely individual. Sam Harris by the Sea of Galilee, sometime in the last decade:

In an instant, the sense of being a separate self – an 'I' or a 'me' – vanished. Everything was as it had been – the cloudless sky, the brown hills sloping to an inland sea, the pilgrims clutching their bottles of water – but I no longer felt separate from the scene, peering out at the world from behind my eyes. Only the world remained.[18]

The teenage Barbara Ehrenreich at a horse show in New England, sometime in the 1950s:

Something peeled off the visible world, taking with it all meaning, inference, association, labels, and words. I was looking at a tree, and if anyone had asked, that's what I would have said I was doing, but the word 'tree' was gone, along with all the notions of tree-ness that had accumulated in the last dozen or so years since I had acquired language. Was it a place that was suddenly revealed to me? Or was it a substance – the indivisible, elemental material out of which the entire known and agreed-upon world arises as a fantastic elaboration?[19]

Both begin with the discovery that there are human experiences that radically refresh perception by getting outside the envelope of our habitual construction of things, and both believe these must be taken seriously. But the differences follow immediately thereafter. For Harris, such alterations of perception are the tranquil, controllable results of a technique which his book helpfully undertakes to teach you, offering advice about posture, breathing and dealing with distractions. For Ehrenreich, they have been startling, unsought visitations, beginning with the vision of the tree in the watery Massachusetts light, and then accelerating when her family moved to cloudless California into unsettling states of rupture.

Consequently, their reflections entail entirely different levels of discomfort and risk, and are written at quite different levels of literary intensity. Ehrenreich wrestles with an angel. Harris puts together some self-assembly instructions for a couch. And experiences so differently weighted, so differently grounded, unsurprisingly are taken to prove wholly different non-religious truths. If we were to emulate Sam Harris, that would be a reason to ignore both. He's very fond of the supposedly knock-down argument that the differences between religions void the case for them all. Sauce, goose, gander, Sam; but actually the issue is too interesting to leave so swiftly alone.

To Harris, meditation teaches happiness by teaching detachment. It shows you how to exist at a calm remove from your own frantic desires and thoughts, and thus to escape the cycles of craving and consumption in which contemporary life promises you may find fulfilment. So far, so Buddhist – in a carefully de-theologised kind of a way. He doesn't, obviously, believe in the inspirited world of Buddhism as a folk religion, or in the Buddha himself as a propitiatory figure, or in specific Buddhist ethics except where they coincide with his preferred, vague, self-evident Golden-Rulery. But he has nicer things to say about the Buddhist tradition than about any of the monotheisms. He praises its scriptures as 'empirical'. They offer intelligible, how-to guides to doing things with your consciousness, from which you can easily snip off the regrettable elements of 'superstition'. He has looked at the Bible and the Quran and discovered that, stuffed as they are with narrative, poetry, biography, law-giving, metaphor and other unsystematic dreck from the Iron Age, they are hardly useful at all as 'manuals for contemplative understanding'. Pick the right Buddhist sutra, however, and it's almost like doing science.

The primacy of science is the main lesson of his account of meditation. When you learn to regard your own anxious self as a fiction, a cobbled-together illusion of control which you need not scurry to maintain, and you dissolve gently into the ocean of consciousness, you are in effect doing neuroscience. Hypothesis, experiment, conclusion. You are obtaining an experiential confirmation of the latest consciousness research, which (he says) suggests that the self as we imagine it is in truth an imperfect post hoc improvisation by our minds, retrofitted to the shoreless ocean within to give us the illusion of being coherent to ourselves. Consciousness is real; the self is not; meditation shows us so; and happiness is to be found in learning to conform to the deep peace of this discovery. Quite how he gets from here to the universal love with 'the character of a geometric proof', 'deeper than any personal history could justify', which he experiences while experimenting with MDMA, is not clear. It's deeply important to him that the visionary should imply the ethical, easily and straightforwardly, but readers who don't share his confidence that virtue is self-evident will tend to think that the step from *is* to *ought* is harder and more puzzling than he allows.

Indeed, a surprising proportion of the latter part of the book consists of fire-fighting, as he endeavours to deal with the frequently erratic and unsavoury and downright unappealing behaviour of some gurus, who palpably know the way to the sea of inner peace, and yet spend their time drunk, or philandering, or collecting Rolls-Royces with their disciples' money. Worriedly reporting a Zen parable in which the master makes a point by lopping off a child's finger with a knife, he trembles on the brink of a whole new way of reading. New to him, anyway: 'Ancient tales of liberating violence . . . seem like literary teaching devices, not accurate accounts of how wisdom has been reliably transmitted from master to disciple.' Hey hey hey: could it be that other ones of these old religious-type documents might be full of complicated non-literal meanings? Metaphors and other verbal gizmos that might stop them just being failures as meditation manuals?

But it's an implication too far for him. He is too wedded to a flat, one-ply account of religion – the monotheisms especially – as a set of falsifiable propositions. And when he tries to summarise what he takes to be theism's essential proposition, you begin to see why faith is emotionally as well as conceptually impossible for him. It's all about coercion, about a scary form of Otherness:

> In Judaism, Christianity and Islam, the human soul is conceived as genuinely separate from the divine reality of God. The appropriate attitude for a creature that finds itself in this circumstance is some combination of terror, shame, and awe. In the best case, notions of God's love and grace provide some relief – but the central message of these faiths is that each of us is separate from, and in relationship to, a divine authority who will punish anyone who harbors the slightest doubt about His supremacy.[20]

He calls this 'dualism', using the term in a distinctly non-standard way to mean not the Cartesian or Platonic soul/body distinction, but the violation of the peaceful ocean by the suggestion that there is another something out there to be discovered. Terror, shame, awe: if these emotions are theism's fundamentals, if being crushed and humiliated is its 'central' offering, then any theistic interpretation of what Sam Harris experiences when he dissolves into transpersonal peace and love and freedom must be threatening. For him, axiomatically, God does not equal peace, or love, or freedom. If He existed at all, God would be a force engaged in a zero-sum dominance game. He'd be a mugger, a pirate on the sea of consciousness. Or, worse yet, he'd make the sea itself angry, and terrifying: not

183

a place where a self-respecting atheist could go to melt away, to lose the illusion of self safely.

There is no safety at all in what Barbara Ehrenreich has to report. Her first visions or revelations of the world's pre-verbal grid, its bare chassis of being beneath all the domesticating specifics of California and Massachusetts, came at a point in her adolescence when she had worked herself into a kind of solipsistic terror over mortality. Stoicism and intellectual honour seemed to require that she dispense with more and more sources of possible consolation for her impending personal extinction, up to and very much including the unprovable reality of other people. On the outside, she might have looked like an averagely gloomy teenager in a plaid dress with lace cuffs, reading Nietzsche in a coffee house and resisting her high-school class in Life Adjustment.

Inside, she was clinging to minute crannies in the walls of a one-person abyss. She wrote in her journal, 'I am Nietzsche's rope dancer and the rope is imaginary. If I look down for an instant and see that there is nothing there, I'm lost.' Not much assistance was to be expected from her parents. 'I understood the family, my family at least, to be a temporary and unstable unit like one of those clumsily named elements down at the bottom of the periodic table, Berkelium or Rutherfordium, for example.' Her father was a clever, angry former copper miner from Butte, Montana, clawing his way up the corporate ladder in a haze of martinis and self-disgust; her mother was a clever, angry reader of every book she could get her hands on, and another heroic drinker, experiencing the duties of 1950s femininity as a personal damnation. Fission loomed.

Ehrenreich renders their portraits with powerful adult understanding, but (again a point of honour) with no more charity than she actually feels. She denies several times that *Living with a Wild God* is anything resembling an autobiography, but of course it is, and a very fine one; a spiritual autobiography, with narrow, sometimes needle-fine focus, recording the isolation and the concentration and the invisible desperation of a mind turning in on itself, and seeming to lose its grip on the world.

Then, aged seventeen, she went on a road trip north from LA – the car driven by a sort-of boyfriend who, somehow inevitably, later turned out to have been transporting ancient, dangerous nitroglycerine in the trunk – and slept the night parked up in a side street in the town of Lone Pine. Walking out the stiffness in the grey early light, she began to have another of her familiar episodes of dissociation. But it turned without warning into something else:

> At some point in my predawn walk – not at the top of hill, or at the exact moment of sunrise, but in its own good time – the world flamed into life. How else to describe it? There were no visions, no prophetic voices or visits by totemic animals, just this blazing everywhere. Something poured into me and I poured out into it. This was not the passive beatific merger with 'the All', as promised by the Eastern mystics. It was a furious encounter with a living substance that was coming at me through all things at once, and one reason for the terrible wordlessness of the experience is that you cannot observe fire really closely without becoming part of it. Whether you start as a twig or a gorgeous tapestry, you will be recruited into the flame and made indistinguishable from the rest of the blaze.[21]

Whatever this was, it was not a gentle experience. Indeed in some respects it resembled the encounter with an irresistible cosmic bully that seems to be what Sam Harris least wants. As Ehrenreich observes now, ' "Ecstasy" would be the word ... but only if you are willing to acknowledge that ecstasy does not occupy the same spectrum as happiness or euphoria, that it participates in the anguish of loss and can resemble an outbreak of violence.' Back then, though, not knowing what to say, she immediately took her own advice and said nothing. She walked the rest of the way up the street to a diner and ate some toast with the sort-of boyfriend, never mentioning that the world had just briefly metamorphosed into immanent fire; and she went on not mentioning it over the decades that followed. She wrote down an account, and then confined the journal pages in question to a folder she never revisited, yet never parted with either, aware that there was something in there that awaited an accounting, that existed in troubling discord with her stated principles. 'The impasse was this: if I let myself speculate even tentatively about that *something*, if I acknowledged the possibility of a nonhuman agent or agents, some mysterious Other, intervening in my life, could I still call myself an atheist?'

Living with a Wild God is that long-delayed reckoning, disinterring the encounter in Lone Pine, adding to it later brushes at Key West with a 'face I could almost begin to make out in the foam', and trying her best to follow out the implications wherever they led, no matter the embarrassment. (She has indeed been pilloried for her apostasy.) It is an exhilarating book to read, for 'vague gurgles of surrender' still never satisfy her, and in her search for exactitude she constantly resharpens the expressive edge of her prose. Where she is headed seems genuinely up for grabs. She is reasoning herself along without a set destination, without the safety net of church or party, and she is as unsparing of herself as she is of her parents. Naught for our comfort, and naught for hers.

One thing she is sure of, though: whatever it is that lobbies for her attention in thunderheads and thrift-store windows, whatever it was that set the world on fire in Lone Pine, it cannot be the God of Christianity and Judaism and Islam. Partly, this is a matter of continuing family loyalty. Whatever her parents' drawbacks, they raised her in a tradition of defiant working-class unbelief which represents to her a precious commitment to this-worldly good. Partly, on the other hand, it's that her experience decisively fails to match what she understands of monotheism. For her, in absolute contradistinction to Sam Harris, *ought* and *is* are entirely separate categories. Religion is pre-eminently the domain of *ought*, of do's and don'ts which her sceptical eye very readily interprets as convenient cover stories for power. Meanwhile she believes that her Other, burning away, is not moral at all. 'My own "epiphanies", to overglorify them, had nothing to do with right or wrong, good or evil, kindness or cruelty, or any other abstractions arising from the human tribal life that I had only recently entered into.' A couple of traditional anti-religious themes play a supporting role, too – an argument from theodicy, a repulsion at the prospect of eternal life – but this is the core of her refusal. 'Whatever I had seen *was what it was*, with no moral valence or reference to human concerns.' With a God of ethics or creed or scripture consequently ruled out, what she is left with is therefore a kind of freelance or zoological theism. The world may be infested with one or many amoral spirit-beasts, bulging under the ontological skin of things. 'Wild' in her title turns out to mean not just unconditioned but actually feral. At this conclusion, of course, monotheists and atheists will swivel round together in rare unanimity to glare at her. Neither side wants this picture she arrives at, by being too honest to deny her experience, and too stubborn to accept any organised, existing description of it.

For a Christian, reading *Living with a Wild God* is frequently frustrating. Despite her brilliance, Ehrenreich makes slow, heavy weather of ideas which for a believer flow together in swift fluent cascades. When she quotes Meister Eckhart saying that God must be born in every soul in 'a sort of nest, or as Eckhart sometimes puts it, a "manger" ' – and calls the result 'shockingly zoomorphic', as if he were proposing that a spiritual parasite will lay eggs in us – can she really not have noticed that he has something Bethlehem-related in mind? A bit of Thomism would help with her firmly post-Protestant sense that a creator would have to be transcendently remote from creation. A familiarity with the Psalms would correlate her startled reflection that 'I was not afraid of dying, because it was obvious that the Other … would continue just fine without me', with the stern comfort of 'As for man, his days are as grass … but the mercy of Lord is from everlasting unto everlasting.' The presence that only '*was what it was*' could be linked with the Presence that announces itself, in a circular affirmation of bare being, as 'I am that I am'. And above all, her insistence on the amorality of the Lone Pine vision, its ethical non-productiveness, seems to rest on a very literal and limited demarcation of what it might mean for an experience to have an effect in a life. Before it, she was a desperate solipsist. After it, she was set on a course that would lead back towards her fellow humans, and eventually, in the second half of the 1960s, into anti-war activism. That sequence again: the bush burns, and sometime later you find yourself trying to guide an unruly crowd towards the promised land. This is not exactly unheard-of as a pattern of events. Oh, come *on*, thinks the believing reader. No need to reinvent the wheel. You would save yourself so much time if you knew how everything was supposed to join up. Quick, someone air-freight this woman a Jesuit!

But this is to let ourselves off the hook too easily, two ways round. If someone as open as this, with such a strong working sense of the tragic possibilities of existence, recognises nothing in the descriptions of faith she has encountered, then we are not describing it rightly. If the 'rage of joy' she has felt seems to have nothing to do with goodness, then we have been misrepresenting virtue. If what we have managed to extend in her direction seems to be only an offer of authoritarian parenthood, or a resistible politics, then we have made a mistake of our own about the place we allow for the wildness of God. Those of us who have a positive theology, populated with the items of the catechism, often treat negative theology – the term for what we don't and can't know about God – as an optional afterthought. But on the strength of this book, negative theology should be getting a much louder say in the public presentation of faith. We should be leaving a humbler, more obvious space for the terrible, the earth-shaking, the category-breaking excess of the Lord, beyond all our systems and descriptions of Him. Everyone who practises a faith, of course, embeds it in one way or another in a set of shared behaviours, in a social and often then in a political vision. Naturally: an occasional experience of ecstasy is not enough, and such embedding is what lets us build out the heart's or the mind's assent into something coherent. But faced with somebody like Ehrenreich, who knows she does not share the conservative politics that seem inseparable from American Christianity as she views it, and therefore is prevented from seeing what essential thing she does have in common with Christians, it behooves us to distinguish much more loudly between theism and the systems into which we build it. If God is universal (if God is God), then He is the God of liberals and radicals as much as of conservatives. Christianity is not just a religion for those temperamentally inclined to be reassured by firm systems, rigorous rules. It is also for the wild at heart. God Himself is both rule-maker and rule-breaker. He is therefore the ground on which human rule-makers and rule-breakers ought to be able to meet.

If we want to talk to Barbara Ehrenreich, we cannot appeal to the naturalness with which, to *us*, our swift cascades of interpretation flow. Least of all can we appeal to the majesty of orthodoxy. (Orthodoxy! Thy very name is like a . . . not very attractive thing!) We would need to be far more cautious, far more fine-grainedly empirical. We would need to dismiss the context that presents itself so readily to us, and say: what is there, in these experiences themselves, which might point a generous-minded seeker towards the Christian understandings? What is there about this Californian flame, which turns its witnesses to flame, that might tentatively align with the strangeness of Pentecost? What is it that consoles, in the thought of this being's permanence, when it makes our temporariness so plain? What wild quality is it, in its seemingly amoral fire, that seems to burn a path to visions of the human good?

And, if we do this, we will also be true to the actual shock and disorientation of such encounters. Anyone who has had anything resembling Ehrenreich's experience – and they are surprisingly common – will tell you that the presence they met did not so much contradict their religious expectations as stand in a kind of orthogonal relationship to them, so much more than and other than

189

expectation, that expectation seemed almost beside the point. Wild justice – justice unmediated and unfiltered – is different from the thing we painstakingly try to make in courtrooms. Wild charity – love unmixed and uncompromised – is fearfully unlike the adulterated product we are used to. It *is* a terrible thing to fall into the hands of the living God. To call the presence you meet 'amoral' is at least to acknowledge its difference; to allow awe and bafflement and uncertainty their honest place.

Three months ago, I was standing in a wood on a hilltop in England with two Anglican priests. The beech trees were in new, intensely green leaf, and the spring sun came through in shifting specklings of brightness; the bluebells were in full flower on the forest floor, and drifted the ground in all directions with a fine-grained blue mixed with the bright white of wild garlic. The silence between the grey uprights of the beeches was expectant, intent, more vivid and demanding than was strictly comfortable. Because we were who we were, and knew what we knew, and believed what we believed, for us it was natural to imply, from the ground we could see, a figure just out of sight: and to name the wild moment by saying, *Surely the holy one of Israel is here.* But if we had been standing in the same wood 2,000 years ago, we might well instead have left an offering to the genius loci. Or, like Barbara Ehrenreich, have improvised an altar to an unknown god.

(2015)

THE PAST AS ZOMBIE HAZARD, AND CONSOLATION

My wife, a parish priest in Cambridgeshire, was doing a wedding rehearsal two years ago in a medieval village church when she realised that the couple's children were hanging about anxiously on the threshold. They had made it across the churchyard with nervous glances from side to side, but the prospect of entering the building was too much for them. 'What's the matter?' she asked. 'We can't go in', they said. 'The zombies will get us!'

If one of your culture's primary associations with old things is pop-culture menace, and its most vivid association with the places where we stow dead people is of the earth splitting, and grey-skinned revenants lumbering out to eat your brain, then it's not surprising that, through the literal eyes of children, *old* should often now mean *dangerous*. It's more complicated than that, of course. Contemporary Britain's relationship with the past, in pop culture and in high culture and in culture in the anthropological sense, has several different strands, with several different moods attached to them. At least one pervasive attitude to history is wistful and fascinated. But the past's difference is taken as a given. Discontinuity, not continuity, is the common experience, except in the narrow channel of people's personal and genealogical connection to past time, and sometimes there too. Whether people go to the past eagerly or nostalgically, with horror or fascination, to deplore or applaud, they tend by definition to be looking for things they perceive as being absent in the present.

The default form of our culture is a hedonistic individualism that takes the test of harm to others as the boundary for acceptable behaviour. Individual moral autonomy is taken as self-evidently right, so long as it doesn't hurt anyone else. (Increasingly, as the effective centre of gravity of British politics moves to the right, this is thought to entail a corollary: not hurting anyone else means you also have a moral obligation not to socialise the costs of your choices. Your drug habit, your housing needs, the welfare of the children in your serial families, are all your problem, not anyone else's.) To criticise the way people exercise their private choices (so long as they pay their bills) comes precious close in our estimation now to criticising their selfhood, their actual free possession of an integral life to call their own, and it aligns you suspiciously with the set of restrictions from which British society is conscious of having only just freed itself, thanks to the social liberalisations of the last four decades.

There is still a shadowy sense that freedom's rivals are lurking nearby, requiring vigilance to be fended off. Indeed, it is part of the culture's mythology of itself, its sense of having a moral purpose, that the enemies of LGBT rights and women's rights remain potent, and are often located in convenient symbolic form in the churches. But for practical purposes, most of the culture's alarms and disquiets are generated by its own success rather than by a real vulnerability to reversal by antique scolds. There is a widespread uneasiness – but a dim one, not organised into axiom or mythology – over the consequences of the morally atomised society. Unresponsive the culture may be to traditional authority figures, but it is becoming clear that it is extremely susceptible to manipulation by expert marketing, guided by the new insights of neuroscience into the predictable bases of our behaviour, and ever more finely grained data. People are starting to wonder how individual our individualism actually is, given that the consensual way to express it is through shopping choices. In the same way, the rather Rousseau-ish picture of inherent human goodness on which the hedonic culture rests, with its brittle insistence that our desires must be harmless unless corrupted by outside agencies, generates anxiety in all the very frequent circumstances of human life where that isn't quite clear. Some of the tools of moral self-knowledge have gone missing, and the absence makes itself felt. Not to know that finding yourself in the wrong is compatible with self-respect is very tiring. Panic is never far away, as demonstrated whenever a particularly barbaric news story brings to the surface the suspicion that all this me-for-myself-alone-and-don't-you-dare-to-judge-me stuff may not be enough to maintain a social fabric. It's not that people crave the return of cultural authority, at all; it's much more that they are agitated by the vacuum where larger-than-individual meaning used to be. They mourn the disappearance of, they worry about the absence of, the social, the collective, the *shared*. They miss shared causes, shared hopes, grand narratives providing maps on which the individual could locate their particular life. At the same time, they are nervously afraid that to share might mean to be coerced.

Not much is to be hoped for from politics, the culture's conventional wisdom declares. The withdrawal of ideology from British politics rid it, for twenty years, of momentous choices, clear divisions between seriously dissimilar visions of the good, and replaced them with a technocratic centrism. It became a cynical commonplace to hold that all politicians are corrupt, and are only pursuing their own self-interest in the public domain, just as the rest of us do in the private one. This may be changing. One of the notable developments of the last two years has been the startlingly instant waves of support for causes that *do* seem to offer significant choices, and new grand narratives: the election of Jeremy Corbyn, Scottish independence, Brexit. There is certainly fuel available for a renewed politics, not least in the deep, deep generational divide of contemporary Britain. Older people who were carried to prosperity by rising property prices can therefore sign up to the hedonic project of a happiness only one social atom wide without too much overt cognitive friction. The young, stranded in bad jobs, renting forever, on the sharp end of inequality, live the hedonic project too, because that's the inherited condition of the culture, but without much ease or optimism; resentfully.

But these are disputes between generations that at least share a set of cultural reference points. Further back in time, beyond the great behavioural shifts of the 1960s–80s, the past begins to grow unintelligible to contemporary Britain, or at least very much harder to understand. And yet it is frequently to this further past that the culture reaches, in a frantic variety of ways, in the search for shared meaning.

Take the newly revivified rituals surrounding the commemoration of the British war dead. As someone who was growing up in the 1970s and 1980s, when it was an undramatic commonplace that most of the older men you passed in the street were veterans of the Second World War, I remember Remembrance Day being scarcely celebrated. There were far fewer poppies, the two minutes' silence was something you could read about in school history books, and there was a general sense of the world wars receding, in time with the receding of private memories of them. Now (not coincidentally) that the First World War has entirely passed out of living memory, and the Second World War nearly has, we memorialise the wars like crazy, in a profusion of public forms. Larger crowds gather round war memorials to people we don't (individually) remember than did in the decades when the British Legion stood there in their berets, mourning remembered, specific friends and comrades. The new wars of New Labour provide part of the cause, giving us new dead to mourn, and new Heroes to be Helped, with a corresponding need to find ways to honour sacrifice irrespective of the new wars' justifications. For this, the First World War can provide a useful context. But most people these days standing serious-faced on

11 November wearing their poppies don't know any currently serving soldiers either. They're there to do some imaginative business on their own account. They're there to participate in a symbolic performance of national continuity, centred round the armed forces as the institution in some ways least corroded by our scepticism. They're there to assert that they *are* joined to previous generations' story of collective sacrifice: despite the fact – because of the fact – that little in their daily experience bears it out.

The same appetite for connection despite and because of disconnection manifests itself over and over again. We are fascinated by the past, puzzled by the past, horrified by the past; we are unable to look away. The stories we tell ourselves at the moment have an avidly historical bent, and I say this as someone who has just themselves published a historical novel. The lawns of twenty-first-century British culture are littered with time machines, dramatised and filmed, broadcast and written, all offering to transport us (but with the option of instant return) out of Now and into Then. The Tardis would be hard put to find a parking space. There's always been costume drama, but a wild multiplication has taken place. We want the wars; but we also want the Tudor past, where the origins of the state we inhabit can be seen in rudimentary, barbarous, unshielded form. We want the past of domestic service, with its deference and its hierarchies and its radically different class destinies running along side by side in single households. Explicit subordination is exotic to us; but troublingly interesting, as we come to suspect that the fluidity of contemporary manners is disguising a return to grotesquely unequal life-chances. We want the past just before we were born, when people like us (but not quite) lived in cities like ours (but not quite) and organised experiences like ours (but not quite) according to rules that seem alien now (but not quite). Ancestors are more of a challenge to British sensibilities than migrants or refugees, because they are so indissolubly linked to our intimate self-understanding. They are where we came from, and yet they cannot be assimilated, they will not conform to the expectations of the present. We have to go to them, trying our best to translate their passions into terms we can make sense of. The historian and critic Alison Light, a professional interpreter of the past's lost social hierarchies, nevertheless came up against an indigestible difference when she discovered in her family history *Common People* (2014) that for a century and more her ancestors had been fervent Baptists. She did her best to view this as a form of social defiance on their part, but something remained stubbornly other in it, impossible to dissolve. Similar challenges await the hundreds of thousands of individuals who do genealogy now as a hobby, creating a private origin story for themselves; their own creation myth, if they could but read it.

The forces making the past illegible are our irreligion, when most of our ancestors, even after the Industrial Revolution, still lived within a domain structured to some extent by the sacred, by Whitsun picnics and chapel-influenced or church-influenced politics and Christian behavioural ideals as a default; and our emotional assumption, because our culture has taken 'the expressive turn', that to be real feeling must be labile and vivid and performative, when our ancestors filtered their equally passionate lives through more stoical codes; and our prosperity, which makes the old poverty of the past hard to enter into, either as a condition of real limit, or as a condition made survivable by resources of tradition, politics, ritual, solidarity and working-class self-organisation. The new poverty of the foodbanked present has the limits but (so far) mostly lacks the resources.

But the past is also, and above all, wicked. It precedes the individualised social liberations on which Britain prides itself, and does so, as it were, defiantly. It is a dark other country of despised attitudes to gender, race and sexuality – many of these, again, seeming to be handily concentrated in the churches, as the past's surviving embodiment. But immediately an ambivalence creeps in. Virtue is a strain, after all, however each generation defines it, and the past is where the reprehensible stuff is at home. It comes naturally there,

196

and therefore in a funny way is not blameworthy. You can go to the past with a sigh of relief, of effort suspended. Or, only one step further, with indulgence; with a gratified sense of the past's naughtiness. Defiant wickedness (even if the defiance is only an artefact of perspective) has front, has attitude, can be seen as strutting its malevolent stuff in an expressive and exciting way. We have a whole little subgenre of visits to the *unrepentant* recent past – *Life on Mars*, *Mad Men* – which let the consumer play on varying terms with the forbidden. Or, if you want your wickedness refined of its historical impurities, the food technologists of fantasy will concentrate it for you in hyperpalatable form, and let you enjoy a history-ish parade of rape and torture and cruelty in *Game of Thrones*, which is not encumbered by the complications of the actual Wars of the Roses.

For most people, though, except for recreational purposes, that's an attraction of the past that exists in tension with its deepest and most powerful lure, which is that it's real. The past is the grand narrative that hasn't melted. There it is, with all its problems, leading up to us. The past is where you go for experience that is non-negotiable, that is not responsive to fancy or to the delicate discrimination between preferences (so long as they are preferences for entirely private tastes). The past is where contemporary Britain goes to taste in virtual form the kind of collective, even coercive, experience that trumps, that renders moot, the autonomous self-definition that is supposed to be the pride of the present. The past is where you go to imagine being conscripted, enduring unanaesthetised pain, having to stay married, being pushed through the weight and dignity and sometimes brutality of the big, shared, involuntary human experiences. The past is our sidelong indictment of the inadequate reality of the present. Till the present grows realer – please God, not by growing poorer and meaner – the past will have to do. Zombies and all.

(2017)

THREE WAYS OF WRITING FAITH

The easy part of representing Christianity would seem to be the part to do with representing it as a human, social activity. Whatever else they are, churches are groups, tribes, institutions, with particular rules and habits of relating, and micro-politics. They have hierarchies both of the formal kind and of charisma and informal authority; and they have demanding ideals of behaviour that most probably will stand in temptingly ironic contrast to the actual behaviour of the people involved. All of which is rich fictional material in exactly the same way that the life of any defined group provides rich material for stories. We like hearing about villages, we humans; and maybe most of all we enjoy villages stirred up by some principle, to give a narrative tug to events, as ironic as you like. This is the recipe for Trollope's explorations of the cathedral close at Barchester, and for Barbara Pym's novels of spinsters at evensong. It would seem that you could enter into this fictional territory without any metaphysical commitments, equipped only with a descriptive curiosity and a broad imaginative sympathy. Representing faith this way would be only as difficult – that is, fiendishly difficult, but let's not be downhearted – as representing any other idea-influenced piece of human activity. It wouldn't pose a particular problem.

But although people go on writing this kind of story of religious life all over the planet, there hasn't been a lot of Trollope or of Barbara Pym produced locally, lately; not in Western Europe, not in England.[22] And I think our position in a culture where the religious tide has gone a very long way out, by global standards – leaving us on these secular mudflats, surrounded by curious shells and rusty bicycles – shows us something that may not be apparent in other places, which is that the apparently descriptive, merely curious, village-life novel of faith, did in fact quietly depend on a metaphysical commitment. It was (is) built on a shared assumption between writer and reader that a disposition of life around religion makes sense. Makes, in fact, such basic sense that the sense it makes can be left off-stage and the author can concentrate on all the secondary human consequences of that sense, ramifying all over the place in lovely narrative patterns. But when that underlying assumption is removed, the village life of Christians stops being just another intelligibly villagey panorama, and becomes mysterious. It dwindles into anthropology, to be explained as it goes; it becomes exotic, science-fictional, a zoo for the bizarre; it becomes a mode of story, often, whose point is to criticise, to indicate a confinement from which the characters could – should – break free.

To say this is not to buy into the legend that some kind of definitive secular disenchantment is available, after which everything will only mean what it really means, and our lives, and presumably our fictions, will stand on the plain, real ground. The Christian mythology may go away, but the mythic dimension of experience will not; any plausible human life will remythicise far faster than Richard Dawkins can keep up with, brandishing the hedge trimmer of 'reason'. The New Atheists are trying to carve the Green Man into static topiary, and it won't work. But particular bonds of sympathy can certainly be severed. The simplest way of putting this is that there won't be much of a market for a book called *Scenes from Clerical Life* if no-one has a fucking clue what the life of the clergy is like.

Oddly, then, the further that Christianity recedes from most people's everyday experience, the less available becomes the apparently most straightforward way of representing it. And the more important become the other ways in which the life of faith can take on fictive life.

There is, for example, the novel that renders, in concrete and particular imagined lives, Christianity's central theological drama of redemption: the story of depravity and grace. I'm thinking of the mid-twentieth-century Catholic novelists here, in whose work that story can often be explicit, appearing under its own name, with clear theological labels attached. Graham Greene, Muriel Spark, Flannery O'Connor: all *demonstrating* the specific gravity of loss, cruelty and destruction within experience, and a redemptive turn towards hope, as being intelligible – intelligibly desired, intelligibly yearned for – within that same experience. The theme was explicitly otherworldly, with the whole story resting upon a possibility for hope not to be accounted for from the usual calculus of events, but it was arrived at in a very worldly and often darkly comic way, with the story's dive into depravity giving it the authority of pessimism, of really well-informed squalor and sleaze and darkness visible. But there is also a version of the novel of redemption that comes without this kind of explicit labelling or theological framing; with the theological motif being, as it were, digested into experience to the point of invisibility. If I was being mischievous I'd call this the Protestant version, with the apparatus of redemption absorbed with no remainder into the sufficient material of the individual life. But I'm not sure that's a fair categorisation of, for instance, the diffused Anglo-Catholic awareness of the possibility of grace that threads through the work of Penelope Fitzgerald; or of, say, Alasdair Gray's *1982, Janine,* which records in frequently pornographic detail the long dark night of the soul of a Scottish businessman, as well as the joy that cometh in the morning. He certainly thought of that book as being locked in combat with his childhood Calvinism, and there's a clue there to the continuing viability of the implicit rather than explicit version of this kind of theologically Christian novel. It can be written without a conscious intention by the writer. Because the narrative of redemption – of the stone rolled away, and the weight of sorrow overturned – still forms one of the deep structures of the culture, hereabouts, it comes easily and, as it were, naturally to the hand of someone who may think that they are merely at work, without presuppositions, in the fields of meaning. I wouldn't want to overstate the unconscious intention, in Alasdair Gray's case, because *1982, Janine* does feature an intervention in the margins by the voice of God, and it does say at the end that it was completed 'on retreat, at the monastery of Santa Semplicità' – but this does seem to me to be a mode in which the novel in Western Europe is likely to go on writing Christian faith unwittingly, for quite some time.

However, as awareness of the Christian nature of the culture's materials dwindles, the third kind of fiction in my rapidly assembled and ad hoc taxonomy seems likely to become most important of all. The kind, that is, that can speak communicatively of faith to readers beyond the bounds of experienced familiarity with it, and beyond the bounds of conscious assent to it, because, rather than exploring the (social) relations of Christians with each other, or showing forth the theological patterning of experience, it takes as at least part of its subject the relationship of Christians with God. The kind that tries to realise, on the page, with the verbal tools of the novelist, the orientation to the world that results when somebody holds that, feels that, behaves *as if* the particular rooms they are in always have another unnumerated door or window, opening onto a different and overwhelming domain. The kind where the particular light of one morning is held to be a manifestation of a general light. The kind where part of the point of what is being carefully reported about everyday experience is that it faces onto something else. That something else, of course, not being a verbal fabric at all. Being made of the Word, that is, not of our vocabulary. As the Reverend John Ames says in Marilynne Robinson's *Gilead*, 'you must not judge of what I know by what I find words for' – except of course that the readers of novels do judge, exactly, by what the writer has found words for. The task of finding expressible language for the inexpressible is inherently impossible. The effort begins in the admission of inevitable defeat.

For me, Robinson's *Gilead* and, in their different way, its successors *Home* and *Lila*, are the best, most grace-touched defeats there have been in fiction for a very long time. And the foundation of their power is their scrupulous fidelity to the integrity of viewpoint. They inhabit the viewpoints of John Ames and then Glory Boughton and Lila Ames with *more*, not less, attention to the particularity and limits of those imagined human selves, because they are trying as well to make an impossible realisation of grace on the page. There is not a word of omniscience, in the narrative sense, in any of them. They do not for an instant exploit the capacity of fiction to condense the hopes of Christianity into direct narrative, on the authority of the author, and to project them onto the screen of the story as if they were present in the same solid way as furniture and trees are present. Which they would be, but only within the terms of the story, only till you put the book down. God would be a special effect. There would be no claim of witness, of observation palpably grounded; only the claim of eloquence. Instead the Christian eloquence of *Gilead* and *Home* is directed towards the resistant reality of experience, and towards what we may find in it, and maybe beyond it.

(2013)

UNAPOLOGETICALLY YOURS (1)

After Unapologetic *was published in 2012, I found myself in blog-dispute with the American biologist and New Atheist Jerry Coyne, professor at the University of Chicago, author of* Why Evolution Is True *(2009) and, later,* Faith vs. Fact: Why Science and Religion Are Incompatible *(2015). This is an edited selection from my side of an impressively bad-tempered exchange.*

Dear Jerry Coyne,

You say, quote, 'Along with many Sophisticated Believers™, Spufford remains ambivalent on the question of the role of evidence in religion.'

Well, no, I really don't think I do. (But let me pause a moment to admire the economical design of the heuristic which divides the religious into unrepresentative 'Sophisticated Believers' and poor brainwashees, neither of whom then need to be taken seriously for an instant. A decision tree with only one fork, and shazam! the landscape simplifies.) I say that the experience of religious emotions causes assent to religious propositions, not the other way around; and then I add that the truth of the propositions nonetheless matters, and that the ultimate test of the value of a religion cannot be how it makes you feel, but whether it does, in fact, correspond to some actual state of the universe. You gloss this as me admitting that faith 'is based on evidence', point to an inconsistency with my wild claim that 'truth is "a willing entry into uncertainty" when we have no answers', and move on instantly to deliver what you take to be the clincher: 'If Christians really respected "truth and logic and science", then they wouldn't willingly enter into the uncertainty of Christianity, for there is no good evidence for its tenets.'

But wait. Without I suspect noticing that you were doing it, you just shuffled the three nouns 'evidence', 'truth' and 'belief', substituting them when convenient for yourself. I didn't say that religion rested ultimately on *evidence*, I said it rested on *truth*. And I didn't say that *truth* entailed a willing entry into uncertainty, I said that *belief* did. Evidence ≠ truth; truth ≠ belief.

This may sound trivial, but it really isn't, because the slippage of terms in your rewrite of my argument has shifted it back towards the picture of the world you prefer. Evidence is a means of ascertaining truth; an organisation of data as part of the human effort to tell what the truth is, through the scientific method. Truth, meanwhile, is just a state of affairs, something which is so whether we currently know it or not. You would *like* it be the case that evidence is the only means of approach we have to truth, and that conversely truth is the kind of thing we can only approach through evidence – in which case you can indeed treat them as terms which are effectively substitutable. But this is a philosophical position, not a scientific one. It is a philosophical picture of the world that gives science a monopoly position as the supplier and definer of truth, but that does not make the picture, itself, scientific. It is only one of several possible pictures, all of which are compatible with the known facts of the case, and all of which are compatible with loyalty to the scientific method. So science does not in itself provide a criterion for choosing between the pictures. Neither does holding to an ideal of fidelity to the real compel one to choose your favoured picture.

The difference between our pictures of the world does not lie in there being different valuations we place on truth. We agree that truth is all-important; that it is the test of all contentions; that it would be shameful intellectual dishonour, *trahison des clercs* or *trahison des savants*, to lie knowingly about matters of fact. Where we differ is in our estimate of the *obtainability* of truth. For me, the things we know – the things we can ever know, even allowing the most generous possible future development of the scope and reach and intellectual power of science, which of course I am in favour of – represent only a fraction of the things that are true about the universe. In particular, we don't have, and aren't ever going to have, access to decisive knowledge about questions of meaning and intention. It may be an anthropomorphic projection to suppose that meaning and intention have anything to do with the state of the universe. Then again it may not. It depends on your picture. But, given my picture, it makes sense to suppose that knowledge cannot reach large and important parts of the true state of things. Knowing has limits. A great deal falls within these limits, but some things fall outside. Those things we cannot *know* are true; and yet, they still are true, or aren't. This is where 'belief' comes in, not as an unrespectable alternative to knowledge, but as the respectable human activity that applies to those areas of truth about the universe to which we *cannot* have access. Within the limits of knowledge, we don't need to believe things. We don't need to believe in gravitation, or natural selection, or the geological history of the Earth. We can just know they are the case, the engine of evidence having brought them within our knowledge. But beyond the limits of knowledge – or rather, beyond the limits of all possible knowledge – radical uncertainty holds, and here believing becomes appropriate, ordinary and essential, and can also be a form of appropriate reverence towards the real. Belief is the condition of holding a conjecture about something which you cannot resolve the truth of; which you maintain in your mind while remaining aware that you may be being absurd, that you may have it got it all wrong. Hence the intimate affinity of belief with doubt, for they share, in two different emotional modes, the same state of not-knowing. Hence the similarity of belief to the state of mind that precedes creativity sometimes, when it is necessary to dwell with, to maintain in fruitful suspension, material you cannot (yet) determine a shape for. (That 'yet' indicates an important difference.)

But I used the word 'ordinary' a minute ago quite deliberately. This is not some tiny residual area of unobtainable truth which is so rarefied that it makes no difference for all practical purposes, and can be safely consigned to the metaphysical junkyard. The truths to which we have no access are a large part of everyday experience. The things we can't know, and must therefore negotiate as best we can by forming beliefs about them, include: what the world looks like for other people; what we ourselves mean by the language we use; how that language is going to be understood; what we ought to do in most situations; what our society should be like; how we ought to vote; what colour we should paint the spare room. Belief in God belongs among this mass of shockingly normal problems, not alongside debates about the value of the cosmological constant. We see 'through a glass, darkly' because that is the nature of our relationship to all questions that deal with 'why' rather than 'how', with 'ought' rather than 'is'. It isn't a situation that can be improved by better lens-grinding. Nor is it 'piffle' to name the situation. It is a matter of paying attention to the experience of being in the world.

We can't verify or falsify our beliefs the way we can our knowledge. But that doesn't mean there are no criteria we can bring to bear to distinguish between beliefs. We can ask whether belief pays due and scrupulous attention to what *can* be known. We can ask whether belief is equipped with, as it were, some of the proper humility owed to the provisional – with a continuing willingness to change, to notice, to be wrong. We can ask whether beliefs are generous or mean, altruistic or self-serving, frightened or hopeful, candid or self-deceiving. We can be intelligent and nuanced about belief. But to do this we need to not dismiss the whole inevitable human activity of belief-formation as nonsense. This is one of my reasons for preferring my picture of the world to yours.

On the particular issue of evidence for the existence of God. You say that 'if there is a God – at least a benevolent and omnipotent and theistic one – we should have evidence of it'. Ah, another one of those 'should' statements. I understand that you would like to pull religion back to where you can hit it with your evidential hammer, but a demand for evidence that's based on a normative claim is a move within the domain of beliefs rather than a successful appeal to facts beyond it. Should we have evidence of God's presence? Why should we? Presumably you mean that a universe featuring God's presence would be nicer than the one we've got; that it would show signs of being unambiguously managed to avoid the dangers, cruelties and randomnesses which palpably afflict the 13.8-billion-year-old place we actually inhabit. Well, it's an opinion. Specifically, it's a theological opinion, in the style of the eighteenth and early nineteenth century, when theologians were big on the idea that the details of the physical and biological worlds should reveal the unambiguous signature of a creator. But it isn't my theological opinion. I hold to the view – very normal in Christianity over the last century or so – that the obviously un-managed, un-regulated, un-nice state of the cosmos poses a never-ending challenge to our understanding of God's benevolence and omnipotence; but that the lack of management-for-niceness in the universe is a given. Amazingly, Christians have actually noticed that the violence and injustice of the human histor-ical experience, and the 'blundering, low and horridly cruel' opera-tions of the biosphere, present faith with a problem. There is a huge imaginative and theological literature about it, many hundreds of years old, under the heading of 'the problem of pain'. I happen to think that almost all of it is unconvincing. But you are making a mistake if you assume that Christians exist in a naive bubble on this score, which can be popped by the mere mention of a difficulty we've never faced. Almost all of us, one way or another, have had to make our individual peace with the issue.

Just to recap, then: believers don't *know* there is a God, God being one of the possible truths about the universe for which there cannot be evidence. We *believe* in Him in the absence of evidence, not in spite of it. We pursue our belief because it matches our experience: our woolly, subjective, untestable experience. Yet we remain aware that our belief either does, or does not, correspond to the true state of affairs, and that it succeeds or fails accordingly in being justified. Since we cannot (as it were) open the envelope that will tell us this truth, our belief requires us to live indefinitely with the envelope unopened, and to enter willingly into the resulting state of uncertainty. Which is not so different from the many other ways in which human beings find it is worth our while to base our behaviour on not-knowing.

Unapologetically,
Francis Spufford

(2012)

UNAPOLOGETICALLY YOURS (2)

A few months later I also corresponded, much less acrimoniously, with the chair of a local British humanist society, who had written to ask which of two theories of the atonement I subscribed to, both of which he thought incoherent or morally repulsive: number 1, in which 'Jesus' death was a death penalty suffered on behalf of the human race', or number 2, in which 'Jesus' death is somehow onto-logically identified with the consequences of human sin: Jesus on the cross is the rape victim, the abused child, the tortured prisoner, the Holocaust victim'. He concluded, 'It seems obvious to me that there is mending and forgiveness in the world whether or not we believe in God. Why can't we just agree on that instead of dragging all of this contentious theology into everything?' Again, I've edited: but not, at least, to make myself wiser or more quick-witted.

Thank you for your email. I am not a theologian, as you know, but I have read a fair bit of theology, and listened to a fair bit more, so I am not coming to the question of what the cross accomplished entirely unprepared. The statement at the back of the book to the effect that I didn't check anything before writing it should not be taken as meaning that I went at the job empty-headed, only that I decided to go with the headful of thoughts I already had.

As I try to narrate the crucifixion in Chapter 5 of *Unapologetic* I am attempting a descriptive balancing act that may not be fully visible to you. I am trying both to give vivid, dramatised form to what I think happened on the cross, and at the same time to point reliably to a wider bundle of interpretations. This double job may well have the effect of making it harder to tell exactly where I stand theologically. As may the fact that I'm storytelling rather than arguing, there.

Your theory number 1 is, of course, penal-substitutionary atonement, beloved by contemporary conservative evangelicals, who often assume that it is the single orthodox interpretation, with nothing beyond but liberal waffle. I've seen it referred to by them as 'the scriptural doctrine of the atonement', as if the Bible unambiguously required this understanding. It isn't and it doesn't. Their picture, of sins as primarily crimes, and of a wrathful God transferring his righteous fury at humankind to a substitute on whom our death penalty is executed by proxy, is a radical modern simplification of *one strand* in traditional understandings of the atonement. As you say, Christians who believe this tend also to believe in hell as part of the same grim theological gizmo. 'Salvation', for them, is indeed principally salvation from being sent to hell: which doubles up, for me, on the morally repellent image of an angry God who needs to be bought off by blood, by adding that He also (if not bought off) is the happy proprietor of a kind of cosmic Abu Ghraib, where the torments last forever. Such a God, if He existed, would not be worth worshipping. People's motives for signing up to penal substitution aren't always hate-filled – they can buy it innocently, as part of a package marked 'Christianity' – but I agree with you that the result is horrible, and morally repellent, and irreconcilable with good everyday understandings of what it would mean to be 'loving', or for that matter 'just'.

For the record, I don't think you're going to hell. I don't think anyone's going to hell, hell being a human construct behind which Christians hide from the alarming consequences of God's generosity.

It is a necessary consequence of human free will that people should be able to say a definitive 'no' to mercy, kindness, hope; but that is not at all the same thing as saying no to overt membership in some Christian church, or to some package of beliefs. I am fairly sure that you are a humanist because you consider that to be a vote in favour of kindness, mercy, love, tolerance, enthusiasm for the richness and potential of human experience. Irritatingly, I consider twenty-first-century British humanism to be immensely Christian in its ethical assumptions.

However, though we agree about the horribleness of theory no. 1, I also have reasons for rejecting it which we don't share, because they rest on theological as well as consequential judgements; and these point me towards an understanding of the atonement which is rather different from your fluffy, ontological theory no. 2.

For me, the other deep objection to penal substitution as a doctrine of the cross is that it implies a character for God which is radically incompatible with the character of Christ as the gospels describe it: a person inclined on occasion to freak out and lose his temper, especially with cruelty or self-righteousness, and serious to the point of horror about human failings, especially cruelty and self-righteousness, but never, never, for a single recorded instant, willing to discard any human soul as beyond the reach of love, whatever the law says. For me, it follows from the doctrine of the incarnation that, if Christ is God-like, God must be Christ-like; the picture of the bloke in the New Testament provides our most authoritative portrait of God, and any theory of God's intentions can be discarded as partial, or incorrect, if it doesn't match the behaviour of Jesus. Therefore the penal-substitutionary picture of an angry dad with a nice son, ruthlessly dispatched to take the bullet meant for us, makes no sense. I do see that, from your point of view, this piece of reasoning is resting on empty air, or rather upon faith. It requires the prior conviction that the beardy rabbi from Galilee is (in some sense) the same as the maker of the universe, before it gives you any traction on the crucifixion.

But my possession of faith, and your lack of it, is a given of this conversation; and you are asking about systems of understanding that all, in any case, depend on faith. Grant me the criterion that faith gives me, then, and what does the death of God on the cross, at the hands of some not-especially-ill-intentioned humans, following out the ordinary logic of *raison d'état*, aim to make happen? It can't be a question of taking a punishment for us, since Jesus was demonstrably not in the punishment business; and it can't be a question of abolishing, or sopping up, human suffering, since, as you point out, 'the rape victim is still with us'. I do see a subordinate function of the crucifixion as being an act of participation by God in suffering, a declaration of solidarity, a willing entry into the costs, not of forgiveness, but of creation itself: the biological realm where life implies death, where all possession implies loss. It can't be the whole point, though, can it?

If I say, he's there to take the blame for human wrongdoing, I suspect you will instinctively collapse 'blame' back into 'penalty', and decide that I'm a devotee of a kind of penal-substitution-lite. (All the moral squalor! None of the gusto!) But 'blame' does not necessarily mean something that has been imposed by a judge; it does not have to denote a consequence of breaching a law code, or having power breathe down your neck with punishment on its mind. Some crimes are sins, but not all sins are crimes, and guilt (though certainly culturally conditioned) also arises spontaneously as a consequence of the shit we humans do. Unless you'll consent to a picture of human life in which guilt is sometimes the appropriate response to our own actions, it will be impossible to tell you any story of redemption that makes sense. The massively misleading present-day association of 'sin' with sexual behaviour no-one should be upset about gets in the way here, which is why *Unapologetic* goes to town on the task of manufacturing an artificial substitute word that doesn't carry sin's frou-frou overtones; but, beyond the argument over terminology, there does in fact still remain – naturally, I'd say – a list of human acts we all agree to take seriously as evils. You mention rape, child abuse, torture, genocidal massacre. I couldn't agree more: but then I'd want to add, as sources of proper and spontaneous human guilt, all sorts of less spectacular cruelties.

It is this mass of guilt that the man on the cross is inviting us to pass over to him instead, not so that he can suffer the penalty for it, not because he becomes the wronged party in all those acts of cruelty (which would be presumptuous indeed), but because he claims the proper, the appropriate, the spontaneous guilt, apart from all law, of the rapist, the torturer, the SS man, the wife-beater, the child-molester; and also the guilt of the everyday lying, bullying, humiliating, and so on, which (if we're honest) forms a fairly standard occasional element of almost all lives. He's there for the wrongdoers, not just the wronged. And since, says faith, he's also God on the cross, he has the reach and the capacity for forgiveness which humans do not.

You ask why we can't just leave forgiveness and mending to people, 'instead of dragging all this contentious theology into everything'. The answer is that people's capacity to forgive, to act for each other, is always limited, is always contingent, always comes up against our needs for self-preservation or for justice. Rape victims should not be asked to forgive rapists. The crucifixion, for far more Christians than sign up to penal substitution, is the site of the outrageous claim that God regards all wrongs, no matter how vile, as forgivable. It does, indeed, represent a breach of justice, but in the opposite direction to the one you perceive (rightly) in penal substitution.

This is not fluffy. It is, however, visibly and centrally present in the orthodox theology of redemption, once you let the language of sin refer to something tragically observable rather than to nasty, antique codes of punishment by a big boss in the sky. I don't always manage to believe that Christ died for the sins of the whole world; I waver and I wobble, and assurance comes and goes, even in Holy Week. But that's what's there to be believed, for me. That's the transmitted, orthodox core of faith.

So, no, I don't think I'll be demoting the atonement to a handy myth or metaphor. I can't banish mystery, though. I feel I can know what the cross did, and why, but not how, since I lack by definition the God's-eye view that would be required ever to know that. Again, faith requires the acceptance of a diagram of the world in which, even after the maximum success we could possibly have in the great war on marshmallow, there would still be things that we, temporary creatures that we are, aren't ever going to be in a position to understand.

I wish you a happy Easter, if only for the chocolate.

Francis Spufford

(2013)

Technical

My experiments in science writing have been centred round my plea-sure in explaining things. To myself first and most urgently, as part of my sense that as an adult and a citizen I really ought to be minimally able to understand the physical (and chemical, and biological) func-tioning of the world I inhabit. Then, if they will sit still and listen for long enough, other people.

My own slowness and mathematical illiteracy have, perversely, been a help here. The metaphors and other mental devices for trans-lating the non-verbal that I need, to get a process fixed comprehen-sibly in mind, often seem to be transferable. And explanation of course is a form of narrative. The flowchart of necessary realisations, to be imparted in the right order and with the right degree of emphasis, is a kind of story, highly specialised. Maybe, with its lack of characteri-sation and vital dependence on sequence, it most resembles Vladimir Propp's bare-bones universal structure for the folk tale. The hero must meet the princess before the villain can threaten him with the loss of her; the reader must grasp the essentials of thermodynamics before a book can get to the difference between a heat engine using the Carnot cycle and one based on the Stirling cycle.

On the whole, I have been more interested in writing about applied sciences than the pure kind. Technology is making, *and therefore has useful affinities with the sort of making I know about, in words. Technological history is the gloriously impure record of science's inter-action with the constraints and possibilities of human societies; and it too is rich in lost worlds, untaken paths, and pasts orphaned by later paradigm shifts.*

DIFFERENCE ENGINE

Despite government grants of unprecedented size, and expectant coverage in the technical press of the day, Charles Babbage did not build the Difference Engine, and he never even came close to realising his plans for its programmable successor, the Analytical Engine. Visit the computing history section of the Science Museum in London to see the Difference Engine, as Doron Swade and his team have made it possible for you to do, and you witness a rich historical paradox.

The handle cranks, and industrialised mathematics takes place before you. The gear wheels turn; sword blades clunk up and snick down, keeping each gear registering a whole, determinate number; at the back the rotors on the main columns turn circles at staggered intervals from one another, sending silvery sine waves rising the height of the engine with each step of the operation. The brass and steel of the engine weigh more than a ton, but at the same time the thing seems curiously insubstantial once you think through its presence on a reinforced upper floor of a South Kensington museum. (In one of the public palaces reserved by the Victorians for just this sort of edifying spectacle – though not this exact one.) It is *so* Victorian in its visual impact; almost exaggeratedly so. It looks like an elaboration, a raising to the nth degree, of every Victorian device you ever saw, from a fob watch with its case open to a steam locomotive whose jointed connecting rods delicately transform enormous linear thrust into huge rotary motion. It expands on every specimen of purposeful nineteenth-century metal. It even delivers a ridiculously clear lesson in Victorian industrial philosophy. It situates its operator, who need only count the number of times the engine has been cranked to produce this or that order of polynomials, in a perfected version of the position labour was supposed to occupy in the Victorian factory system. Here is an abstruse operation of the calculus, previously the province of a trained mathematical mind, made over into a job of machine-minding, at the cost of perfect alienation from the task. Yet you are seeing a quintessentially Victorian object on which no Victorian ever laid eyes, including Babbage, whose craftsmen could not cut gears to the necessary fine tolerances.

What can you call it? A fictitious antique? In one sense, it is the relic of a non-existent history, an artificially created survival from a past in which Babbage, after all, succeeded. Babbage faced tangible and intangible obstacles, both problems with materials and problems with ideas. Having conceived a machine some technical stages in advance of his era's power to manipulate metal, he lacked a whole set of supporting technologies for the Engine, which was why he was constantly sidetracked by questions that had to be answered first, about alloys and temperatures and brass-turning equipment. His design was balanced, so to speak, on the single pole of his own determination, instead of fitting comfortably atop a pyramid of assured skills. Likewise, he could not refer the intellectual endeavour represented by the Engines to any established context of ideas. There was the analogy (beloved of his mathematical collaborator Ada Lovelace) between the Analytical Engine's proposed card-storage for information and the card-hopper of a Jacquard loom, but analogy – individual illuminating comparison, constructed for the occasion by a specific effort of perception – was about the limit of what the Engine could draw on from the culture. There existed no shared vocabulary available to describe Babbage's intentions, and make them obvious; no already existing notation, no convenient mathematical shorthand, no canon of procedures. The Science Museum's department of computing history found itself in a position to remove both obstacles, supply both lacks, solve both problems. Supervising the production of several hundred identical brass gears only proved to be interestingly tricky for them. And so far as ideas went, they possessed the very significant power to name Babbage's enterprise as part of, well, the history of computers, in which his thinking made perfect, retrospective sense. They furnished him a belated context from current computer science – they could simply refer (a tiny illustration in itself) to his hardware and software difficulties.

So the Engine is in effect a collaboration between times. Its functional, successful existence here and now vindicates Babbage's design, but the *design* alone. The Science Museum did not mean to test the Engine's feasibility then, only its feasibility now. They abolished, rather than recreating, contemporary constraints. They acted on their own power to complete what had been uncompleted, to realise what had been unrealised. The object in the gallery therefore says nothing decisive about whether Babbage could have succeeded. Instead it pays a tribute to a man who has been retrospectively organised into being an ancestor; and it brings the might-have-been to the surface, all the more powerfully for not being decided one way or the other. When we look at it, this synthetic thing made from now's response to then, we are dealing with a relationship to the past, with our own ability to imagine and retrieve, and with the fluctuating process by which, at different times, different parts of history seem to come to prominence as we recognise unfinished business there. In fact we are seeing a peculiarly concrete, peculiarly provoking exercise of the historical imagination, something just as alive in the history of science as in the history of manners or the history of speech. And the imagination we use alike to 'enter' the past idly, and to reason about it carefully or proportionately, does not possess the history it works upon as some uniformly dead or distant object. There are constant transactions involved, like the transaction between Babbage and the museum: exchanges and barters in a sort of imaginative economy. We nominate some times as livelier than others because, like the living present, they seem to contain unexhausted possibilities, of which our sense that at a certain point things could have gone otherwise gives a perverse sort of index.

The Difference Engine still radiates a feeling of possibility which cannot easily be accounted for. Certainly not from the functional point of view: by any modern standard of comparison, the Engine has negligible powers. Any programmable pocket calculator can be instructed to calculate the polynomials, and it can solve any other equation you program it to as well; while Babbage's metal beast is a one-task tool, hard-wired or rather hard-cogged for its single purpose. The shining, immovable architecture of the Difference Engine actually embodies its program. The thing's beauty in fact declares how thoroughly it is obsolete. But even if it were the open-ended Analytical Engine we were looking at, the same functional comparison would produce the same result. It is not what the Engine can do that is really at issue, but some quality of promise we see in it independent of its actual function. This quality, interestingly, the established and ordinary technologies of the present completely fail to produce. Neither a calculator, nor – say – the motherboard of an office PC (a piece of kit infinitely removed from Victorian tech in complexity and performance) promise anything except that they will perform the tasks we know they can. The Engine, on the other hand, obstinately promises wonders, and the domain of wonders is the domain of the unspecified, the rich-because-uncertain. In part, perhaps, this only amounts to an old delusion about complex systems. Unlike printed microcircuits, the components of the Engine fall within the range of scale at which made things can be readily admired. A cog of the Engine is accessibly fist-sized; yet there are so many of them that the eye cannot immediately tally the total, a much more aesthetically impressive bemusement when you lose your way in an object the size of a small bathroom. And the same sub-rational hope begins to operate that alchemists felt when they had multiplied the rules and formulae of their craft beyond the mind's capacity to hold them all at once: that the whole may magically become greater than the sum of the parts, and complexity tell on itself to secrete the philosopher's stone.

But the promise we perceive has another side, tied to the development of technologies and the juncture in their development when wonder plays a proper part. It is the promise of beginnings. As a technological vista opens for the first time, before the journey into it has really begun that will prove each step to be prosaic, one by one, the possibility of the whole line of development can be felt at once. Often the anticipations turn out to be inaccurate, but that knowledge has not yet been forced upon us, likely and unlikely consequences have not yet been sifted apart. For a brief moment, for that very reason, modest results of an invention and frankly utopian results can have equal likelihood in our minds, and are rolled together intoxicatingly, almost lyrically.

If the Difference Engine had been built, it would have represented that phase in the development of computers. Since it now has been, it enables us to glimpse the chance for the same information technology that we actually have as it would have appeared from the vantage point of anticipation – as a wonderful prospect, an opening box which could contain anything. The Difference Engine re-enchants computers. It doubles our vision: all the while word processors and accounting software go on being dull and familiar, yet simultaneously we sight on them as shadowy promises at the edge of plausibility. We can look forward to the present (a mental sleight rather like Flann O'Brien's 'art of predicting past events') in the spirit of the 1840s manual of technical breakthroughs, written for the use of alert artisans, which described the Analytical Engine even in the absence of a working model as bringing 'metal close to rationality', bounding on towards artificial intelligence at the slight hint from Babbage that such things could now be hoped for. Wonder includes terror as well as delight. It isn't the sleep of reason that brings forth monsters after all, but reason's first confused awakening to a line of inquiry. Mary Shelley wrote *Frankenstein* from the equivalent tangled moment at the birth of the life sciences. 'Perhaps a corpse would be reanimated; galvanism had given token of such things; perhaps the component parts of a creature might be manufactured . . .' Perhaps, perhaps. If we want to find the present counterpart to the Difference Engine, we have to look not at the achieved technologies it might have pointed towards, but at technologies now passing through the same phase, where the perhapses still cluster and the dispensation of wonder still obtains. Virtual reality, say, or the internet, though the bloom of unlimited possibility is already passing from them. The internet begins to shrinks back from its ecstatic characterisations (a web for democracy, a surfable sea of data, an instrument of expanded perception), and settle down as a very large database-cum-techie salon.[23] The smart idolatry is moving on. Nanotechnology, maybe? Still, whatever should be the next locus of wonder, the Difference Engine will resemble it more than it resembles any strictly comparable device for crunching numbers. Phases of change remain curiously *in* phase with each other, where the imagination is concerned.

But the history the Difference Engine stands for is of course an imaginary one.

Imaginary histories offend against seriousness. They lead the mind away, most historians have thought, from what can be studied into what by definition cannot; from solid actuality, quite difficult enough to document and comprehend, to a terrain of nebulous possibility governed by wishes and other illegitimate impulses. We humans can know history in a profound sense, argued Vico, because we made it, in however complex and collective and half-intentional a way. What did not happen, we did not make, and cannot know from within, as we can know (or grope towards knowing) the acts and omissions even of the most distant and different peoples. This leaves thinking about them as a hobby at best, a peculiarly ethereal recreation, a confessed preference for unreality. Yet it must be admitted that the foolish question of how things might have happened is certainly involved with, attached to, the sensible question of how in fact things do happen: how necessity and chance, the quick foreground incidents of history and the slow background shifts in the regimen of human societies, luck and weather, material factors and intellectual factors, the sequence of scientific discovery and the effect of popular novels, all combine – differently, according to different contending theories and understandings of history – to shape an outcome and produce this event rather than that one. Only a belief that all events are rigidly predetermined can entirely exclude the possibility that things could have been otherwise. And most historians are not pure determinists. So the same qualities that make imaginary histories ridiculous have occasionally commended them, and made some people wonder if they could be useful.

For a while in the 1960s and 1970s a fashion waxed among statistical economists for 'cliometry'. It was a beautiful and arrogant term meaning 'history measuring', after Clio, history's muse. What do you measure history against? It is a permanent problem in all studies of unrepeatable phenomena (in geology and epidemiology as much as in the history of humans) that you must make inferences without being able to set up controlled experiments. Shifts in the Earth's crust, outbreaks of plague and industrial revolutions cannot be run through to order in the laboratory. There are no control groups, no test cases, only the single pattern of raw data provided by events as they fell out. It's like being asked to come up with an account of a whole game when you can only shake the dice once. The cliometrists tried to get around the problem by referring the real world to hypothetical worlds – 'counterfactuals' – where there had been other outcomes. One study, for example, tested the effect that railroads had had on the nineteenth-century American economy by modelling a railway-less version of it and then comparing the two, in the hope of being able to tell apart those developments that were, and those that were not, the economic consequences of railway building. Objections to cliometry came from those who pointed out that the fundamental difficulty still applied. A statistical model of a different history is a grossly abbreviated, simplified thing. To keep it coherent you had to choke back its implications; you had to set arbitrary limits on how far economic behaviour might branch away; you might be able to cope with the consequences of there being no railways, but you had to leave out the consequences of the consequences. Statisticians already made a beeline for any case where economic behaviour was different enough from the norm, and simple enough, for it to approach the conditions of a controlled experiment. Therefore in cliometry you arrived at a model which gave you no more purchase on the totality of the true historical record than you could get from a look at some real deviant group (say, the buggy-driving Amish), and which would be considerably less rich and reliable besides. Cliometry did not die. It lost its glamour and its name, and became a method among others, to be brought into play in those circum-stances when real history has accidentally produced the chance for comparison. A humbled form of cliometry happens when medical historians model the effects of the Japanese taking to a meat diet sooner, by investigating the homogeneous group of Japanese emigrants to Hawaii, who munched beef decades before the first McDonald's opened on mainland Honshu.

Around the same time, however (you see that imaginary histo-ries themselves have a history), the idea of other, differently ordered worlds came to seem philosophically fruitful. In 1973 the logician David Lewis published *Counterfactuals*, a short provoking book which claimed a semantically watertight (and very technical) argu-ment for, as he put it, 'realism about possible worlds'. His central chapter gleefully hinted that people kept coming up to him at Oxford parties and asking what he thought he was playing at. In the face of 'incredulous stares', or more rarely questions about what he *meant* by possible worlds, he wrote:

I cannot give the kind of reply my questioner probably expects: that is, a proposal to reduce possible worlds to something else.

I can only ask him to admit that he knows what sort of thing our actual world is, and then explain that other worlds are more things of *that* sort, differing not in kind but only in what goes on at them ... It is said that realism about possible worlds is false because only our own world, and its contents, actually exist. But of course unactualized possible worlds and their unactualized inhabitants do not *actually* exist. To actually exist is to exist and to be located here at our actual world – at this world that we inhabit ... It does not follow that realism about possible worlds is false. Realism about unactualized possibles is exactly the thesis that there are more things than actually exist.[24]

This was not only a bravura demonstration of philosophical wit, though it is that, and curious-sounding as ever to non-philosophers who expect that discussion will strike out from roughly agreed terms into the material of evidence and opinions. It was a deliberately extreme statement of a belief about possibilities which a much wider range of philosophers and social scientists only feel compelled to reject when the possibilities are solidified into complete possible worlds. Those interested in how historical explanations work – how something we recognise as a satisfactory description of cause emerges – have been especially willing to admit hypothetical outcomes into the argument (so long as they stay hypothetical). It has been argued, for example, that a whole class of explanations turns on an 'implied counterfactual'. I employed one earlier in this essay. I asked what conditions would have had to be fulfilled for Babbage to build the Difference Engine, in the hypothetical case that he succeeded; pointed out that those conditions were not in fact fulfilled; and gave that as my reason why the Engine was not built. But in a general sense, everyone concerned with explaining and describing history has a practical stake in the 'thesis that there are more things than actually exist'. There has always had to be some conceptual scope found for potential, though no such *thing* as a potential can conceivably be identified in the finite world of objects and people, or else we allow no room for change and becoming. There have always had to be ways found for giving an account of a situation's potential for change, and in the social sciences attention to might-bes and might-have-beens has sometimes seemed like a promising source of tools. It need not be 'dispiriting', Geoffrey Hawthorn observes in his recent *Plausible Worlds*,[25] that possibilities 'are not items . . . about which [we] could be said to be certain, and thus to know'. 'On the contrary. It promises that kind of understanding . . . which comes from locating an actual in a space of possibles', sighting the real and single course of history among its attendant fuzz of counterfactuals. Hawthorn's proposal for using imaginary history aims, modestly, at illuminating where we are, and how likely it is that we find ourselves here. It does not aim, like cliometry, to make comparisons outwith the real world.

All these, though, are ways of making imaginary history serve real history. In one way or another, they raise the ghost of another possibility in order to investigate the groundwork of the real; they raise it in order to lay it again. They treat the possibility like one of those incalculable quantities that can nonetheless be used in mathematics because it will be neatly cancelled from both sides before the equation reaches its final form. The specific imaginary histories they put forward have only the status of an illustration, or a model, or an example. But it is noteworthy how much nearly every author of a rare, serious inquiry into counterfactuals enjoys the opportunity to play at changes. Often they embroider their exemplary counterfactual to pleasurable excess: certainly far in excess of the strict needs of an example. They invent sly details. Geoffrey Hawthorn, for instance, kicks off *Plausible Worlds* with an updated variant on an old speculation about what would have happened if Ferdinand and Isabella of Spain had failed to conquer the Muslim emirate of Granada in 1492. Because he then has his independent Granada add early factory chimneys to its skyline of mosques, shifting the whole industrial focus of Europe south-ward, he can send ripples of revision through the learned literature of his own discipline which deals with industrialisation. Foundation texts of the social sciences shimmer into slightly different form. Weber's *The Protestant Ethic and the Spirit of Capitalism* becomes *The Kharejite Ethic and the Spirit of Capitalism* by 'ibn Weber', delicious to cite.

Some things are good to eat. Others fall into a useful parallel category invented by an Amazonian tribe, and are 'good to think'. That is, they feel good when you think them through, they give a pleasure like the pleasure of eating. And indeed you are consuming something in this kind of thinking. Rather than pursuing a thought to a conclusion, you are dining on its aspects, guzzling its ramifications, digesting it gourmand-style. The issues and concerns that would structure your thought if you were in search of conclusions do come in, but like a menu. When Hawthorn gives himself the incidental pleasure of an altered book title, or when David Lewis picked out for use such propositions as *If kangaroos had no tails, they would topple over*, they are switching for a moment into this other style of thinking. They taste, in passing, the pleasure that the topic of different worlds proffers, quite independently of whether it can be turned to philosophical account. Where imaginary histories are concerned, of course, utilitarian thinking counts as the rare exception. Almost all the thinking people do about them is of the edible kind. Which does not mean that it is negligible, for it can be as alert as serious thought to a difficulty or an intellectual knot, only to different ends. It uses imaginary worlds for the sake of imagination, and because it can draw on so much that the imagination understands about history, it can be extremely revealing.

Words, which summon worlds, are its proper medium. If the money could be raised, the Science Museum would like to go ahead and build the printer Babbage envisaged for the Engine, to tabulate the results of the Engine's calculations, stamping them – almost incising them, in the manner of an old-fashioned railway ticket punch – into broad fillets of pasteboard: which raises the bizarre prospect, at least in my mind, of the museum following through the next stage, and then the next, and in effect launching a Victorian Age of Information Technology in the upstairs gallery. Why stop? Presumably they would have to when they reached the limit of Babbage's own designs. To start improving on the Analytical Engine would be to leave the province of museums altogether. And it will take a sobering sum even to assemble the printer. But what it is formidably expensive to execute in metal, words can perform at no cost at all, except imaginative effort and historical sympathy.

William Gibson and Bruce Sterling's SF novel *The Difference Engine*, published in 1990, contains a world of the 1850s altered by the rampant success of Babbage's computers. To bring about this state of affairs, preceding history has been adjusted as far back as 1815, so that the ground can be prepared, politically and economically, for Babbage's little metal shoots to flourish. The ironmasters and the savants have taken unequivocal control of Britain, as they were prevented from doing in fact by orchestrated, conserving reforms. Instead of fissuring under pressure of diverging interests, the pro-industrial coalition of capitalists and workers and scientists, which in our world only preserved a frail existence during the 1830s and 1840s, overthrew the Duke of Wellington in a revolution around 1830. Now reason rules triumphant. It is the Young Men's Agnostic Association which proselytises. Babbage and Lyell and Brunel sit as 'Merit Lords' in Westminster, influential, idolised, masters of the public purse. Data dances unimpeded across the land by telegraph, on punched cards, on spools of ticker tape. In the bowels of the monstrous Egyptianesque pyramid of the Central Statistical Office on Horseferry Road, serially connected Analytical Engines process dossiers on every man, woman and child in the country. 'How many gear-yards do you spin here?' 'Yards? We measure our gearage in *miles* here ...' Smaller Engines check customers' credit on the counters of smart emporia, automate manufacturing, perform mathematical reconstructions of dinosaur skeletons. The Irish potato famine has been avoided by rational relief measures, but London groans beneath an overload of smoke and fumes, tottering towards systemic crisis. We recognise this city. It's a Gustave Doré drawing made more so. It's Dickensian London subjected to an exponential growth in both wonder and horror. It's the ville of penny-dreadful night, coloured in shades of mud and India ink, stage-lit by gas for melodramatic glare, abounding in spectacular villainy, fantastically a-swarm. In broad outline it's also, since Gibson and Sterling make amazingly conscious and resonant use of genre conventions, somewhere that cool American practitioners of the 'steampunk' SF subgenre have visited several times before. A rejigged Victorian London seems to serve (it's been observed) as a favourite kind of artificial unconscious, where anxieties can be condensed, and discharged, on the understanding that this lurid place is definitively *other*.

But genre is chiefly a consideration here because science fiction, by nature, offers both surprises and guaranteed pleasures. SF, no matter how good it is or how individual, tends always to hold out more specific and more predictable promises to the reader than fiction per se. To a much greater extent than the literary novel, it allows you to select the pleasures you plan to have in advance. This concentration, this extra single-mindedness, is what makes it the pre-eminent form in the culture for exploring ideas that are 'good to think'. Sometimes SF does little else. Gibson and Sterling, interestingly, come down emphatically on the side of genre convention in their choice of a precise moment for their alteration of history to begin. SF 'alternative history' uses a very simple rationale: events branch at points of decision. It shows audacity to nominate some juncture as decisive that doesn't especially look it. Despite research so thorough that historians of science who read *The Difference Engine* feel they are breathing air thick with allusions to their own work, Gibson and Sterling did not opt for a metallurgical breakthrough, or a paradigm shift in mathematics. They had Lady Byron decide she would stay with her husband in 1815, however disgusting his taste for practices expressible only in Latin. And the *imagination* is tickled, outraged: satisfied.

A partial bibliography of imaginary histories drawn up in 1980 lists about 175 fictions of one kind and another, not counting films, plays and board games. By now the number must have multiplied many times over. Alternate history has been one of the boom areas in the genre since the (relative) decline of 'hard', starships 'n' rayguns SF. Branching-points have multiplied correspondingly, but the most popular probably remain the fall of the Roman Empire, Columbus's arrival in the New World, the Spanish Armada, the American Wars of Independence and Civil War (the latter much-revised at every stage from Fort Sumter to Lincoln's assassination), and the Second World War. The pronounced bias towards American history of course reflects the predominantly American readership and authorship of English-language SF. Almost all these most-favoured junctures for historical alteration are military events, because a war going the other way provides the most blatant and immediate possibility of change. Usually, though, a technological shift follows. It's rare for a surviving Roman Empire not to have mastered steam power and the printing press at least, and more often machine-guns and television as well. Success for the Spanish Armada on the whole signals an aborted Industrial Revolution in Europe, with the connection between Protestants and machines, Catholics and obscurantism taken as read: under the thumb of the Popes, ox-carts generally lumber along rutted roads carrying cargoes of illuminated manuscripts. Similarly, unless the author happens to be a committed Dixie partisan, the result of a Confederate victory in 1862 or 1863 tends to be a backwoods, tar-paper-shack North America, stuck with clunky telegraphs and puffing billies, the internal combustion engine nowhere to be seen. German victory in the Second World War, on the other hand, can offer the prospect of accelerated but malignant technology, Gruppenführer Wolfgang Something replacing Neil Armstrong on the moon as he steps from his swastika'd V10 rocket years before 1969. It is impossible to exaggerate how routine these manoeuvres have become in science fiction; but equally important not to assume that the conservatism, the recourse to stereotype manifested in them, is purely a generic thing, a sign merely of a genre *running* according to type.

With a few exceptions, people first began to play at altering history in the first decades of the twentieth century. The two collections of essays most commonly quoted as the foundation stones, F.J.C. Hearnshaw's *The 'Ifs' of History* and J.C. Squire's *If It Had Happened Otherwise*, were published in 1929 and 1931. (Interestingly, many of the contributors belonged to that governing caste in British society which had reason, by 1930, to wish that history were working out differently, yet could still, if barely, believe that decisive moments were formed by the decisions of people like them. One contributor to Squire's collection was Winston Churchill. Another speculated about what would have happened if the General Strike of 1926 had not been defeated by the then Home Secretary, Winston Churchill.) But some of the attractions of altering history had been identified centuries earlier, at the point when fiction of any kind, with its sober relation of non-existent events, seemed itself to hold out the problem of a counterfeit reality. Francis Bacon classed the invented people and invented emotions of poetry as a category of 'feigned history' in *The Advancement of Learning* (1605). Poetry's root in the Greek *poiesis*, making, was uppermost in his mind:

> The use of this FAINED HISTORIE, hath beene to give some shadowe of satisfaction to the minde of Man in those points, wherein the Nature of things doth denie it, the world being in proportion inferioure to the soule ... and therefore it was ever thought to have some participation of divinenesse, because it doth raise and erect the Minde, by submitting the shewes of things to the desires of the Mind, whereas reason doth buckle and bow the Mind unto the Nature of things.

Imaginary history – applying Bacon's terms as he certainly never intended we should – is poetical history, *made* history; and it too gives the shadowy satisfaction of raising 'the Minde' higher in importance than 'the shewes of things'.

It can be everybody's mind that imaginary history bestows this satisfaction on. Especially when a story of what might have been plays up the extent to which history is chance-made, and therefore turns on accidents and on choices as opposed to laws or necessities, it pays in one sense a warm tribute to everyone's powers of decision. 'There is no history', Gibson and Sterling have their scientist hero Mallory shout provocatively, '– there is only contingency!' Which seems to promise that the course of events is a piano and not a pianola: we too can sit and pick out a tune that pleases us. If history is not inevitable, and does not operate by general rules, then it may really matter whether we turn right or left when we leave the house in the morning. In a much more obvious sense, and simultaneously, sovereignty over the imagined order of things belongs entirely to the mind of the author, and the reader participates far less than she or he does in real history: the reader can contribute nothing from memory or shared inheritance of the past. Imaginary history makes its author's mind the sole arbiter of chance and likelihood; it makes over the superlatively intractable stuff of what has been into material; it turns history plastic and sculptable; it seats the author in the office of time. Spare kingdoms and republics fall out of the author's pockets like loose change.

Neither the sculptural satisfaction nor the privileged authorial position are entirely denied in the writing of real history. Inevitably, narrating the real past is also a matter of interpretation, and tacit modelling, and when the history in question is perceived as having a conclusion which touches on the present position of the narrator, then the historian, too, has a seat in the midst of history; it flows towards her or him. Michelet, for example, included his own birth in his annals of the French Revolution, where it was indeed a significant event, because the Revolution led to the possibility of Michelet becoming what he was. The rise of 'the people' from subjection to power was also, as Michelet saw it, his own rise from poverty to learning. The Revolution created the conditions for a republican intelligence like himself to grasp the times, and tell them. Imaginary history exaggerates, and literalises, this role. The tacit becomes the explicit. A maker of imagined history has all the powers of a real historian to impose a narrative on events, tamping this and that into place in an intelligible design, with the additional power of adding or inventing the pieces to be tamped.

The heady ability to create worlds brings in its train the equally heady chance of criticising them, as you can only criticise *made* things. When the fabric of history becomes a chosen arrangement, it can be savoured like a picture (or like the book it actually is), assessed for consistency, admired in some parts but regretted in others. An imaginary history is open to criticism from base to crown. In John Crowley's *Great Work of Time* (1989), an exquisite and paradoxical fable about the defects of granted wishes, the 'President *pro tem*' of a society dedicated to the preservation of the British Empire by altering history wanders the streets of a place his society has, in a strange half-accidental way, created. This 'capital city of an aged empire' answers his desires uncannily, though he never anticipated a class structure contrived from different species: saurian butlers, maned Magi as subtle and gentlemanly as Sherlock Holmes, tubby hominids to do the heavy lifting, and sexless angels annunciating in the public parks. But do the pieces fit, the President wonders. He studies this world as if it were a set of nested fictions of differing, and perhaps incompatible, moods and styles:

The lives of the races constituted different universes of meaning, different constructions of reality; it was as though four or five different novels, novels of different kinds by different and differently limited writers, were to become interpenetrated and conflated: inside a gigantic Russian thing a stark and violent policier; and inside that something Dickensian, full of plot, humours, and eccentricity. Such an interlacing of mutually exclusive universes might be comical, like a sketch in *Punch*; it might be tragic too. And it might be neither: it might simply be what is, the given against which all airy imaginings must finally be measured: reality.[26]

The sting in the tail, as the President finds, is that inconsistency has no force as an objection against what actually is, if with sudden doubt and bewilderment you should find yourself in the posture of a connoisseur before that real order of things which cannot be accepted or rejected, appreciated or deprecated. What Crowley makes happen to the President *pro tem* within the kaleidoscopic precincts of *Great Work of Time* can also happen in our solid and consensual world to the reader of imaginary histories. They can have a temporarily estranging effect on your perception. As you close some story in which matters are otherwise, you can catch yourself regarding the real course of history, by a kind of persistence of vision, in the guise of an equally gratuitous arrangement. If imaginary histories have any radical quality at all, it's this momentary gift of the feeling that real history might well be done better. It takes mountainous effrontery, though, to mark reality low for inventiveness and coherence. For that reason Madame de Staël reserved it as a role for the Devil, God's would-be competitor at world-creating, who in Goethe's *Faust* she said 'criticises the universe like a bad book'.

But the pleasures of upset, inversion and irony are quite as attractive in the writing of imaginary histories as the chance at omnipotence. If they are a game, they are one with peculiarly loose rules. Probability is a consideration, but the decisive factor is what you can get away with, while retaining a sufficient *atmosphere* of probability. Strictly speaking, in *The Difference Engine* Gibson and Sterling cheat. They have invented a world of sluggish mainframe computers, analogous to the IBM-dominated globe of say 1960, yet wanted to infuse it with the cyberish attitudes of the present, and people it at least in part with the denizens of the hacker subculture of the 1980s and 1990s. They want youths in frockcoats who feel the same covetous delight about what they can do with a pillar of gears that youths in baseballs caps feel about the havoc they can wreak with a modem. Hence the constant tug they exert on the Babbage technology towards devices ever further out of developmental sequence. Their cinema-screen-sized 'kinotrope', with its tens of thousands of mechanically rotated pixels, lets them have Victorian computer graphics despite the absence of the cathode-ray tube. Hence too the conceptual shove in the novel which makes 'catastrophist' interpretations of evolution shade over into chaos theory. Accelerated modernity and accelerated postmodernity are all mixed up; but then buttressed by matter-of-fact storytelling, and defended by jokes and subterfuges that deliberately blur period. Gibson and Sterling work tricksily at the reader's belief. They are both keen to have you credit their alterations (though the kinotrope may be nearly as functionally implausible as Fred Flintstone's rock-hewn TV set, it exudes the same ingenuity as real Victorian optical toys) – and eager to trap you, if they can, into spurning unlikely but genuine Victoriana. Surely calling the radical governors of this England 'the Rads' is an obvious exercise in forged slang? It hints at radiation. It sounds off-key, an unwise attempt to make Victorian politics sound zippy and streetwise. Nope: louche politicos drawl the word in Disraeli's *Sybil* (1845), one of Gibson and Sterling's chief sources, a book whose plot, characters and even author all appear here in mangled form.

Like most of those in the world-revising business, Gibson and Sterling are fascinated by the encapsulated meanings of words and habits and objects. Really perfunctory stories in the genre will indicate a different world by looking at banknotes, coins, flags, stamps and military uniforms, the most concentrated tokens of a course of history. (Even the most economical fiction featuring an American stamp with Hitler on it can't match mathematical logic for high-handed brevity. 'Possible worlds are mentioned by means of the lower-case letters h, i, j, k', runs one of David Lewis's footnotes; 'sets of worlds by means of capital letters; and sets of sets of worlds by means of script capitals.') Such self-contained signs, above all, are portable. They work as counters that can be moved elsewhere, still meaning what they mean, so the expectations they represent collide. Imaginary histories offer the pleasure of seeing familiar objects in unfamiliar settings: a revolver in Julius Caesar's hands, a word-processor on Disraeli's desk. And the contrary tickle of satisfaction when unfamiliar circumstances lap a familiar scene: J.F. Kennedy trundling across Dealey Plaza in a cart pulled by donkeys. Likewise, imaginary history can confirm, or reverse, our sense of a historical character, either extending a person as we already imagine they were into new but suitable contexts, or using the revisionary power of the genre to force an incongruity. The latter ploy comes accompanied by the cynical suggestion that character and role are themselves accidents, and could have been otherwise. A story published around the time of the Rolling Stones drugs trial in London played with a counter-world where Victorian manners, social deference and cold-bath culture still ruled. It therefore contained a fresh-faced detective constable from Scotland Yard by the name of Michael Jagger. 'This', as Merlin remarks bitterly in T.H. White's *Once and Future King*, when his familiar spirit supplies him a sailor hat to wear, 'is an anachronism . . . That is what it is, a beastly anachronism.'

Most imaginary histories use anachronism in one way or another, though perhaps it is too broad a term for the variety of switches and swaps that are possible with the capsuled material of history. When a tract of time can be made to appear, like a hat out of thin air, in the form of some typical thing, anachronism itself can be a form of wit; of the kind of conceit-building wit which involves finding an unlikely affinity or point of comparison. Anachronism dispenses with the time between what it brings together in the same way that calling love a pair of compasses dispenses with every obvious dissimilarity. Your surprise is the object of the exercise. A medieval magus in kiss-me-quick headgear, the Emperor Caligula riffing away on a cherry-red electric guitar, John Keats loading every rift of a *graphics program* with ore: all these exemplify the quality defined (disapprovingly) in the eighteenth century as 'the unexpected copulation of ideas'. Interestingly, it was around the same time as the rejection of conceited wit that 'anachronism' first entered the vocabulary of literary critics. A growing awareness of historical difference led to stringent displeasure at current poetry, and translations of ancient works, which broke the decorum of period – by inaccurate dress on Roman orators, impossibly modern sentiments in the mouths of Celtic heroes. Writers of imaginary history have returned the compliment and largely ignored the eighteenth century. Hardly anybody has thought it worth altering the seventy-odd years before the French and American revolutions. Somehow, before the revolutions brought in their unpredictable fire, the eighteenth century seems too primly stable; somehow its events seem to be of the wrong kind. Nobody has ever bothered to make the War of Jenkins' Ear come out the other way. Imaginary historians prefer times that teeter between possibilities: wig-less days when it seems anything might happen. They have a vested interest in flux.

All the same they surprisingly often have the people who inhabit their different history sense that something is awry. 'It has come to me', says a scruffy aristocratic communard in *The Difference Engine*, a boy doubly opposed to Babbage's world of capitalist merit, 'that some dire violence has been done to the true and natural course of historical development.' On the words 'true' and 'natural' red flags signalling dangerous irony snap to the top of textual flagpoles. It's a remark laminated with intent, and it goes to the heart of Gibson and Sterling's alterations, for the talk, just before, has been of poetry. Their 1855 is indeed founded on an imbalance between reason and imagination; they've deliberately enthroned science at poetry's expense, starting with Byron's new career as politician and working on down through instance after instance in which those qualities that cannot be quantified or analysed have been scrubbed out of daily life. The result is polarisation. Their London streets are so dark because they've become the repository of all unacknowledged desires. The repressed must return, and it does, it erupts in the form of a Blakean insurrection scattering prophetic gibberish through the poisonous fog. A world 'unnaturally' divided tries convulsively to reunite. Other imaginary histories register their own artificiality in passages of unease, or in premonitory dreams sent by the author to warn a character that the world is less solid than they think. Quite frequently, the Caesar of a surviving Rome gets visions of a tumbled Colosseum: Lincoln, retired and disgraced in 1870, senses that he has outlived his proper span. The weirdest ripple of doubt probably passes across the Axis-occupied America of Philip K. Dick's *The Man in the High Castle*, when the yarrow stalks of the I Ching are made to deliver the plain message that the world is not true, an oracle very puzzling to the people of Dick's most tautly realised novel, who must continue to live all the same where the punctilious agents of the Greater East Asia Co-Prosperity Sphere rule San Francisco, delighting in Mickey Mouse watches and other remnants of Americana. It's as if the deviance of imaginary histories from the truth were a pervasive wrongness you could feel, infiltrating everything; as if what is not true was also out-of-true, subtly misshapen throughout its fabric.

No contradiction is necessarily involved when a genre devoted to change also throws up these momentary confessions of inadequacy. The characters may grow uneasy but the authors are not. Such nods back towards the unaltered world cheerfully acknowledge, in fact, a truth about the making of false realities. They are one manifestation of real history's paradoxical conservation by the process of chopping and changing it. Some authors like to conjure plots from a cod 'Law of the Conservation of History' which makes events right themselves no matter how hard you try to force a detour. That way they have their cake and eat it too; they get to tamper without disturbing a comfy Panglossian belief that everything is as it is for good reason. But a more fundamental kind of conservation is written deep into the structure of imaginary histories, and unites their ploys with the transactions that go on during the ordinary exercise of the historical imagination. Altered histories work with, work *on*, the sense of the past that readers bring to them. They operate upon what we think we know about Victorians or Romans or Christopher Columbus; their raw material is real history, not as real historians study it or understand it, but as a ready pack of characteristic images – the reader's mind's stock of associations between Victorians and crinolines, Romans and bloodstained togas, Columbus and cockleshell voyages off the map. They rely on the expectations they disrupt. History, joked *1066 and All That*, 'is what you can remember'. What you, the reader, can remember furnishes all that the imaginary historians have in the store cupboard once they have vanished the actual record. Of course they can invent; they can tell you things you didn't know; but they can never go beyond that point of invention where contact is lost with your original sense of history, or they also lose the point of making an alteration. If everything changes, then the changes are no longer measurable against the real past, and can no longer be enjoyed. An imaginary history which forked off into a completely unrecognisable sequence of events would have no resonance at all.

And what first loaded meaning into the capsule props beloved of imaginary historians, except our customary understanding of history? Imaginary history needs the real past to instil such hybrids as the US Hitler stamp with reflexive, immediate significance. The same applies to human population of altered worlds: the memory of real history acts as essential preservative for the stated identities of the cast. The less 'Victorian' the things people are shown to be doing, for example, the more exaggeratedly Victorian in manners and outlook they have to be. Detached from their setting, they have to possess their Victorian identity as a concentrated essence of period, and the only source from which it can be pumped is our pool of shared expectations. So in undistinguished books you get an unusually high proportion of inevitable characterisations, characterisations done by numbers (though the numbers are scrambled). Predetermined bundles of mutton-chop-whisker and check trousering masquerade as human. Even excellent authors in the genre cannot ever quite invent from scratch. Person-building must always happen on a grid of references. The scope for surprise and sympathy that does remain stems from the diversity of references available, which can become a sort of palette. The inhabitants of invented worlds can be tinted to flesh colour with shades extracted from here, here and (unexpectedly) *here*. Gibson and Sterling were able to find out-of-the-way and almost novel stereotypes for *The Difference Engine*. They give us, in the underworld adventures of Mallory the savant, not the gestures and speaking voice of Victorian prudery (the popular choice of period trademark) but an active and half-shamed sexual hypocrisy like an outtake from *My Secret Life*. In the cloak-and-dagger part of the plot, they give us, rather than Sherlock Holmesery and predictable gaslit mayhem, an amalgam whose constituent parts could be listed like movie credits. Feel for detective procedure: Wilkie Collins. Criminal mastermind supplied by: Jules Verne. Action sequences: Spring-Heeled Jack, of Limehouse. Apocalyptic lighting effects: the painter John Martin. Et cetera.

Still the most obvious aspect of their 1855 is its premature, its blatantly precocious, similarity to our own time. Their updating is not always smooth, and when Gibson and Sterling tweak overhard to align 'clackers' with 'hackers', or to make London pavements into mean streets the *Neuromancer* audience will like, it can seem that the past is just being invested with arbitrary cool. Hey, these aren't dull Victorians. These are hip Victorians! Turbo Victorians! Victorians With Attitude! But modernising the Victorians can also mean discovering a modernity in them that was really there. Gibson and Sterling are frivolous *and* serious here: travesty is mingled with an operation on our sense of the Victorian past that – like the slang 'Rads' – only looks like travesty. They have an agenda. Gibson, for one, has long been interested in pushing back the starting dates for the communications phenomena that fascinate him: he has argued before that access to the unsituated dimension of 'cyberspace' really began with the telephone, and now it looks as if the Morse key of a telegraph apparatus is being saluted as an even earlier gateway. He exaggerates, of course, but the effect of this kind of exaggeration is to render an element of the past visible. The same is true of *The Difference Engine* in sum; a wholesale device, after all, for solidifying theories, completing abandoned Engines, and turning wispy speculations into a visible manifold of events. More: it pursues a kind of secret, unlikely fidelity to elusive strains of genuine nineteenth-century technological feeling, by exploiting our ability to recognise them as familiar once they have been transposed into current terms. The cartoonish enthusiasms for machinery in *The Difference Engine*, and the gothic apprehensions, are both blatant versions – therefore visible versions – of real feeling. The book is filled with disguised continuities. This is Gibson and Sterling's subtlest use of imaginary history's constant return upon the real. Imaginary history's prime material, the consensual vision of what used to be, is generally a sluggish thing, fond of its segmented sense of period, slow to register a new thought; but it can be hoodwinked into expansion. Gibson and Sterling's imaginary history returns the past to us, garishly refurbished, loudly wonderful; but those prove to be the terms on which, as when we look at the ranked cogs in South Kensington, we can glimpse the past's possibility alive.

If the Difference Engine re-enchants computers, *The Difference Engine* refreshes the nineteenth century. Let me give the best illustration. The Central Statistical Bureau of Gibson and Sterling's 1855 is a special effect, with its pyramid walls pierced by smokestacks, its polished halls of pandemonium within. The spinning Engines, multiplied in row upon row of 'majestic gearage', are 'like some carnival deception, meant to trick the eye'. In our 1855 a 'computer' was a person who did bulk arithmetic. But the unsettled admiration the Bureau provokes had an exact real-world counterpart. The *Quarterly Review* of June 1850 contained forty-six rapturous pages devoted to the 'Mechanism of the Post Office'. There were no literal machines at all in the giant sorting halls the article explored, stacked one on top of another out of the reach of daylight – except a lift, described with estranged wonder as 'a very ingenious contrivance suggested by Mr Bokenham'. Instead they presented a 'mechanism' built from human components, each class of whom broke down the 'multitudinous mass' of the post by one specific stage: the red-coated postmen 'like a body of soldiers playing for their very lives at cards' who face all the 2,288,000 weekly letters in the same direction; the clerks who pass one verifying finger over each stamp with 'rapidity ... most astonishing'; the postmarkers whose right hands 'destroy from 6,000 to 7,000 Queen's heads in an hour'; the twenty-one sorting clerks through whose sets of fourteen tiny identical pigeonholes pass 'the whole of the correspondence of the United Kingdom, not only with itself, but with every region of the habitable globe, primarily arranged!' Except for the packages gingerly removed from circulation because they enclosed gunpowder or leeches or 'a human stomach &c', and the odd letter addressed only to 'sfromfredevi' (Sir Humphrey Davy), every item, rejoices the *Quarterly Review*, departs again in its right direction 'by two great pulsations', 'diurnally directed along six arterial railways to about 600 principal towns'. It was all 'very strange' but 'magnificent'.

Since the real years between have abolished the strangeness, it takes the replacement of the GPO by a mirage of the Babbage Engines, the morphing of the human circuitry into impossible metal, to remind us that what the *Quarterly Review* is describing is – that thing whose promise comes and goes in different lights – data processing.

(1996)

BOFFINS

Five years ago I was on the Isle of Wight making a radio documentary about the British rocket programme of the 1950s and 1960s, and while I was there I realised something. Well, several somethings. I discovered, for example, that although retired British rocket engineers tend to live in neat, unremarkable semis, you can often tell their houses apart from other people's because they will have one or more astonishingly competent pieces of DIY on display. DIY that towers in scope and ambition over other people's sets of shelves or scumbled paint effects. In one case literally. I went to a house where the engineer in residence – who'd been in charge of rocket development at a firm called Saunders-Roe Limited – had strung the clothes-line in his back garden between two steel pylons about twenty-five feet high, with a ratchet system and a little crank, so you could load up the line with your washing and then winch it to the top. Because, he said, he'd worked out that if you could get the laundry into the quicker flow of air over the roof of the house, it would dry much more efficiently. So I learned that. And I learned that towards the very end of Britain's participation in satellite-launcher building, in 1971, when the programme was cancelled while the very last Black Arrow test vehicle was already on its way to Australia, and the engineers were given their last chance to prove their system on the understanding that, succeed or fail, Black Arrow was cancelled anyway – one of this bloke's colleagues at Saunders-Roe had suggested that it might be nice to paint a Union Jack on the side of the last British rocket. 'Oh no', he was told by the powers that be. 'Why would we want to do that? We don't put the name of the country on the stamps, you know . . .'

But the larger thing I realised, put together from all the anecdotes like this, and all the testimony we got down on tape, was that I was dealing with the remnants of a lost world. Although Black Arrow's sad ending at the moment of its triumph happened in my own lifetime, the world it came out of had vanished so completely during the great deindustrialisation of the 1970s and 1980s that it was now hard to believe that the events I was hearing about had really happened. They didn't fit with British reality as I had got used to it being, coming to adulthood in the 1980s, when the UK was phobically averse to getting involved in any grand technological projects, and certainly in European rocket-building. This was another world, with different assumptions and expectations; where, although the UK was only a minimal and half-hearted participant in the space race compared to the US and the Soviet Union, with the French coming up behind, nevertheless it was still a player; and there in the geography of the Space Age, alongside Cape Kennedy and Baikonur, there was still the faint presence of Woomera, on the Nullarbor Plain of South Australia. The last scraps still lingered in that world of the great-power military-industrial mindset that had held in Britain during the Second World War – the attitude that, if space was the next item on the technological agenda, a country like Britain would *of course* be involved. Probably this attitude hung around longest among the rocket engineers themselves, because they were so focused on the technical challenge. And on the technical level they couldn't see why not, they couldn't see why, with a bit of ingenuity and a bit of deft exploitation of some of the cheaper and more peculiar technologies in the rocket engineer's cupboard, there couldn't be a viable British rocket industry.

They weren't expecting the future that actually arrived. By 1971, not many people were still entertaining the dream of a British space programme in its full-on, full-blown romantic form; the form that the British Interplanetary Society had dreamed it in not long after the end of the war; the form of it that Dan Dare acted out in the *Eagle*; the form of the dream in which, one day, an RAF squadron leader would drink tea beside the Sea of Tranquillity while getting a crackly congratulatory radio message from the Queen. 'Good hivens, I should think this must be the most expinsive telephone call iver made . . .' The tea, presumably, in some sort of self-heating aluminium canister invented by the boffins at Lipton, and available on earth for thirty guineas a time in Fortnum & Mason. *That* dream was never likely, because Wernher von Braun had been essentially right about the facts of the situation when he chose the Americans for him and his Peenemunde colleagues to surrender to in 1945. 'We feared the Russians, we despised the French, and the British could not afford us.' But other more modest dreams *were* possible. For instance, the one in which Britain built up the kind of profitable specialised competence at building rocket motors which Rolls-Royce presently has at building jet engines. Or the one in which Britain collaborated whole-heartedly in European launcher development, and ended up manufacturing half of every Ariane. All of these possibilities, romantic and sensible, likely and insanely unlikely, disappeared together. They popped out of existence like a soap bubble when Black Arrow was cancelled. And what struck me, doing the radio documentary, was that as a result it wasn't just the squadron leader on the moon that belonged in the domain of alternate history. From the point of view of the world that replaced it – the world whose dimensions and expectations I'd learned to take as normality, growing up in the 1980s – the world that these retired rocket engineers really remembered, not very long ago in the grand scheme of things, itself seemed almost counterfactual, seemed to belong to a different strand of history. To the other leg of the Trousers of Time. Which seemed to me to be a wonderful index of just how drastic the change had been when the old industrial tradition fractured in Britain.

I was fascinated. I decided I wanted to write about the change, about this enormous phase shift that had happened so recently, but so *thoroughly* that the world before it now looked as if it belonged to a different history. I wanted to know about what had happened, not just in the specific little territory of rocket-building, but in lots of other technologies. I wanted to know how the vanishing felt to the generation of engineers I'd been interviewing on the Isle of Wight. But then, as I looked around, I started to see transformation as well as disappearance; I started to see quiet ways in which there was unexpected continuity between this lost world of technology and the new world that followed it, after the crash, after the industrial landscape shattered, when technology in Britain reconstituted itself, both in completely new areas, like the videogame, and also around ancient competences in music, in genetics, in pharmacology. I realised that, if I could just work out how to tell it, how to pick the right bits from a profusion of material, there was an enormous story here. And at its centre would be the figure of the engineer, first of the rocket engineer but then also of the software designers and the biotechnologists and the people who laid out the mobile phone network, and and and. People whose experience got hardly any attention in mainstream culture. (SF is the grand exception, which is one reason why SF was a vital resource of ideas throughout the whole project.)

If you think about it, although there's now a lot of critically acclaimed popular science writing, and a good thing too, there is hardly any ambitious and inventive writing about engineering out there. Which seems to me to be perverse. My theory is – and I want you to know that I'm beating myself up here as much as anyone else – my theory is that in a culture still dominated by the assumptions of the liberal arts, it's far easier to assimilate the importance of the abstract idea-driven things that scientists do, than to pay proper attention to the muddy, kludgy, impure, *applied* activities of those who wrestle with steel, string and software and actually construct stuff. Particle physics and chaos theory get subtle, adventurous coverage, and writing about evolutionary biology has virtually taken over the slot in the culture that theology used to occupy. But few writers have put serious literary effort into conveying how a Formula One engine works, or where the beauty lies in object-oriented programming. Even the glut of 'technology' books inspired by the late-1990s bubble economy mostly told business stories, about technology lending money new mobility and velocity. There's nothing wrong with that in itself – the story of the money is always a part of how something concrete gets created – but again, explaining technology's finances is the easy bit, the bit that's least of a challenge, that causes least culture-shock for verbal types like me, with my college degree in literature and my D at Physics A-level.

Yet engineering ought to be a deeply sympathetic subject for writers. It's *like* writing; in many ways it's more like writing and the other arts than pure science is. It too is about *making*. It too is a mode of imagination, working concretely in the world of things. To represent it on the page, you have to come up with some sort of necessarily artificial verbal counterpart to its non-verbal processes: but if you can contrive to do that, you gain access to an activity which makes deep, immediate human sense, because it's part of the grappling with the physical world which we've been doing as long as we've existed as a species. And also to an activity which is gloriously interconnected with area after area of the rest of human life, precisely because getting things made is not pure. It's an art of the possible two ways round: it happens at the point of intersection between what's technically feasible and what a particular enterprise in a particular society in a particular time in a particular place is willing to do, can manage to do, wants to do, can afford to do. Looked at right, technology tells you about history, about politics, about economics, and about the dimensions of human character. It has universal themes, and it tells a thousand local stories. Often it tells a local story most pervasively when it believes it's being most universal. At the height of the internet bubble, when I was thinking about different ways to talk about technology, I spent a lot of time reading *Wired* magazine,[27] and all of the stuff I found in it about the abolition of place breathed out an intensely local understanding of place, and all the stuff about atoms becoming bits made it clear that these were Californian atoms becoming Californian 1s and 0s, and all the stuff about real life being just another window made it clear that said window opened on a view of the Bay Area of San Francisco. It wasn't a palette of shades that was very well adapted to technology's other histories in other places.

Which brings me to the British boffin.

Different countries have different folk-myths by which they understand technology, and different iconic figures to embody those myths. In America, the mythological engineer is a polymath and an entrepreneur, someone who can turn their hand to anything and turn it into a saleable product. Pre-eminently, Edison, the human cornucopia from which lightbulbs, telephones, sound recording and movie cameras all gushed out. The Russian or German one is an imposing visionary in danger of losing his soul to power by making a Faustian bargain. Wernher von Braun, Korolyev. The Italian one is a designer of temperamental genius. The French one is a technocrat. And what do the British have? Well, close your eyes and look at the picture that forms. (I absolutely swear that I won't ask you to clap your hands if you believe in boffins.) Probably what you're seeing is a middle-aged man of mild demeanour with an absent-minded expression, wearing some sort of white or brown lab coat. He works for the government, and though he wouldn't hurt a fly personally, he spends his days creating weapons of mass destruction: bouncing bombs, jet fighters, exploding toothpaste, death rays. He is, in short, a stereotype straight out of the same Second World War setting that produced the fading impulse behind the British rocket programme. I'd guess that the stereotype was established because, at the time, the war was such an intense experience of technological acceleration, and because it made people aware of depending very directly on technology for survival. The black-and-white war-film boffin put a comfy, manageable face on military tech; like a lot of stereotypes he provided a sense of familiarity that let you stop asking anxious questions. I'd guess that the stereotype is still around, amazingly, when it's decades out of date, and actual British engineers are more likely to be smoking a spliff than a pipe, and wearing a black T-shirt that says Plus Plus Ungood on the front instead of a lab coat, and even from time to time to be women, exactly *because* the post-war industrial tradition in this country crashed without leaving a culturally obvious successor. The rival figure of the geek started to make inroads in the 1990s, but it still hasn't displaced the older stereotype. Recently there's been a very welcome rediscovery of the world-shaking powers of Victorian engineers like Brunel: but, still, our mental boffin endures. I don't, myself, *like* the word 'boffin' much. It seems to me to be an alibi for incuriosity about what's actually going on, stuffing present-day reality into a nostalgic container it doesn't really fit. Newspapers use 'boffin' as one of their special headline-shorthand words which are completely divorced from ordinary speech, like 'love nest' and 'probe', whereas in British playgrounds 'boffin' is a term used to oppress speccy gits who do their homework, which as a speccy git myself, I object to.

So is the stereotype completely without meaningful content? Nope. Like clichés, stereotypes go on circulating because they also embody recognisable truths. If you discard the bits of the picture that are just anachronisms, and just patronising, and just borrowed from Q in the Bond films, you are left with something that does, sort of, correspond to the peculiarities of the particular, local history of technology, here. When I went looking for the new technologies into which our local urge to build the future migrated, in the 1980s and 1990s, I kept finding patterns that repeated, even when, as with the subculture of programmers writing the early videogames for the BBC Micro and the Commodore 64 and the Sinclair Spectrum, the big draw of the technology in question was that it offered a clean slate; that these twenty-year-olds in their bedrooms were joining something so early in its life cycle that anything could happen, and anyone who wanted to make a difference in them could, without any money, without anything much but the determination to do it. Yet these repeating patterns were still there. And one of them was to do with the element of truth in the stereotype; with the temperament encouraged in British engineers by the local technoculture. If the iconic French engineer is a technocrat, and the iconic American one is an entrepreneur, then the iconic British one, and quite often the *actual* British one, is an enthusiast. He (or, increasingly, she) is usually an employee rather than a lone inventor in a shed, these days more likely an employee of a company rather than the government – but he brings to his work a passion which has almost nothing to do with the bottom line (except as a means of going on doing what he loves doing) and almost nothing to do with dreams of personal glory (except in terms of winning the good opinion of other enthusiasts like himself). This kind of attitude to engineering is very strongly associated with informal, self-constituting networks – with clubs, and hobbies, and wet Saturday afternoons in garages, and midnight emails. It also has, often, very strong connections to a childhood fascination with constructing things, which in turn steers it as an adult activity towards the types of making which you can use your hands for; towards messing about, and getting dirty, and being rewarded by feeling the project developing intricately under your fingers. Interestingly, this seems to be true of software too, which you'd think would be too disembodied to offer that tactile satisfaction, but which exists quite firmly enough in the minds of some of those creating it to feel to them like a sculptural, textural thing, something with extension and weight and different degrees of smoothed-out done-ness, which can therefore be tinkered with to your heart's content. I kept finding parallel formative experiences in the lives of the people I interviewed. For example, there was the old-fashioned metal construction kit Meccano buried way down in the decision by John Sulston, the director of the British end of the

Human Genome Project, to become the kind of biologist who wanted to touch things; and then there was Meccano again in James Dyson's evolution towards being the king of the bagless vacuum. (Interestingly, Dan Dare was also a big influence on Dyson. In his autobiography, he describes reading the *Eagle* as a child in deepest Norfolk in the early 1960s, and naively assuming that, way out there in the big cities, people really were getting on with building the Dan Dare future. He says he was genuinely angry when he found out that the world wasn't going that way. I suppose you could interpret the vacuums as small yellow and purple plastic contributions to making the dream come true. Dual Cyclones against the Mekon!)

Anyway. Unfolding from this idea of what an engineer is comes a set of characteristic ways of doing engineering. Technology projects in Britain have tended to be executed by small groups of people, informally organised. They've tended to depend on people educating themselves in specialist skills, or picking up their knowledge on the job. They tend to be strong on lateral thinking and improvisation. They often have recourse to brilliant simplifications which let them sidestep around issues that other people are pouring time and money into. At the same time, they are strongly attracted to the notion of the one-off, smooth, bespoke, high-end technological marvel: to building the kinds of machine that promise a technological leap. These last two qualities sound contradictory, but they do go together. The belief in making things cheap because simple, and the desire to build one-off marvels, combine to produce projects in which British engineers try to deliver marvels on budgets so small that no-one else on the planet would even dream of making the attempt.

And sometimes succeed. As a demonstration of all these qualities operating at once, consider the true story of how British engineers took over motor racing in the 1960s. At the time, the incumbents who dominated Grand Prix were the Italian car companies, and of course Ferrari in particular, which treated racing as an advert for the road-car business and subsidised it accordingly.

They had massive investment in design and manufacturing, and they remorselessly produced generation after generation of expensive, ever more powerful engines. Meanwhile, in Britain, a completely different style of race engineering had come out of a pair of clubs founded in the years just after the war for skint racing enthusiasts. The 750 Motor Club taught weekend racers who couldn't afford a car off the peg to build one from Austin 7 parts, and the 500cc Club specialised in cannibalising motorbike engines. Between them, these two clubs produced a network of homebrew engineers who concentrated on aspects of car design where cleverness without a budget would be rewarded. Eventually, they started getting their hands on good engines – the Coventry Climax (wonderful name) and the first ever Cosworth – but the engines were never the main point. During the era of their breakthrough, British racing cars were characteristically underpowered compared to the competition. Instead the attention went into the dynamics of the vehicles. John and Charles Cooper worked out their thoughts about weight distribution by sketching in chalk on their workshop floor, and moved the engine back behind the driver: their rear-engined cars won their first Grand Prix in 1958. Colin Chapman focused on aerodynamics, and his exploitation of ground effect to stick his Lotuses to the track abruptly produced another paradigm shift. Suddenly cars that neglected the influence of the air they travelled through were as obsolete as front-engined cars. He started winning in 1962. Both times, oblique innovation, smart thinking on a neglected and unprestigious flank, beat superior power and resources. A pissed-off Enzo Ferrari said of the British club constructors (in French, because he was being pissed-off in France), 'Ils ne sont que des garagistes.' They're nothing but a bunch of bloody car mechanics. And from that beginning came a near-total British domination of Formula One that has lasted to the present day. A network of tiny, specialised tuners and component manufacturers in 'Grand Prix Valley' in Oxfordshire supply McLaren and so on, lavishly resourced now thanks to sponsorship money and advertising and TV rights. There are people out there whose lives are devoted to getting a single carbon-fibre widget thinner and thinner, lighter and lighter, closer and closer to being a pure streak in space of force-transmission. There's a critical mass of race-engineering expertise in Britain which makes it difficult for anyone, anywhere in the world to operate at the highest competitive level without coming here. Most of the cars for the roaring, snorting, all-American Champ Cars racing series in the US are actually imported from Lola of Huntingdon.

On the other hand, look at what there isn't in Britain. McLaren has a profitable business manufacturing six, eight, ten astonishingly high-specified vehicles a year for Formula One: they make a living from the entertainment value of the highest of automotive high technology. But since Chapman and the Coopers started the winning streak in racing cars, the rest of the British car industry, the part that did mass production, has virtually ceased to exist, at least under British ownership; this during the most explosive growth of car ownership in history. No more Austin, no more Morris; no more Rover, Humber, Hillman, MG, Sunbeam, Wolseley, Riley, Bristol, Alvis, Talbot, Singer, Triumph. Go back to that list of the idiosyncrasies of British engineering. Those technological folkways are in fact symbiotically linked to industrial weaknesses, both as causes and effects. They're both ways of making the best of a bad job, and also contributing factors in the way things turned out. British boffins partly believe in improvisation because the institutional backup available to them is so feeble. They're self-taught in specialised skills a lot of the time, because our system of technical education is crap. They resort to lateral thinking because we don't have an industrial culture that lets us benefit from steady, incremental product improvements. They use personal commitment to get quality control because we're not good at building it in and making it automatic. And they're attracted to the task of creating the individual, bespoke marvel because we don't do very well at turning out anything complicated by the thousand or by the million. As I say, these are symptoms – but in their turn they're also influences, shaping our future sense of what's possible and what isn't.

We maybe need to be a little bit nastier to ourselves here. Look at the kind of story about British technology that tends to give us a lump in our throats, that moves us, that makes us want to cheer. In fact I'll tell you one. In the 1950s, Saunders-Roe, the same company on the Isle of Wight that had the contract to build the Black Arrow satellite launcher, designed a rocket-propelled interceptor in answer to a Ministry of Defence request for a plane that could get off the ground fast enough to have a chance at shooting down incoming high-altitude Russian nuclear bombers. What this thing chiefly needed was to be able to climb like a bat out of hell. Saunders-Roe actually constructed two working prototypes. Their SR.53 was a beautiful and terrifying object with stubby little wings, a bit like the X-plane Chuck Yeager broke the sound barrier in. Since the Russians then switched to missiles as their nuclear delivery system, the mission the plane was intended for stopped making sense, and it wasn't commissioned. But a couple of years ago I heard the retired engineers who built it give a talk; and they explained that Saunders-Roe ran out of money just before the first prototype was complete. They needed a fire-suppression system, and they also needed a pyrotechnic igniter for the De Havilland Spectre rocket engine. So they took the petty cash and they went to a yachting supplies shop in Cowes. They bought a self-inflating life raft, and they used the little CO_2 cylinder it came with for the fire-suppression, and the igniter was a cartridge from a flare gun, stuck in a hole under the tail. It's crucial here to remember that these people were not amateurs: this was a professional, extremely serious project based on very high-level aerodynamics. And it worked. The cartridge sparked, and the plane performed as specified, roaring 50,000 feet into the stratosphere over Wiltshire in about one minute, and then returned the test pilot to the ground alive and in one piece, reporting that the aircraft was 'docile and exceedingly pleasant to fly'. When I heard this, I thought: yay! Then I thought, hang on: I'm being moved here because this is a story about success against the odds, and why should a major defence procurement exercise have been this kind of threadbare struggle? Too many charming stories about British technology are like this, when you look closely. We're in danger of telling ourselves a national story about technology which is a story of only just being able to do things, of teetering desperately on the line between success and failure, and only just managing to fall onto the 'success' side by performing an ingenious last-minute backflip. But should we actually want technologies – and this is the implication – technologies which only just work?

(2004)

Printed

From 1990, when I gave up my day job in publishing, to 2005 when I acquired a new one as a writing teacher, I made most of my living as a book reviewer. The internet had not yet reduced the marginal cost of opinions to zero, and newspapers would pay you well enough for one day's work to subsidise two or three days on your own project, as long as your overheads were low. But the couple of hundred thousand words of literary journalism I produced are only very lightly represented here.

This is not because, in Orwell's words, I was 'pouring my immortal spirit down the drain, half a pint at a time'. I rather enjoyed being randomly educated by whatever dropped onto the mat in a jiffy bag, though I was glad when I could stop. (As a non-fiction writer, I tended to be sent non-fiction, on subjects which nearly-sorta-kinda abutted on areas I nearly-sorta-kinda knew about: books about the Iranian Revolution, cave-dwelling bacteria, gout, Stonehenge, amateur rocketry, map theft, the genesis of the footnote.)

Instead, it's that I was never very good at declaring sufficient independence from the book at hand, and producing something that said what I wanted to say, in a form worth keeping. So the pieces here are those in which I was able, from time to time, to make an accounting with a writer I particularly cared about, or to reflect on the processes of reading and writing themselves.

HALF IN PRAISE

One way and another, reading takes up so large a share of my existence that I have to praise it. It is what I know best, it is what I know how to do best, and the riches it brings me are always under my eye, undeniable. I know that the discoveries I make as I read are real and substantial, and so I insist that my switchback progress from left to right, left to right, left to right along lines of printed prose represents a genuine mode of experience whose integrity I have to defend if I'm not to be untrue to the hours and years I've spent engaged in it. This makes me, on an instinctive level, reading's advocate. I'm in favour of it for myself, and I'm in favour of it for other people. Whenever I hear about another child converted by J.K. Rowling to the joys of story, I can't help but be glad. I know what's in there, and I want other people to have it too. But over the last few years I have also found, as I tried to explore reading through its role in my own childhood, that there is an ambivalence in my perception of it which demands acknowledgement. Taken seriously, every quality in fiction that makes it powerful seems capable of being taken another way, not as revelation, but as revelation's cheap substitute. With that doubleness in mind, I found I couldn't write – or couldn't *only* write – a celebration. The best I can do truthfully is a kind of balancing act: half in praise of reading.

To start with its greatest power: fiction builds bridges between people. To know someone is not a straightforward act. It is to enter into a mutual negotiation, to find a way through the crusts of opacity represented by all their differences from us, and there is always the consideration that a person may not wish to be known. He or she may look back at us and form a judgement in the negative based on whatever degree of success they have had in decoding us. Tact, empathetic imagination, desire and the other tools of connection remain complex things even if they are in successfully workaday operation; even if instinctive, still complex, because of the multiple codes they work on and furnish translations between. Two people can be divided by temperament, by gender, by class, by nationality, by culture, by race, by religion. Fiction has the power to lift our gaze beyond our own particular set of categories, because it preserves those acts of understanding that have succeeded. All but the most consciously momentous conversations vanish into breath and oblivion, but when a fruitful foray across the space between selves is written down, it becomes permanently available. It adds to fiction's great, cumulative effort to do justice to the selves not our own, in which (as Dorothea famously recognises in *Middlemarch*) 'the lights and shadows must always fall with a certain difference'. So books are tools of understanding. From a book you can borrow percipient powers you lack yourself. You can take up a greater intuition about motive or a more unwavering compassion as if they were prostheses.

From a book, too, you can learn of people beyond the scope of your single, limited life; people you'd never meet. A book is a great liberator from the tyranny of given circumstances. The propagandists of the Enlightenment said that the free flow of writing would expand human sympathy beyond the local cramps of prejudice and limited vision, out of the choking hands of kings and hierarchs. And they were right: it is an essential function of writing that it widens our vision beyond the evidence of our own senses. William Hazlitt rhapsodised on the free press as the 'remote but inevitable' cause of the French Revolution. He said:

> Books alone teach us to judge of truth and good in the abstract: without a knowledge of things at a distance from us, we judge like savages or animals from our senses and appetites alone; but by the aid of books and of an intercourse with the world of ideas, we are purified, raised, ennobled from savages into intellectual and rational beings.

This is why a novel is often the fastest guide to a country we know nothing about. Read Márquez, and you receive a vivid intelligence of Colombia. Read di Lampedusa's *The Leopard* and Sciascia's *Day of the Owl*, and you take the royal road to knowing Sicily. Not its dimensions, exports, geography, economics, train timetables – though that kind of knowledge accretes from novel-reading with surprising density – but its typical forms of human encounter. The novelist took them for granted, since the novel was written from within the culture it described, yet they are sufficiently explained for the stranger-reader in the process of articulating them on the page.

What gesture does a Colombian make when inviting you to sit at an empty place at a café table? How does a low-level Sicilian 'man of respect' conduct himself when talking to a naively zealous policeman from the north of Italy? The author's answer reduces the multiple codes of human distance and human difference into coherent story, thus into the single code of written language. Some cultures, some novels, are much harder to enter into than others, but every book can be read by everyone who can read, and there is always *some* gain in comprehension. Of course you have to bring sufficient emotional experience of your own to the reading. If you've never seen a Colombian, or even a café table, you're OK, but if no-one has ever invited you to sit down your reading will be crippled. Conversely, the more perceptive you are in life, the richer your reading will grow. But the kitty of understandings necessary to crack the code of writing in a minimal way is not large, and you still gain an extraordinarily intimate access to people whose living counterparts would never be transparent to you. You can shadow the thinking of a Berber chieftain, a Japanese department store lady condemned to bow at opening elevator doors, an Appalachian miner, a primary-school teacher in Dundee. You can read them without necessarily having an inkling (fatally textual word) how to 'read' them off the page.

For the other side of fiction's loan of wisdom is the fact that the knowledge it brings is not necessarily transferrable to the realm of experience. The world is not narrated as you pass along it. Compared to fiction it can seem *unlabelled*. No authoritative voice tells you what the person you're talking to is thinking. Consequently, as well as a supplement to our real knowledge of other people, fiction can also offer a substitute. It can be used as an alternative to the work of really knowing people. To a certain kind of reader, like myself, it represents a permanent temptation to bypass the difficult process of getting sustenance from human encounters. After all, you arrive at the same place, don't you?

But maybe not. Maybe the means whereby we come to knowledge of other people in the world are indispensable sources of that knowledge's strength and value. Perhaps the friction of meetings, the meandering development of a friendship, the sudden demolition of a tower of supposition when a misunderstanding is exposed, the resistance of a hostility that won't diminish, the limited transit through the outworks of a personality permitted by some specific act of trust, love's opening of the membranes of private memory – perhaps all these textured efforts are more than processes. Perhaps in themselves they constitute a dimension of understanding, because all those negotiations actually map the other self we're approaching. With each motion they tell us that the other person is there, and how they are there. Some novels do enact this resistant journey to understanding, whose qualities condition the understanding arrived at. Proust wrote characters who have to be attended to at the pace of experience. But it is much more usual for novels to name the difficulty of judging people than actually to recreate it. Most fiction exploits the power to move between selves without any resistance at all, making many characters in turn the centre of perception, laying out many points of view. Long before the reflex shots of cinema, novels could cut like lightning between the marquis looking at the waiter and the waiter looking at the marquis. This is an essential freedom of the form. But again though, it puts it in the power of a reader who is so minded to use novels to circumvent the drudgery (and the reward) of striking out into the world, as we all do in life, from our one centre, our single lifelong point of view.

Take what happens what you stop reading. When you begin a book, your adaptation to its world is usually gradual. You have to learn its rhythm, you have to feel your way in. It would be a rare book in rare sync with a reader that absorbed you instantaneously at the first words. I always feel that a book has a kind of inner seal that has to be broken, like the drum-tight circle of waxed paper inside the lid of a jar of instant coffee. For the first ten, or twenty, or thirty pages, I'm still reading tentatively, like someone tapping on the paper seal; only then does the novel truly come open. But at the end of a book, however well prepared you have been for the ending by the down-shifting cadence of the narrative, the text simply runs out, and you find yourself for a minute still in the emotional state the book has aroused, without the book to sustain it. It's then that the difference between the two states of reading and living becomes palpable as a sudden contrast. Sometimes it can feel like running off a cliff in a cartoon: your feet keep pedalling until you notice there's no ground beneath them. Sometimes the scrim of the book – which has been between you and the input of your senses – thins and fades patchily, a tapestry becoming a veil in places, then scrubbing away altogether while other parts still linger, so that you see the real face of someone in the room with you appear through the persisting green and gold of a heraldic forest. Sometimes, though the scenery of the story is quite gone, its mood or tone persists and alters how you see your exterior surroundings; and the people in them. Although you do not see a lover, parent, child, friend, acquaintance, associate or stranger the same way that you see a character, from the moment of ceasing to read until the unpredictable moment when the book fades sufficiently from your imagination, the frame of your mind as a reader is going to alter your literal vision, telling you (among other things) how the you that responds to characters differs from the you that responds to people: what you do in the different arenas of living and reading, what you are capable of doing in them.

Not many records have been made of these moments of transition. Trying to describe the life books have in your mind when you're not actually reading them is a rare project, on the edge of conventional criticism or perhaps over it. One such rare description was given by the critic Sven Birkerts in his recent *The Gutenberg Elegies*. Here, a Patrick McGrath novel, *Dr Haggard's Disease*, is on his knee:

> In the course of a fifteen-minute subway ride I drop into Haggard's world as into a well. I heed the outside signals only enough to insure I don't travel on past my stop. Not until I feel the train decelerating do I close the book and look up. For an instant everything swims in a milky sort of haze; then the eyes readjust and the sensations of reading begin to ebb. I look around at the other passengers – the student, the mother fiddling with the strap on her child's knapsack – and I feel irradiated with a benign detachment. The inner and outer are, briefly, in balance. Haggard is as present to me as these people. And that specious equivalence brings me closer to them, though I'm not sure why. Their boundaries seem porous; I have the illusion that I could enter and understand their lives. The feeling passes. The life of the book dims out as I get to my feet and jostle through the doors.[28]

Birkerts is very sure that the result when his reading ends is a gain in perception, just as he is sure that while he is reading, 'reconnoitering between inner and outer focus … enriches my overall responsiveness'. He says 'illusion', he says 'specious', but he is very tender towards his subway epiphany. This is a triumphant affirmation of literature's power to help us perceive, by encouraging us to adopt the equivalent in real life of a reader's 'benign detachment' while reading. Notice, though, that Birkerts is not saying that his taste of reader-like understanding for the people opposite has given him any ambition to get to know them in fact as opposed to theory. He is attending to his sensation of knowledge *as* a sensation, one which has continued the sensory properties of reading into a batch of seconds in the life of a car of the A-train, bound for Brooklyn. The student, the mother, the child seem for a moment to be open to the switch of viewpoints which would let him look back out of their eyes at the guy opposite holding the Patrick McGrath novel. Yet all the while, since he has no means of knowing them as all real humans have to know other humans, from the outside in, they remain total strangers. A cynic might say that with no foundation in accurate this-worldly insight, Birkerts' benign detachment is not very different, functionally, from a beery glow. It's a very sophisticated glow, but then literature makes a very classy drug.

And Birkerts' sensation represents only one end of a spectrum of possible sensations generated by the return from the labelled world of text. Different drugs in different consumers produce different after-effects, umpteen temporary alterations of the eye. Birkerts in effect describes a brief illusion that the world is mimicking the book. The passengers in the subway car exhibited an openness to being known as characters, and specifically as *Patrick McGrath characters*. I imagine they looked incipiently gothic, prone to pitiably violent passions. If he had that moment closed the text of an Oscar Wilde play, they might have seemed less provincially solid, more posed in a set of attitudes. *I live in Coney Island: that is my tragedy*. Yet the dominant perception at the end of a book can also be that the world contradicts it, or exceeds it. A very cerebral, abstract fiction, far from imposing a tracery of pure idea on your vision in its aftermath, can make all that you see and hear seem intensely particular and vivid. Or, if you are rebounding from some story whose characters have had to obey a demanding set of manners, if it has been hard to imagine controlling your elbows and your language in a text's genteel ballroom, then what's real can proclaim a kind of cheerful *heaviness*, the lumpy Rabelaisian assertiveness belonging to all those things that just *are* whether anyone likes it or not. Elbows also rest on tabletops, you remember: whoopee cushions are bought, dogs attempt to have sex with the legs of respectable strangers.

But the most common aftermath for me has been a feeling that the world simply contains less than the book. I get a hangover, not a glow. Instead of Birkerts' elated confusion of real people with characters, I get a disappointment that real people are not characters. That their behaviour is not plotted. That you cannot have the quick flush of unnegotiated knowledge of them. That no selecting intelligence is pruning their qualities to produce a consistent effect.

When in December 2001 I read the obituary of the historical novelist Dorothy Dunnett, I remembered the morning after a night I spent ten years earlier with one of her books. The light was grey in the room. Dawn had come on at the same rate as the traffic noise increased from the South Circular Road beside the house, as if someone were pushing up a slider switch controlling several of the urban elements together. On the floor by the ruptured sofa my ashtray was full. I had the taste in my mouth and the brittle energy in my brain of the twenty cigarettes I'd rolled since midnight; rolled steadily, smoked steadily, as I moved through the long book at steady high speed, my eye pole-vaulting across each opened duo of pages, from a jump-point on the left to a landing on the right, the text between taken in whole. Dunnett's world absorbed me, but she wasn't a descriptive writer, as such. She never created a past that took hold as a persuasive environment. Rather than any moment-filling

shimmer of silk or thump of believable Flemish floorboards underfoot in the year 1460, she offered the labyrinthine behaviour of
Machiavellian heroes: two of them, Lymond and Niccolò, each with
a cycle of novels to his name. She constructed these Renaissance
demons of subterfuge to a patented plan of her own, by breaking –
habitually, continually – the rule of narrative which states that in
circumstances of mystery the reader should be supplied with all
relevant information, so you can at least have a try at working out
what's going on. Dunnett deliberately withheld basic plot details,
putting the reader into the same position of thwarted dependence as
her heroes' entourages, or the women who loved them. Heroes and
author alike never explained, never apologised. Like all descendants
of the gothic incorporating relishable bad behaviour into romance,
these fictions exploited the illusion that to be horrible to someone
shows strong feeling about them; is a sign of intense involvement
with them. And the reader was brought within the circle of intensity.
The endlessly drawn-out, opaque situations secreted for the reader
too a powerful set of emotions in the key of frustration. Loyalty, jealousy, curiosity, rebellion, indignation: a fibrous mat of feeling that
constituted Dunnett's characteristic world.

And it stops. I stopped. I levered myself off the sofa, with the
sensation that my mind had been used to plant, grow and harvest
a crop of passion, and then been burnt off, to a dead level of stubble.
Now it felt scorched, like my palate from the smoke. I fancied
something sweet to eat, suddenly, to fill that space, and to set me
along the route to a physical comfort, a sugary bodily security.
They sold doughnuts at the newsagent's. I drifted out of the house
and up the street on unstrung legs. People were going to work, the
side streets carrying little tributaries of commuters towards the
bus stops. My drift took me across the line of the main, deep current
flowing down Brixton Hill into central London. But I didn't feel it;
it didn't pluck at me. The grey of the light extended to the humans.
They looked hollow, artificial, incomparably less alive than the
inhabitants of a fiction. I could tell from the sample I saw that

nowhere in the whole waking, moving city would there be anybody walking whose face conveyed the organisation of a plot. Nobody would give me the story's tug on my glands. Logic said that these faces all fronted experience more complicated than narrative, but that seemed like a statement of chaos to me: and not a loud overwhelming chaos either (William James's 'booming, buzzing confusion') but a chaos of vanishingly faint signals, dimming towards entropy. Luckily there was an apple doughnut in the chill cabinet, my favourite. Twenty minutes later I was asleep, curled around a bolus of carbohydrate.

(2004)

KIPLING'S JUNGLE

Rudyard Kipling began *The Jungle Book* in the spring of 1893, in Bliss Cottage, a little house near Brattleboro, Vermont, leased from his wife Caroline Balestier's mother. They had only been married for a year. He was twenty-seven: soon he would be a father, and paternity was much on his mind, along with the revolution which every generation turns a child into a parent. *The Just So Stories*, later, would be for his own children to hear: these present ones, his first stories for a child audience, celebrated the change in his life, and meditated on pedagogy, for though Mowgli's biological father plays a tiny and ignoble role in one episode alone of *The Second Jungle Book*, in another sense the wolf-boy has a plethora of fathers. Baloo, Bagheera, Kaa, Akela: all fathers in all but name, alive in a magical space both like and unlike a late-Victorian nursery. Moreover he drew for his jungle creatures on his own father Lockwood Kipling's *Beast and Man in India*, finding anecdotal sketches there of the mongoose, the python and the jackal. Thus he loyally incorporated his own tutelage by Lockwood into the book even as the times revolved and he moved, for Josephine Kipling (b. March 1893), into the place Lockwood had occupied for him.

Kipling wrote books, but not novels – with the exceptions of his single best work, *Kim*, and his single worst one, *The Light That Failed*. It was not simply that he was a 'short-breathed' writer, attuned to the needs of a short story with its relatively swift closure and peremptory insights into people via single, dazzling details; as opposed to the 'long-breathed' writer of novels, with their extended arc and their patient attention to the processes of growth and development. He wrote short stories, but he conceived them by the bookful. As a young man in India, and a brilliant apprentice to literature, he had worked in brief because that form best suited his pell-mell exploration of his powers. (And, of course, because it allowed him to conceal, beneath a quickly sketched worldly wisdom, those many things he did not yet know.) At this stage he expected to progress to writing novels, following the conventional writer's path. But by the time he came to write the two Jungle Books in the 1890s, with the disgruntling experience of *The Light That Failed* behind him, the volume of linked narratives had become his consciously chosen form – his metier, the particular field for his talents. Here, large design and short effect co-existed; and he was able to attain a loose, suggestive richness. Loose, because it was not his way to accumulate episodes amounting to one continuous narrative. The Mowgli stories are the core of the Jungle Books, but they are not printed in chronological order, and they are actually outnumbered by the other pieces. 'Rikki-Tikki-Tavi', 'The White Seal', 'Toomai of the Elephants' and 'Her Majesty's Servants' make up more than sidelights. Though recurrent themes connect them to Mowgli's Jungle, these are not connections of a rigorous order. Kipling made two books'-full, and was content to let the stories settle into place in the reader's imagination. By design the stories tell upon one another. The individual precisions of the telling enlace. Kipling was acutely aware of the shape he hoped would coalesce after reading: the didactic intentions are plain and obvious. Equally, he was unwilling to pre-empt the imaginative response, or to offer lore and symbolism that could *only* resolve in one way. Some of the imaginative afterlives of *The Jungle Book* have been very public.

We can imagine Kipling hating Disney's singing version, which prettifies all the cruelty of the Jungle, and turns his lessons on growing up into a glib romp. We can know for certain that he approved Baden-Powell's borrowing of key elements for the official mythology of the scouting movement. But we aren't obliged to follow him in either position, and the purposely loose weave of the stories – their quilted arrangement – actually helps to free us of that obligation.

Why are the most sympathetic inhabitants of Kipling's Jungle its predators? The wolves who succour Mowgli are pack-hunters, and Akela holds his position as their grizzled chief only while his jaws are still capable of the death grip. They can be corrupted by the insidious words of the tiger Shere Khan, but at their best they prove their status as 'the Free People' by an untameable tenacity. Mother Wolf, Mowgli's foster-parent, 'was not called The Demon for compliment's sake' in the days when she ran with the pack. Bagheera the panther is a lithe, magnificent slayer, 'and nobody cared to cross his path'. His physical beauty, his black-on-black markings that show up 'in certain lights like the pattern of watered silk', cannot be separated from the threat he exudes. His voice 'as soft as wild honey dripping from a tree' is after all a hunter's tool. Kaa the python – whose coldness and menace we are never allowed to forget, while we admire his wisdom and subtlety – has the Jungle's deepest gullet, its most capacious swallow. Of course, there is also 'old Baloo, who can come and go where he pleases, because he eats only nuts and roots and honey'. In his company Mowgli does learn 'that honey and nuts were just as pleasant to eat as raw meat'; but the vegetarian example Baloo sets weighs lightly beside the education the bear imparts as tutor to the wolf-cubs, and judge of the Jungle Law. That Law is concerned with survival, with the proprieties to be observed when eating and being eaten. Baloo has a boxer's strength when occasion requires it. Biffing Mowgli black and blue in the boy's own interests, he counts as a proud observer of the hunt rather than a dissenter from it. '"Well said", growled Baloo', when Mowgli offers Kaa a grand massacre of goats by way of return for the python's part in rescuing him.

The period in which Kipling wrote the two Jungle Books saw a growing appreciation of predators in general and wolves in particular: a sort of imaginative rehabilitation of creatures that had formerly served as symbols of chaotic appetite and destructiveness. In part the cultural backwash of Darwinism was involved. Evolutionary ideas had enabled mid-Victorians to discover pattern in animal behaviour that had seemed chaotic before. An efficient, instinctual killer no longer looked quite like an agent of mayhem, but took a role in something like a natural economy, where eating and being eaten supported each other. As Kipling's parents' generation gave way to his, other, more crudely 'Darwinian' ideas also came into circulation. These drew parallels between natural selection in biology and the struggle for survival in human society, making it appear that predatory humans had the force of nature behind them. Kipling never assented to this debased (and extremely unscientific) vision, but he did believe in the necessity for toughness, of which the turn-of-the-century vogue for animal stories was partly a symptom. It was an old truth, of course, that the imagination is attracted to strength, to the stealthy step of a hunting cat. The essayist William Hazlitt wrote in 1817, 'A lion hunting a flock of sheep or a herd of wild asses is a more poetical object than they; and we even take part with the lordly beast, because our vanity or some other feeling makes us disposed to place ourselves in the situation of the strongest party.'[29] But the animal fictions of the 1890s and early 1900s actually set out to place the reader 'in the situation' of their animal heroes. Some made their animals speak, some did not; almost all tried to look out on the world through the eyes of wolf or eagle or bear. From being fearful objects, powerful animals became sympathetic subjects. For a child reader, of course, living a life governed by adult decisions, it was always specially attractive to slip into the skin of a lion, wild and self-sufficient. Kipling's own genius as a writer for children sprang in part from his sensitivity to this attraction.

The wider culture was also disposed towards the idea, though; Kipling's age liked the chance to identify with predators, in accordance with new ideals of masculinity that were shaping literature and society. Thirty or twenty years earlier, a wolf-child's adventures in the jungle would not have been plausible subject-matter for ambitious writing. Then, the settings for serious litera-ture had been primarily domestic, its most influential authors as likely to be women as men, its audience assumed to be mixed; the novel itself had been acknowledged to be a form moulded by female experience and female sensibility. Since the death of George Eliot in 1880 (to choose a date that contemporaries sensed might represent the end of an epoch) a pronounced, masculine revolution had taken place, whose effect can be measured by comparing the old and the new sets of luminaries. Eliot, Elizabeth Gaskell, Dickens: as against Robert Louis Stevenson, Kipling, Conrad. A genre that one critic calls 'the male romance' had been launched, or rather retrieved from the ghetto of writing-for-boys and shifted into the centre of current literature, where stories of ships and the sea, or work and machines, or animals, gained unprecedented degrees of psychological subtlety, without losing their masculine emphasis. The human types thought worth investigating changed; became more extroverted and reticent, more occupied by toil, shame and vigorous activity. Kipling himself reserved a special admiration for wily, capable men. His heroes in India had been the young, close-mouthed colonial officers who administered districts remote from formal laws and the trappings of power. In his mind (he never joined the company of his idols) these men had the stature of myth; and his version of admirable masculinity accordingly referred again and again to the qualities he thought he had glimpsed. Strength, for him, involved the possibility of violence. So it should not be unex-pected that in his Jungle (where almost every creature is male, except Mother Wolf) the predators should furnish the eyes through which we watch and pounce. He expected his readers to covet, as he did, the chance to identify with 'lordly beasts'.

Yet nature in the Jungle is not a gory ruck, a perpetual munching scrimmage. 'The law in this world', wrote Angus Wilson in his biography of Kipling,[30] 'is far from Darwinian . . .' Kipling wants us to come to a sensuous realisation of ferocity, and accept it as a badge of realism, a sign of things-as-they-are. But the violence of the Jungle is rule-bound, constrained by the Law (though the Law never protects the weak from the strong as such), and constrained too by the Aesopian, fabular quality of the stories. Only Shere Khan, that shabby tiger, is an indiscriminate killer, the wrong sort of predator in the predatory fantasy. It is important that Shere Khan arouses the fear we don't feel for Mowgli in the jaws of the wolf, the coils of Kaa, the claws of the panther or the paws of the bear. In fact we notice how often the memorable tableaux of Jungle life approximate to the traditional images of the peaceable kingdom of the beasts. With a certain difference, of course: here the lamb *would* be snapped up if it lay down with the wolf, but predator and prey, killer and killed, all form a community of tough laws and tough loyalties, with Mowgli's safety expressing the trust it is right to feel in the nobility of all the killers bar one.

On the other hand, we learn something quite different about Kipling's preference for predators from his rejection of the monkeys in 'Kaa's Hunting'. Here he departs for once from the characters of species given in his father's *Beast and Man in India*. Lockwood Kipling observed the 'sudden petulance' the bandar-log were prone to, reported their skill as 'daring and mischievous pilferers' – he tells the story of a complete wedding cake removed from a reception in Simla by a chain of monkeys who passed it down the hill piece by piece. He also commented that 'the sudden flash of interest in a triviality and its abrupt cessation remind one more of lunacy than sane humanity': yet his dominant impression was melancholic. *His* monkeys were trailing, 'wistful', patriarchal bands, sitting impassive in the rain. Rudyard takes only the playful portion of the characterisation, then makes it malevolent. 'They have no law', Baloo explains:

> They are outcaste. They have no speech of their own, but use the stolen words they overhear when they listen, and peep, and wait

up above in the branches. Their way is not our way. They are without leaders. They have no remembrance. They boast and chatter and pretend that they are a great people about to do great affairs in the jungle, but the falling of a nut turns their mind to laughter and all is forgotten.[31]

The worst of the monkeys seems to be their pretensions. From the borrowed collapsing grandeur of the Cold Lairs, the ruined human city they have colonised, they 'pretended to despise the Jungle-People because they lived in the forest'. Again, 'they scratch for fleas and pretend to be men'. No other animal feels this wish to seem more than it is; no other animal possesses so threateningly unstable an identity. The monkeys' dual refusal of the stately register of the Jungle speech, and the immutable imperatives of the Law, remove their chance to own the splendid self-possession of a Bagheera or a Baloo. One might have thought that their anthropomorphism – their manlike shape, their clever hands – would make the monkeys the natural companions of a wild child: after all, in Edgar Rice Burroughs' *Tarzan*, a sort of pulp derivative of the Jungle Books, they were to have just that role. But it is the anthropomorphism that is the problem, the point of maximum instability, for Kipling can only see it as anarchic and presumptuous, and even parodic, as if the monkeys were debased copies of humans who violate the proud sufficiency the other beasts feel in being themselves. Even Shere Khan has more dignity than they.

Kipling was never especially interested in the real details of natural history; but here it seems that natural history is left behind altogether, and we need to think of the implicit parallel between the animal cast of the Jungle Books and the dramatis personae of Kipling's Indian Empire. He consciously conceived the Jungle as a microcosm. The lessons Mowgli learns are transferable to the overtly human society at the periphery of the stories which he must one day return to, because the society of beasts is also a disguised vision of human society, seductive yet schematic. And his lessons (though this description strips away their richness unfairly) revolve around the question of power, and the place he is to find for himself on the ladder of power. As he grows, Bagheera cannot meet his gaze. Baloo, sage of all the Seoni, master of local wisdom, defers to him once Mowgli has understood his teaching and gone on where Baloo cannot follow. Given the purpose as an idealised allegory of empire, it is hard to avoid the conclusion that, on the magical ground of the forest floor, the Indian boy stands to the beasts as, on the real ground of British India, the white man is supposed to stand in relation to Indian men. He must give the respect commanded by the proper denizens of a wild place, but knows that it requires his own greater vision to complete the local lore. To be able to do this, he must humbly absorb all that the Jungle has to offer; live by its rules and honour its ways; yet in the end the roles allotted to him and them are utterly, satisfyingly distinct. Which is only right, according to this vision of empire, for the animals are proudly content to be different from the boy. Baloo, Bagheera and Kaa exhibit, so to speak, the *right* difference from him: but what of the monkeys, who wish to close the gap, who claim to resemble him?

In other stories, Kipling wrote Indian characters he admired as he admired the dignified ferocity of Bagheera. *Kim*, for example, has Mahbub Ali, the scarlet-bearded horse dealer from the north, a man of honour and of honourable violence. He preferred these human predators, so securely different, so rooted in the Indian environment as he envisaged it, to Indians who troubled the distinctness of rulers and ruled by resembling Europeans in unexpected ways. Kipling had known India at the time of the Raj's maximum placidity. The memory of the 1859 'Mutiny' (a bloody uprising against the British) had receded to a safe historical distance, and Queen Victoria's pomp-swathed installation as Empress of India in 1877 seemed a promise of permanence. Mass nationalist agitation had scarcely begun, but though they did not challenge it effectively yet, the chief internal irritants to British rule were the assertive Hindu intelligentsia of Bengal, who had just founded the Congress movement. These Calcutta journalists, advocates, functionaries, landlords, doctors and poets – lumped together as 'Babus' – argued law and literature, policy and government, sometimes on Western terms, sometimes in the light of Hinduism. Derisive remarks about their comical English and their absurd pretensions formed a staple of Anglo-Indian conversation, as Kipling heard it among the armchairs of the Lahore Club, at home with his family, and on his journalistic travels. Ever more intelligent than his prejudices – able to send one part of his mind scouting beyond the limits of his own fixed views – Kipling did, however, share in this communal contempt. Bengalis who presumed to meddle in public affairs were, he agreed, merely denying their Indian identity on the strength of a veneer of Western education. 'They talk too much, and do too little', Kipling wrote in 1887, sticking to the stereotype while selecting the (supposed) failing that most contravened his personal gospel of stoical industriousness. In the analogy between Jungle and Raj, the bandar-log surely correspond to the Babus.

It is important to realise, though, that Kipling did not intend a racial caricature. He was concerned with transgressions against good order, as he understood it, and against intelligibility, order's equivalent in language. The monkeys' sin lay in crossing the boundaries of identity. Kipling's world had many necessary boundaries – between the public and the private, for example – which the individual neglected at his peril, and, once formed vividly in his mind, he used the symbol of the bandar-log promiscuously, for whomever he distrusted. At one time it was the London literary scene that habitually called to his mind the image of an ape troupe: metropolitan chatterers (thought Kipling, recoiling) whose light talk and dinner-party intimacies obscurely threatened the springs of creativity. He had packed such mythic potency into his animals, he produced such a strong and immediate sense of their physical existence, that they could never serve as simple shadows of his opinions. The game of spotting real-world counterparts to the Jungle creatures went on inexhaustibly among Kipling's readers, even after his death. During the Second World War, General Wavell identified Shere Khan as a premonition of Hitler, and the jackal Tabaqui with Mussolini.

'Now these are the Laws of the Jungle', runs Kipling's verse digest of Baloo's teaching in *The Second Jungle Book*,

> and many and mighty are they;
> But the head and the hoof of the Law and the haunch and the
>   hump is – Obey!

If the Jungle Books were merely fables of hierarchy and proper subordination, they would not offer the sense they do, to adult readers as much as children, of a palpable enlargement of possibilities. Mowgli's experience of the Jungle is our gateway to it, and Mowgli's anomalous position, poised between two worlds, is the crucial thing here. Not only is he far freer physically than any human-reared child could ever be, swinging along the 'tree-roads' with the monkeys in a dizzy rush, or bathing in deliciously cool brown forest pools; he experiences the lessons of power as a dimension of his self-discovery. His is not the story of a life lived within the strict confines of the Law. In the Jungle, but never entirely of it, he learns how the Law does *and does not* contain the actions of an unprecedented being like himself. What code will govern him, he must decide for himself – twice over, because there is also the village to be considered, where at first, as he says to himself in 'Tiger! Tiger!', 'I am as silly and dumb as a man would be with us in the jungle.' The Jungle Books speak to the fluid condition of learning the world and its laws, rather than the static one of obeying them. In the same way, *Kim*, with its child-hero able to dart and forage at will through multiplicitous 'native' India, yet destined to join the ranks of India's governors, only narrates the first wondering discovery of the secret means by which the diverse splendours around Kim are maintained. Moving freely himself, Kim does not see the structures of rule as an iron lid over the country, but as aspects of his own complicated nature. *Kim* and the Jungle Books alike give a poetic view of power – power still as dewy, flexible and exciting as adolescence.

Most important of all, again like Kimball O'Hara whose famous cry 'Who is Kim?' expresses the void left untouched by the learning of many rules, Mowgli is mysterious to himself, mysterious beyond the powers of his pedagogues to explain, though Bagheera can tell him (like a naturalist) that the water on his face is tears 'such as men use'. He asks unanswerable questions in his song of himself that he chants at the Council Rock:

The water comes out of my eyes; yet I laugh while it falls.
Why?

The Law cannot help on this brink of emotion. It never can, in Kipling, whose lifelong belief in the necessity of law grew, precisely, out of his awareness of the inward confusions it cannot regulate. Notoriously reticent in his private life, Kipling was also notoriously and remarkably unwilling (for a major writer) to probe or fathom his characters' psychologies directly. He would take them to the brink of turbulent feeling, then specify only that cliffs of fall had opened beneath them, leaving the job of communicating the crisis in the hands of brilliantly suggestive external description. He conceived the Law defensively, as a forever insufficient bulwark against the consequences of questions like Mowgli's. It was something to hold on to, rather than a cage. Accordingly, his sense of the direction in which danger lay was quite different. The danger in the Jungle Books, as in *Kim*, is less that the Law will prove intolerably harsh and confining, than that a sensory overload – in the calling, populous Jungle or among the endlessly varied crowds flowing with Kim along the Grand Trunk Road – will press intolerably on the lonely individual.

The state of being suspended between worlds, neither an insider nor an outsider, furnishes one of the threads connecting the three

Mowgli stories to the four other tales in *The Jungle Book*. Kotick, the albino-pelted hero of 'The White Seal', is separated from his gregarious, complacent tribe both by his colour and his unwillingness to accept the customary decimation of the seal people. He sees the Aleut hunters plain, as they club the tranquil seals, instead of 'staring stupidly'; and undertakes a solitary odyssey among other sea species in order to change what only he can understand is changeable. Small Toomai in 'Toomai of the Elephants', son of a government mahout or elephant driver, will soon have a place in the scheme of things, but does not yet: and he, loose where the adult drivers and even the sage Petersen Sahib are fixed in the firmament of tradition, alone rides into the midnight forest on the wrinkled back of Kala Nag to see the rumoured dancing of the elephants. The grateful English family in 'Rikki-Tikki-Tavi' feed 'their' mongoose banana and boiled egg at the breakfast table. His other existence, exploring the intricate animal societies of bungalow and garden, is largely invisible to them, except when it results in a dead snake; yet he is a newcomer to his wild role as much as to being petted, intensely curious, exploring the customs, the alliances and the hostilities of his two domains. 'Her Majesty's Servants' lets the reader overhear the night-talk of bullocks, camels, horses and elephants whose animal natures have been recruited to the different ends of the Indian Army.

This last story, however, so neatly productive of an imperial moral, is also the least successful in the book, because it *regiments*, it tidies to the point of imaginative death, another important common strand of *The Jungle Book*. 'Her Majesty's Servants' only collects the supply-beasts' views of human warfare. Their independent existences have been reduced to a set of routinely different reactions, sometimes comically partial ones, to the moment when the big guns go off, or 'the red stuff' soaks into the ground. His dog lies beside the listening narrator: and you might say that the entire animal cast have been spanielised, turned into spaniels with humps, spaniels with horns, and large grey spaniels with trunks. Elsewhere in the book, it takes a very special kind of fool to draw a human-centred conclusion from the wild world – like Buldeo the hunter, confidently announcing Shere Khan incarnates the soul of a lame money-lender ('cobwebs and moontalk', says Mowgli), or the Aleut seal-clubber who thinks Kotick 'is old Zaharoff's ghost. He was lost last year in the big gale.' The English father in 'Rikki-Tikki-Tavi' is wiser. He knows Rikki is to be treated with respect, and his cobra-killing services accepted as the voluntary, inexplicable gift they are. The idea that Kipling patterns into triviality in 'Her Majesty's Servants', and otherwise deploys throughout *The Jungle Book* with seductive vigour, is that it is wildness which gives obedience – or service – its value. A tamed animal has no gift to give, no dignified self-possession from which to act in chosen obedience to an order it thinks is worth obeying. Kala Nag, on the other hand, the great bull elephant, master of the government herd, serves with such force (paradoxically) in the round-ups of his wild cousins because there are inviolate parts of his nature which captivity has never altered; those same parts that respond to the summons to the secret dancing. 'And we will hunt with thee', offer Mowgli's four wolf-brothers at the end of 'Tiger! Tiger!' The same principle is at work, of course, in Mahbub Ali's decision in *Kim*, from out of his own stylishly murderous nature, to serve the Raj in the Great Game against the Russians – for we return here to the human underpinning of the animal tales, and Kipling's ideal portrait of imperial relations.

Mowgli's future among men can be imagined. In fact, it does not need to be: as the envoi of 'Tiger! Tiger!' suggests ('But that is a story for grown-ups'), Kipling had already written it. 'In the Rukh', the story in question, never appeared in any of the editions of the Jungle Books. Kipling conceived it first, before any of the famous Mowgli stories, and, looking at it and his next work, 'Mowgli's Brothers', realised that the latter had the germ of imaginative growth in it, while the former did not. Though good in his vein of adult colonial tales, it had to be kept apart from the two collections because it abolishes Mowgli's gloriously unresolved state in the Jungle. It shows him entirely from the outside. A young Englishman, Gisborne Sahib of the Indian government's Department of Woods and Forests, is tending to his lonely woodland patch when an angelic visitant arrives at the scene of a recent tiger kill. 'A man was walking down the dried bed of the stream, naked except for the loin-cloth, but crowned with a wreath of the tasselled blossoms of the white convulvulus creeper.' Mowgli's physical beauty – only implied previously, until his mother Messua applauds it at the very end of *The Second Jungle Book*, in accordance with Mowgli's dawning adolescent self-consciousness – becomes explicit here, is insisted on and pinned down in European terms. '"He's a most wonderful chap," thought Gisborne; "he's like the illustrations in the Classical Dictionary."' Like the Greek god Pan, that is, or one of the pantheon of wood spirits. What strikes Gisborne most of all, especially in comparison to his wheedling Muslim butler, is Mowgli's total, oblivious ignorance of 'the proper manner of addressing white people', 'of all forms of ceremony and salutations'. 'His voice was clear and bell-like, utterly different from the usual whine of the native ...'. Gisborne finds the godling's combination of uncanny woodcraft and undeferential speech irresistible. 'I must get him into the Government service somehow', he thinks. And indeed, once the mystery of his origins (a soluble, short-story-sized mystery) has been solved, Mowgli elects of his own free will to join the hierarchy that defends the forest, and be Gisborne's man. He ends married to the butler's daughter, with steady pay and a pension. If a certain ignominy attaches to being a myth *with a pension*, the story's gratifying demonstration that the wild peg fits exactly into the official hole brings a much greater imaginative loss. Kipling could not begin the Jungle Books here, nor even end them with this drab disclosure of Mowgli's role in the imperial scheme. It's one thing to have Mowgli's fate implied, another seeing him dwindle to match it, as if he could only see his true reflection in the mirror of a white man's gaze.

Instead, you might say, Kipling wrote the Jungle Books in the spirit of that folk tale about the farmer returning from market who takes shelter from a storm in an abandoned barn. There, a hundred cats are slinking shadowy to and fro along the rafters, murmuring to each other over and over again, 'If you see Simble, tell him Samble is dead.' 'Whatever is the matter, my dear?' asks the farmer's wife when he returns, shaken. But no sooner has his explanation reached the words 'Tell Simble that Samble is dead' when the old familiar farmhouse tabby leaps up from his place by the fire. 'Then I'm the king of the cats!' he cries, and leaps up the chimney, never to be seen again. Cats have kings, a boychild can become a wild wolf, the jungle hides a whole unsuspected mesh of secret lives. While Kipling could not doubt that in the end the wildest find a proper place in the great world's hierarchy, he chooses to look instead at the wild freedom of the search for it, at liberation from the familiar hearth. And worlds within worlds open.

(1993)

ROBINSON'S MARS

Hidden among the many juggled, intermitting aims of Kim Stanley Robinson's colour-coded Mars trilogy,[32] I think there is a secret ambition, to exhaust the topography of Mars, to describe (with meticulous justification) every single one of the planet's landscapes. He pays out his determination like a planet-girdling rope through the long journeys that figure over and over in the books' plot. He has, in spades, the necessary land-sense, the feeling for the particular quiddities of rock and desert. He turns his flat starting-data on craters and canyons into writing of such sensuous exactitude that ever after, anyone who reads these books is likely to think of his Mars as the real place, and NASA photographs as sadly inadequate snapshots of it. Beauty abounds. *Red Mars* gives us the waved black dunes and stepped terrain of the North Pole, the sublime volcanic heave of the Tharsis Bulge (which rears out of the atmosphere), the brittle regolith walls of Valles Marineris; *Green Mars* continues the unobtrusive drive for completeness with tours of the wind-blasted chaos around the southern pole, the serrated Hellespontus peaks bordering the Hellas basin, the western escarpments of Olympus Mons. As the series goes on, of course, the changes to the face of the planet wreaked by Robinson's own terraformers threaten to make the task never-ending. New greens and whites creep onto his original thesaurus-beating palette of red shades: scarlet, crimson, maroon, rust, plum, violet, mauve, cerise, indigo, dry-blood brown, ochre, sienna, cinnamon. 'Persian carpet shreds' of vegetation grow at the foot of new glaciers, the Hellas basin refills with a warm blue sea, though both square nicely with Robinson's fundamental sense of the planet as Mediterranean or Levantine, put through a slight Californian filter; a feel which rubs off on his Martian cities, named Odessa or Nicosia or Cairo, nanotechnologically efficient yet also the kind of clove-scented places where coffee cups empty slowly while the world goes by.

But there's one region he cannot visit. In a riddle whose answer is 'chess', wrote Jorge Luis Borges, what is the one word you must not use? The word 'chess'. The particular plain of volcanic rubble christened 'Utopia' by astronomers goes artfully unmentioned here, except when the characters quietly crack open 'a bottle of Utopian zinfandel'. Kim Stanley Robinson's Mars comes closer than most new worlds in science fiction to the dream of a just no-place. Only in its premises, to be sure: in a firm belief that a 'net gain' is possible from history, that human virtues exist which contest the dismal, downward entropic spiral of things as they usually turn out. Murder, disaster and common-or-garden unhappiness are not excluded. By the end of the first volume of the trilogy, the quarrelsome 'First Hundred' colonists on the planet have already seen their visions busted, and Realpolitik seemingly triumphant. The 'blank red slate' that Mars appeared to be to one character has been scribbled over with the usual messages of power and profit; this new beginning has not proved, as the same woman half-hoped it might, 'the golden one at last'.

But still the hope animates the series that people will be remade in the unprecedented act of conjuring up a biosphere from scratch. Delicate desert Mars, arid, chilled to minus 50 degrees centigrade, thinly veiled in poisonous carbon dioxide, challenges its shapers to live up to their own powers. Robinson assumes a sorcerer's box of technologies which can do almost anything, if the task can only be framed. They amplify human wishes, throwing back inescapably loud the question of what, good or bad, people can manage to wish for, given their own ambiguous selves to work from: what laws, what ecology, what life, where there are as yet no rules, no ecosystem, no patterns of love and work. So the opportunity of Mars is double from the outset. For Kim Stanley Robinson, equally, to build a world (SF's enormous routine possibility, usually frittered away on hyperbole and clumsy gigantism) without developing the hope implicit in so large a beginning would waste the scope of his planet-sized project. The chance at the good place is half his subject.

Often, the worst of utopias is the way they curtail characterisation. Authors produce serenity-by-numbers, snipping and chopping until they arrive at the radically simplified species of human who can inhabit ideal terrain without spoiling it. That doesn't happen here. The First Hundred, at the heart of Robinson's cast, are preselected for utopia to the simple extent that all are clever, all scientifically adept, and all are by definition doing what they most want to do in coming to Mars. Within this initial uniformity (and there's no doubt that universal vocational passion does help utopia on its way) wild heterogeneity reigns, a planned largesse of outlook. Robinson's optimism has led him to take for a form not a tract, but something like a nineteenth-century novel of ideas, witty and earnest at the same time; a three-decker with generous room for debate and development. The question *What is to be done?* rings explicitly through it, but is enacted so diversely, and with such an appetite for character, that the people never become dully representative. It progresses by braiding viewpoints. We see the planet through an engineer's delight in her tools; a psychiatrist's heartbreaking nostalgia for Provence; a blinking lab-rat of a scientist's clinical enthusiasm for the biggest lab a scientist could have; a geologist's reverence for rock; a politician's disenchanted sense of opportunity; a visionary's passion for new beginnings; a would-be goddess's worship of the force that through the green fuse drives the flower; a happy man's talent for spreading happiness; a manic-depressive's need for a great stage.

The hopes aroused by Mars don't compose into a utopian tableau. They vary individually, diverge individually, sometimes bitterly contradict each other. *Red Mars* was structured, marvellously, by one such tension, a rooted murderous antipathy which spreads to take in the whole contest between innocence and experience on the planet. This too might seem diagrammatic, were it not that the two men in question, John Boone and Frank Chalmers, are such large creations, not coarsely inflated by their Martian circumstances, but sized for tragedy from the outset: positively Greek, ample far in excess of Robinson's tactical interest in undercutting the buoyancy of the first with the saturating rage of the second. (The very first voices we catch out of the future ether are theirs, a folksy political speech annotated by a sour internal monologue. '"On Mars we will come to care for each other more than ever before," John said, which really meant, Chalmers thought, an alarming incidence of the kind of behaviour seen in rat overpopulation experiments.') The blatant corn-fed good looks and glad-handing charm of Boone disclose the portrait of a genuinely good man deliberately mimicking the behaviour of a pasteboard American hero; Chalmers' necessary awareness of every difficulty Boone laughs away masks a man gripped desperately tight inside, intractable to himself, and once he has contrived Boone's death, so terrifyingly guilty that his own body becomes an automaton to him, to be guided through the world by a constant vigilance of will. It's a sign, not of reductiveness, but of Robinson's success at taking hold of something elemental here, that the pair can be remembered later as the happy man and the angry man, simple names for complex inventions. Their expansion to mythic stature comes about through the processes of time and memory, in which – since no unequivocal voice of the author can be heard – the reader has a decisive role, judging, fitting together, assisting the composition of the picture. The same expansion marks other characters too, because of

Robinson's decision that some of the eyes that witnessed the start of Mars's transformation should also see its completion. He invented a longevity treatment in *Red Mars*, with a rich psychological side-effect. By the time his people hit 110 or 120, they can barely remember the years from their 40s to their 90s; history is spiced with amnesia, and the reader frequently knows more of their past than they do. The reader becomes a repository of lost time for these ancients, whose lives have expanded to the scale of the novel, but no longer contain themselves. Time makes giants of them with the reader's collaboration.

Even so, it looked at the end of *Red Mars* (500 large-format, closely printed pages) as if the First Hundred were on their way out of the centre of the narrative. The survivors were last seen beetling wearily away into hiding up the Martian canyons, once more isolated in the wilderness, amid a sort of mineral *Götterdämmerung*, the landscape itself going to wrack as frozen water erupted from deep aquifers onto the surface, tearing a tumbled, yellow-white path. A generation shift seemed in prospect: time for the spindly young Mars-born men and women to step forward from the background, onto a cleared canvas. In fact *Green Mars* shows great continuity, holding close to the original narrators, and even to the original sequence of events, for *Red Mars* has set a pattern of story. Middles are difficult things. Robinson exercises his determination to make each panel of his triptych a fully shaped novel rather than a mere instalment, not by the separate development of a new plot equal in force to *Red Mars*'s, but in a technique of mirroring that he has used before in his trio of Californian futures, the Orange County trilogy. There, a utopia, an extrapolation from the smoggy present and a Mark Twain-like post-holocaust novel shared a common story of youthful confusion, right down to parallel scenes and common characters, shuffling difference and sameness. Now *Green Mars* parallels *Red Mars*, from the mutation of deliberate plans through time's changes to the final dice-throw of a revolution, only in a new mood, more patient, more inward, more chastened.

The grand sweep of terraforming continues, but a sense of cautious movement now prevails.

No longer movers and shakers, his ancient protagonists emerge from the underground after twenty-odd years to slip back under assumed names into smaller roles: designing a single plant, for example, or rationing the water for a new sea. For the former head of the scientific effort, a blinkered cerebral gnome, pretending to be someone else becomes a tragi-comic education in human behaviour. 'He had never danced in his life, so far as he could recall. But that was Sax Russell's life. Surely Stephen Lindholm had danced a lot. So Sax began to hop gently up and down in time with the bass steel drum, wiggling his arms uncertainly at his sides ... in a desperate simulation of debonair pleasure.' Some of the best writing in the book comes in the melancholy reach of it devoted to the struggles of Maya Toitovna, the hawkish Russian *grande dame* of the piece, against the strange limbo of her unprecedented age: a wonderful appreciation, in the face of endless time and tormenting fragments of memory, of the fragile shield offered by 'the ordinary days of an ordinary life' in an apartment. Yet the caution of *Green Mars* prepares for things to go right at the second attempt, at least in some ambiguous form that tempers utopia with necessity. (An alliance grows with a slippery, seemingly friendly corporation called Praxis – theory into practice, indeed.) A sense is also building of the accelerating remoteness of what Robinson describes, however acclimatised to his Mars the reader has become. Unlike the First Hundred, born in the 1970s and 1980s, who therefore see with something like our sense of wonder, the Mars-born begin from altogether elsewhere. When, in *Blue Mars*, their moment finally comes, the break is conclusive. The Mars of the settlers' seven-foot, polysexual, unwittingly aristocratic grandchildren is an admirable place, but maybe not somewhere we would be at home. Robinson, though, insists on negotiating the explanation that utopias, almost by definition, tend to avoid: how careful steps across the teetering fulcrum of the historical see-saw might get you *there* from *here*.

Where *Red Mars* ends with a dreadful flight through ruins, and *Blue Mars* ends with a day out at the beach, the trilogy's public business all done, *Green Mars* at the midpoint of the journey to utopia climaxes on a hopeful exodus. It's a set-piece scene: thousands tramp away from a drowning city in filtered masks, like something out of an Eisenstein film. Yet – typically – Robinson pulls off this classic coup of large-scale writing without fanfare, without formality, without throat-clearing announcements of imminent grandeur. Somehow he furnishes epic scale and epic satisfactions without epic emphases. His language is always direct, like the best mountaineering or nature writing; and though never casual, unattached to literary etiquette except as a source of ideas. He exploits, in particular, the power of ingenuousness to lead one into mood without heavy cues or visibly elaborate artifice. As a result, maybe, his manner always comes across as slightly boyish; yet he uses it to work to an ideal of unobtrusive transparency. His range of sympathy is enormous, and mature. He observes from very close to: hence the unemphatic presence he secures for the reader at the core of a jealousy, in the midst of crowds, at the midpoint of a discursive train of technical thought, on the crest of a black Martian dune under a violet sky.

At the same time he is fascinated by the absurd simplifications and distortions that occur when the same things are seen from outside, when they transmute into public possessions and produce meaning of a different kind. The events of *Red Mars* become the 'red soap opera' of TV reports, instant kingly legends spring up in John Boone's footsteps, and furnish a sort of choral farewell to him on his death. Maya discovers she's been made a character in an opera, 'Meaning some villainous coloratura was down there on Earth, singing her thoughts.' This outer crusting of rumour and glamour is the level on which bad science fiction operates all the time, continually flogging at heroic appearances, pumping the language uselessly for excitement, trapped in the cycle of diminishing returns. About the time *Red Mars* was published, Ben Bova's

Mars put a rival expedition on the planet. There were thrills galore. In his spacesuit – Bova reported – the first astronaut to step down from the pod 'looked as he had been swallowed by a robot'. Robinson, by contrast, likes two-word sentences sometimes, plain fresh exclamations: 'It's funny!' 'It hurts!' 'It's beautiful!' They aren't facile. They're a sign of justified confidence in his powers: which can take on the intricate long haul of the task he has set himself without getting lost in histories or technologies, which can manage the incorporation of all this into imagined bodies thick with age and complicated memories, and then still find the moments of direct response. You assent. In fact you can only respond in kind. Robinson's Mars? It's good!

(1994)

THE AMAZING TERENCE

A talking rat is fighting for his life against a terrier, inside a circle of excited men who whoop and roar and snarl. Another rat bungee-jumps down from the rafters to rescue him. In the instant of astonishment before both rats are whisked skyward, the human onlookers just have time to notice that the rescuer is wearing a tiny straw boater on his head. He lifts it. 'Good evening!' he squeaks.

This is a scene from *The Amazing Maurice and His Educated Rodents*, which won Terry Pratchett the Carnegie Medal for children's literature in 2001. (Astonishingly, up to that point, the first book prize he had ever won. 'They've never given me anything for my writing', he told the press. 'Apart of course from a pile of money big enough to fill St Paul's Cathedral.') Maurice is a cat; the rats are accidental beneficiaries of a magic spillage; together with a daft-looking human boy who plays the flute they travel from town to town, working a Pied Piper-related con on the unsuspecting inhabitants. Ethically challenging, beautifully orchestrated, philosophically opposed (like all of Pratchett's books) to the usual plot fixes of fantasy, *The Amazing Maurice* deserved its medal. But as usual, there was a certain arbitrariness about which one of a good author's good books an award goes to. *Johnny and the Dead* (1993) and

Johnny and the Bomb (1996), the two high points in Pratchett's series about a melancholy thirteen-year-old assailed by supernatural troubles, were just as amazing as *Maurice*.

Actually, there was a further arbitrary element at work, specific to Terry Pratchett, when he won a prize for *children's* books. The truth is that he wrote in almost exactly the same way for children as he did for adults. There have been other writers, like Peter Dickinson, who wrote for both and drew on aspects of the same sensibility to enrich both; but Pratchett essentially worked in exactly the same mode for both audiences. The qualities in him that might be thought of as ideally suited to children's books, like his unembarrassed pleasure in wordplay, his easy access to polymorphous messing around with words, were equally central to his adult novels. Whichever audience he was talking to, he was always engaged in a kind of comic explanation. He had something he was interested in, in his head, and he was sorting it out for himself and his audience in the form of a story – a story with jokes, which for him, as for all serious comedians, he set off like explosions of discovery, each revealing a relationship between things, underlining an uncertainty, warming an idea so it showed its human meaning. He always wrote streamlined sentences, easy to assimilate, because he had *plans* for the reader's attention, and wanted to lead it along twiddly inventive paths without wasting any on unnecessary obstacles.

To be sure, the adult Discworld novels were all comedies of recognition. Part of the point was always to spot which thing in our world the Discworld was refracting in satirical form, from *Macbeth* to email. Pratchett's children's books took exemplary care to contain in themselves everything you needed to understand what was going on, to be their own completely adequate guidebook. But then they, too, offered the pleasures of recognition. *The Amazing Maurice* provides pleasingly sharp reminders of the whole, frequently icky tradition of humanised animal stories, not least because the rats are in the process of constructing a religion around a discarded picture book about a rabbit in a waistcoat called Mr Bunnsy; and it gives you foolish behaviour to recognise that will be as familiar to readers of ten as to readers of forty.

Terry Pratchett was always writing the same kind of satire, one whose picture of human (and rat) nature his readers tended to cherish, whether child or adult, because it was fundamentally hopeful. In Pratchett's eyes, people were ridiculous, but often kind; deluded, but good-hearted; irrational, but in consequence also strangely innocent. Even his thugs often had a sheepish simplicity about their thuggishness. He genially accepted that people are self-interested brawlers locked in a Darwinian scrum, but he didn't think we should find it too hard to forgive ourselves for that, so long as we don't claim we're allowed to behave badly because we're better than other people. Pratchett hated condescension. In fact, taken to its extreme, condescension becomes the one unforgiveable sin in Pratchett's world: treating other people as things. Characters who do that aroused his sense of real horror, and are the true villains of his novels: the elves in *Lords and Ladies*, the vampires in *Carpe Jugulum*, Mr Teatime the assassin in *Hogfather* (pronounced Tay-at-im-ay, if you please).

By choice, he did popular art, and he had a quite deliberate sense of what that entailed, if it was to mean more than art that happens to have hit a fashion, or art that gets a big audience as a nice bonus. It means using the common language, it means deliberately working on the huge areas of emotional experience that overlap for all of us. One of the reasons he was so interested in stories as such is that the famous stories, the urban legends, the central stories of religion, the fairy tales everyone knows, tend each to record a way of making sense of exactly one of these areas of shared experience. It's not an accident that his books so often took on an existing story – as *Maurice* does with the Pied Piper. Where there's a story, there's sure to be a rich deposit of stuff-we-all-care-about. He trusted the accumulated wisdom of storytelling to point out what's really important. Then, of course, he reshaped the story, because he combined a remarkable ability to access shared, generic imaginings, with a very idiosyncratic imagination of his own. He campaigned against the idea that stories offer a reliable guide to reality: but he still thought they were essential maps, and that it was important to get the right story, the right map, because it affects how generous and tolerant you can manage to be, really.

Some things he couldn't do (which is a bit of a relief). He didn't do beauty. He didn't do epic. With him, large-scale scenes came out more like the big numbers in a musical, or like the synchronised swimming that the rats do in bowls of cream. He did sadness, but he didn't do tragedy, because tragedy puts things beyond the reach of the comic recuperation of sadness which was his writing's big gift. It's typical that in *Maurice*, when the kid with the flute confronts a professional rat piper, Pratchett endorsed the common sense of the watching crowd, who 'were rather attached to the experience of real life, which is that when someone small and righteous takes on someone big and nasty, he is grilled bread product, very quickly'. And still arranged for the small person to win. He bungee-jumped into the midst of grim things, and lifted his hat. Good evening!

(2001)

YOU COULD READ FOREVER

The chances are, if you've bought a Companion to Tolkien, or a Guide to *Finnegans Wake*, or the encyclopaedic *Quid de Proust*, that you've read the original books to exhaustion, fat though they are. The spines are broken, the page corners are waxy. Still you want to linger just a while longer, in a kind of lean-to extension built around the back of the house of the book. Companions blunt the realisation that even the longest fictions have a last page, a back cover, and therefore a definitive back door through which you must step out.

Ordinarily they do, anyway. Robert Irwin's companion to the *Arabian Nights* can't.[33] It accompanies a book no-one except the most persistent scholars can be said to have exhausted – a virtually unknown book, despite the ingrained familiarity of some of the stories it contains. We know it as the source of stories, almost always four or five removes distant from the 'Aladdin' or the 'Ali Baba' we have at hand: not as a succession of pages. In a way this familiarity without effort or direct acquaintance is a tribute to the vitality of the *Nights*, whose tales hop borders and cultures and centuries, endlessly mutating, yet persisting in recognisable forms. (At one point Irwin experiments with the biological conceit of stories as 'selfish word strings' like 'selfish' genes, always pressing to be reproduced. Terry Pratchett, as it happens, used the same idea last year in a story: a good paradoxical argument for its being correct, since the book in question has reproduced all over the place.)

Alf Layla Wa Layla, the *One Thousand and One Nights*, Irwin quotes Borges as saying, is 'so vast that it is not necessary to have read it'. He meant that the enormous collection of tales has so settled into overlap with the grand collection constituting Western culture, that we are all, effectively, *in* the *Arabian Nights* already. But however pleasing the idea might be of a limitless book, a world-sized and world-shaped book, the literal bulk of the literal *Nights* is no joke. Talking for her life in the bed of King Shahriyar, Scheherazade subjects her twitchy, murderous listener to eloquence on a scale which over-bears and oppresses the imagination. In the longest versions the book of her talk holds 480-something stories, distributed unevenly over the 1,001 sessions. The local pleasure you may take in the appearance of one genie desiccates at the prospect of a multitude more of them. You don't exhaust the *Nights*: it exhausts you.

Then there is the question of what, exactly, you would be looking at if you set out to 'read the *Arabian Nights*'. As Irwin explains, in illuminating chapters exploring the translation history and textual history of the monster, when *Alf Layla Wa Layla* was first translated into French in 1704, no single authoritative version of it existed in Arabic to be referred to. Related collections called by the same name have ballooned and contracted in different parts of the Arab world since the tenth century – probably. There is no certain date of composition, certainly no chance of identifying one author. The 'frame story' of Scheherazade may be Persian, or Indian, and much older. Many of the tales may have passed back and forth between writing and oral performance several times over, leaving the marks of successive erosions and embroideries. The translations, in turn, have added to the vagueness; they follow a scattering of fairly recent Arabic manuscripts, or a foursome of printed Arabic versions from the early nineteenth century, one prepared for the East India Company to help its cadets learn the language. A collated canonical text is only now appearing, and, for a final deterrent, the fullest English translation, which Irwin quotes perforce, remains the maddening sixteen-volume edition by Sir Richard Burton.

Irwin's account of Burton's 'kinky, obtrusive' editorial methods is a dry comic triumph. 'In a note in the fifth supplementary volume, he cites Swedenborg on how there will be no looking at the backs of people's heads in the afterlife.' Less engagingly, Burton inserted slobbering and eye-rolling whenever a black character appeared. The only nice thing you can say about Burton's handling of the sex in the *Nights* is that his style ensured the erotic passages would be virtually incomprehensible, because, above all, Burton rendered his sixteen volumes in a jumbled archaic diction of his own devising. When a king is sad, in Burton, 'there betided him sore cark and care and chagrin exceeding'. With terrifying industriousness, Burton gothicised every part of Scheherazade's night-talk, lending curlicues, not to a single house of fiction, but a whole city of it, a sort of sprawling Cairo of story, now styled by Burton as a voluptuous, contorted vision of the Middle East rather like contemporary European paintings of the real Cairo.

What a metropolis like this needs is a crisp, reassuringly finite guidebook. Irwin provides it. As an academic Arabist and an adventurous remoulder in his own right of the *Nights* (he wrote *The Arabian Nightmare*) he can cite erudite chapter and experienced verse for the double status of the book. It *is* both an Arab literary monument and a prime vehicle for Orientalist projections. The incalculable extent of the *Nights*, he shows, has actually served the more fluid ends of Western writers, who have pinned its name to their own dreams and hallucinations. He discusses a glorious description by De Quincey of his opium-induced thrall to the Nights, perhaps the most marvelling and marvellous passage quoted in the book. But the story De Quincey thinks he remembers, about a magician who can distinguish an individual's footsteps on the far side of the globe amidst the drumming of a million other feet, lacks an origin in any known variant of any *Nights* tale.

Irwin cannot, of course, give a fixed or straightforward picture of the 'original' *Nights*, as it was written, read and recited in Arabic before Antoine Galland first adapted it to the taste of Versailles. He can, though, open it up boldly as a box of Egyptian and Syrian social history, an implicit record of manners and expectations. The audience of the *Nights*, he argues, were the confident petty bourgeois of the medieval Islamic cities. They were shopkeepers who enjoyed the fantasy of miraculous wealth at the rub of a lamp. They were citizens susceptible to beggars' operas and low-life exploits. Irwin reconstructs a world where burglars would case a house by sending in a tortoise with a lighted candle stuck on its shell, where slum gangs were available for war against the infidel, mounted piggyback on other homeboys in horse costumes. In the market, actors played ancient farces inherited from the Roman and Byzantine theatre; amazing cons trapped the unwary; male picnic-parties improvised poetry in the public gardens. Despite the evident pride in 'urban Muslim know-how', as Irwin puts it, this small-time life scarcely participated in the high culture of court and university. Learning could filter down into it, as in the case of the ingenious law code devised by the jurists to govern sexual relations between humans and jinns, and the occasional scholar took an interest in the popular arts. Ibn Daniyal, a thirteenth-century ophthalmologist, wrote shadow-puppet plays which sound rather like Ben Jonson comedies. But for the most part, educated opinion regarded stories as *khurafa*, or lies, vulgar shallow stuff. Hence the low critical valuation put on the *Nights* in the Arab world right up to the present day, a low opinion now reinforced by the *Nights'* unsuitability as Pan-Arab reading (too much dialect), and by the childish image of Arab culture it has spread in the West.

The tenth-century bookseller Ibn al-Nadim attempted a universal bibliography. He included prose fiction but, says Irwin, called it 'cold', in distinction to 'warm' poetry, thought of as the expressive outpouring of noble hearts. It's a judgement that keeps coming back to you, in a larger sense, as you read Irwin, especially when he arrives in his excellent final chapter at modernist appropriations of the *Nights*. The use of the book as a formal grid, as a treasury of 'early and exotic examples of . . . self reference . . . recursion and intertextuality', may invent an emphasis strange to the early audiences. But it matches the *Nights'* abiding fascination with wonders instead of with individuals, or shaded motives. So far as characterisation is concerned, the *Nights* rests content presenting chunks of destiny in roughly human form. A cruel man 'is cruel because he does cruel acts, and does cruel acts because he is cruel'. The *Nights* does marry well, sometimes, with the novel's interest in individualised people. Its wonders can be metaphors, an appetite for those wonders an indication of what heats somebody. A steam hammer, in Elizabeth Gaskell's *North and South*, recalls 'to Mr Hale some of the wonderful stories of subservient genii in the Arabian Nights'; the genie's power to fill the sky, then to shrink 'into a vase small enough to be borne in the hand of a child', takes on an industrial, a sexual, a *personal* significance. Which is never true of the impersonal perceptions of a tale. Like fairy tales of every culture, read end-to-end the stories of the *Nights* make you profoundly glad novels exist. All those thousands of pages, all those heroes and villains: you could read forever, and never get warm.

(1994)

THIS GRAND CAUSE OF TERROR

The Half-Made World and *The Rise of Ransom City*, Felix Gilman's pair of fantasies transmogrifying the mythologies of American history, are both rich books, full of pleasures for the reader. But the pair of them are also, to an unusual degree, in the business of being deliberately frustrating, of withholding from readers a set of expected pleasures that seemed to have been virtually promised us. I mean pleasures that are usual to fantasy as a genre – pleasures, even, that are usual to the implicit contract a plot makes between writer and reader. And yet what Gilman holds back, what he refuses to deliver, is essential to the power of the effect he does create.

There's a sense, of course, in which refusing to provide the expected is absolutely basic, phrase by phrase, word by word, to all writing which aspires to be adequate at all: to fulfil Operation A of any newly made row of words, which is to convince us that *is* new, or at any rate new enough to persuade us that it has some particular effort of communication behind it. A cliché by definition is a lump of expected language. All writers of narrative prose who wish their stories to live – at least, to twitch from time to time on the slab – must therefore be engaged in a ceaseless low-level effort to keep refreshing the unpredictability of the surface of language. Even just at the level of gesture. As Gore Vidal (I think) pointed out, while crapping from a height on some bestseller of the day, it doesn't do *much* to write 'by crook or by hook' instead of 'by hook or by crook' – but it at least shows willing. Since Felix Gilman writes taut, witty, lexically adventurous prose in a variety of voices and registers, he is necessarily signed up to denying expectation in this minimal sense.

His characteristic and individual refusals, though, start to come into view when you look at his attitude to describing the central inventions of the invented world of the two books. At what he will say, and what he won't, about the mythic linchpins of his own creation. Gilman's world is demon-haunted. Beyond the mountains that stand in for the Atlantic in dividing old settled kingdoms from new territories, in a West where colonisation literally fixes the terrain out of the primal murk, two sets of dark powers rule. The demons of the Gun literalise the anarchic violence of American expansion, and the demons of the Line literalise the devouring order of industrial mass society. Far more than merely metaphors, these beings are central to the books' translation of history into fantasy. They imaginatively reconfigure the qualities and consequences of human history into its independent drivers. Causation has been upended. From being merely epiphenomena of unpoliced spaces full of firearms, now massacre and mayhem have become the point, the goal, the chief delight of Marmion and Belphagor and the other spirits of the Gun, muttering in their blood-warm Lodge somewhere between the stars. From being merely side-effects of the Industrial Revolution, now noise and sickness and ugliness and uniformity have become the positive vision, the plan for the world, of the thirty-eight unkillable Engines who travel the network of the Line. Humanity's relations with these rival lords of destruction are fully Faustian, and where they and their human followers collide, catastrophe spreads. Reading *The Half-Made World*, we hear quite a lot of the voice of the particular Gun that speaks in the mind of John Creedmoor, one of the novel's three protagonists; and we see (since hearing would destroy human ears) the telegraphed orders of the Engines, as they drive onward their representative in the plot, the matchstick man Lowry and his army of lurching, coughing, bullying, agoraphobic little grey-clad followers. But it's all consequences, it's all secondary. Of the Guns and the Engines themselves we get only the most minute and occasional glimpses. Their motives and modes of existence are said to be beyond human understanding, not as the preliminary build-up to some full-on evocation, ripe with paradox, but as the plain warrant for the book not including them: there they aren't.

The nearest thing in either book to a visual description of an Engine is this, significantly enough given us indirectly, through a character's journal entry:

> What did the Engine look like? I saw it on the Concourse, but only in shadow, and besides, the memory fades. I cannot quite express it in words. I might try to sketch its machinery, as I have sketched in these pages the neuron, the cerebellum, the pituitary gland – but to do so, I think, would miss its essence. I can say that it was long, very long; it was four, five men tall. It was jet-black and it smoked. It was plated with extrusions and grilles and thorns of iron that might have been armor, and might have been machinery, but which in any case made it rough, uneven, asymmetrical, and hideous. It reminded me somewhat of the ink-blot tests devised by Professor Kohler. It reminded me also somewhat of storm-clouds. From the complex cowling at the very front of the engine two lights shone through the gloom and the smoke of the Concourse. The light was the gray of moths' wings or dirty old ice.[34]

Liv Alverhuysen, doctor from the East, voice of civilised neurosis and of mercy in the books, has passed the Engine at a run a few pages before, 'and perhaps that was fortunate, too'. Now, in an icy black compartment within the beast's mile-long body, she struggles to remember it. The first-person filter is a favourite device of Gilman's – he is going to use it continuously, on the grand scale, in

The Rise of Ransom City, where the world of the book is passed to us exclusively through the unreliable voices of Harry Ransom and his editor – and there is certainly an element of pure gameplay to his preference. He likes the tricky and the partial for their own sake, just as (as in the passage above, and in all the oblique descriptions of the 'half-made' chaos of the West) he is interested for their own sake in things of uncertain shape. But we can see that his objection to reliable description isn't a reservation about vividness, perhaps a sign of a non-visual sensibility at work. Far from it. Vividness, he likes: the dirty ice eye-beams here, the comparison soon after of the train racing across salt flats to a line of ink running across clean paper, are brilliant, if carefully minimal. He doesn't mind allowing himself the occasional wild pulp ululation, either. '*Their boiling black blood, their breath!*' the novel suddenly cries out, Lovecraftianishly, as the Engine's smoke billows back at Liv.

No; the objection is surely to definiteness. Take it away, Edmund Burke, theorising the sublime in 1757:

> But let it be considered that hardly anything can strike the mind with its greatness, which does not make some sort of approach towards infinity; which nothing can do whilst we are able to perceive its bounds; but to see an object distinctly, and to perceive its bounds, is one and the same thing. A clear idea is therefore another name for a little idea. There is a passage in the Book of Job amazingly sublime, and this sublimity is principally due to the terrible uncertainty of the thing described:
>
>> In thoughts from the visions of the night, when deep sleep falleth upon men, fear came upon me and trembling, which made all my bones to shake. Then a spirit passed before my face. The hair of my flesh stood up. It stood still, but I could not discern the form thereof; an image was before mine eyes; there was silence; and I heard a voice – Shall mortal man be more just than God?

We are first prepared with the utmost solemnity for the vision; we are first terrified, before we are let even into the obscure cause of our emotion: but when this grand cause of terror makes its appearance, what is it? Is it not wrapt up in the shades of its own incomprehensible darkness, more awful, more striking, more terrible, than the liveliest description, than the clearest painting, could possibly represent it?

'Terror' for Burke was a pleasure to be found here and there in literature as the Book of Job, or Milton, pushed particular psychological buttons for particular momentary effect. But it was about to start being produced deliberately, generically, in bulk, in the emerging Gothic; and the whole cluster of twentieth-century popular literatures of the fantastic, fantasy/SF/horror, are among other things deliberate factories of grandly indefinite Burkean terror; to an extent therefore routinising the sublime, making it over itself into a predictable clause of the writer–reader contract of expectations. And there are certainly aspects of Gilman's use of sublimity which might seem to come under this kind of good-management heading, to be routine and (as it were) tactical. For a start, Gilman has a strong negative motive for not letting us know too much or see too much about the Engines. As Burke goes on to point out, both literal pictures and writing that is too pictorial tip over easily into 'the ludicrous' if they try for terror. The danger of bathos yawns very nearby in *The Half-Made World*. Gilman is writing villains (as he's said himself) who are 'Giant Evil Trains': he really, really needs to avoid specifying himself down into writing a kind of satanic Reverend W. Awdry adventure, featuring Belial the Bad Engine.

But I would argue that he belongs in the much rarer category of fantasists for whom the Burkean sublime still retains its original expectation-confuting power, and with it its power to shock and confuse. He is interested in it for the sake of its disruptive potential, not for its efficiencies as a recipe. If there is, so to speak, a 'normal' sublime lodged in fantasy now, it comes with a promise that what is withheld in one way will be restored in another. If writers have learned from Lovecraft how to milk the terror of the not-quite-seen, of monstrosity asserted to be unimaginable yet equipped with a few delicately phobia-inducing qualities of texture, then the implication is that a compensating resolution will be supplied in plot terms. We won't ever quite see Cthulhu, but we'll be led through a narrative catastrophe which is very clear, very definite, very distinct. Resolution will *not* be withheld.

In Gilman's case, though, the pulp energy and violence are there (the body count of the two books is enormous) but the delicate non-resolution of the sublime descriptions – the way in which stormcloud, Rorschach blot, hint of a crown of mechanical thorns, all become visually active without settling into visual coherence – is, instead, matched on the scale of narrative by a particular kind of non-resolution there, too. The monsters you can't quite see are, if anything, metonyms for plots you can't quite declare finished.

Gilman rules one plot closure out in *The Half-Made World* before he even begins. The war of Line with Gun is a fantasticated version of the Matter of America, yes; but the consoling, canonical reconciliation of America's violences and America's masses within America's civil religion has been pre-sabotaged. The Red River Republic has already risen, failed, and vanished from the scene. The remnant of it in the wilderness that Liv and Creedmoor stumble on is a repellent, simple-minded little Sparta. Then, in *The Rise of Ransom City*, Gilman brings the Republic back, but casually, almost dismissively, without ever letting it occupy the focus of the book. I don't know which is more successfully shocking: the original abolition, or the Republic's return on terms which make it clear that Gilman cares far more about not providing a conventional sequel, in which we might have seen the double possession of the land by Line and Gun exorcised within our view. He's willing to reverse the political withholding of the first book, but only because it has been trumped by another opportunity for withholding resolution that he cares about more.

For, meanwhile, he has lured us with the MacGuffin of a secret weapon possessed by the land's indigenes, and led us out into the wilderness while Liv and Creedmoor develop a relationship of considerable conflicted intensity, but no conventional romantic form; and then stopped, at the moment when we're told the search for the weapon against the demons is just beginning; only to resume again in the second book through the eyes of a minor character who seems to be coming along on the search, but then doesn't, and follows a destiny of his own irresolvably suspended between innocence and con-artistry, with the consequence that we *never find out* what the MacGuffin was, or how Creedmoor and Liv ended, or how, with the maximum ironic tidiness, the world of the books seems finally to be converging with, secularising and dwindling into, one much more like our own. Boxes that won't close are his specialty; beautiful discords; inventions that, having taken the licence of fantasy to curve away from our world, then refuse to curve reassuringly back again.

One possible analogy that strikes me is with David Foster Wallace's explicit promise, in *Infinite Jest*, that the parallel lines of his two plots would eventually meet, only for the novel to end with them still as separate as ever. But that, I take it, was a high-modernist point being made about the real, and about its unrepresentability except by means that included the mimetic sensations of not-fitting, not-solving, not-ending. Whereas this is –

[I had a beautiful formulation of what this is, but alas there is not room for it in this margin]

(2013)

BATS OF SOME KIND

Books that make you laugh out loud; books about the Russian novel. In the grand Venn diagram of literature, these are usually thought of as non-intersecting phenomena. Wholly separate soap-bubbles of literary content, in fact, bobbing about autonomously with a continent's-worth of space in between, probably filled with wolves and pine trees. Yet Elif Batuman's *The Possessed*[35] is set firmly in the impossible overlap of the two. It really is, seriously and perceptively, about Russian fiction, and it really is funny. Not surprisingly, the ease with which Elif Batuman has conjured this domain for herself has had critics in the US predicting great things for her. Hardly anyone can pull a life-sized Dostoevsky out of an opera hat. Frankly, hardly anyone would have thought of stuffing him in there in the first place.

The trick is that *The Possessed* is a book about reading much more than it is one about writing. It is about the way that a passionate reader's encounter (or reader's passionate encounter) with *Anna Karenina* or Chekhov's 'Lady with the Little Dog' or Isaac Babel's *Red Cavalry* always happens in a particular time and place in a life, and therefore joins the mood you find on the page with the mood of that moment. If your life happens not to be in the groove of intense moral seriousness, or tragic delicacy, or revolutionary metamorphosis just then, then the more seriously and intelligently you read, the worse the disparity gets. Or the better, for the purposes of comedy. Batuman reads *Red Cavalry* while trying to cook a Black Forest gateau. 'As Babel immortalised for posterity the military embarrassment of the botched 1920 Russo-Polish campaign, so he immortalised for me the culinary embarrassment of this cake, which ... produced the final pansensory impression of an old hat soaked in cough syrup.'

But it isn't (just) a recipe for being silly about Russian lit. She is interested in finding words for a whole array of disparities, for the different emotional mixtures that coalesce when her teenage self reads Tolstoy in her grandmother's house in Turkey, when she's studying in Samarkand one hot summer where she has to pick ants out of the jam, when she's experiencing a collective infatuation at grad school that mirrors her understanding of Dostoevsky's *Demons*. Funny is a constant but it isn't the goal. It's her means, her method, her chosen form of conversational naturalness, and her palette of intentions is much wider. From the Samarkand sections, spread out through the course of the book, you remember the disastrous Uzbek medieval poem she reads:

Was it my heart – a bird – that was caught in your locks
    that unfortunate night,
Or was it bats of some kind?

Indeed, I think I'm never going to forget it; but you also retain an elegantly, lightly expressive portrait of a post-Soviet city, where she had hoped to find a meeting ground between her ancestral Turkish and her chosen Russian, between the who and the what of her identity, and instead discovered that places and languages don't work like that.

The disparities between reading and its circumstances stand in for, provide the local embodiment of, the difference between novel-shaped experiences and life-shaped ones. This is her serious theme; and her comic one too, both at once. 'Unknown parties had strongly impressed upon the camp organisers that I, as an American, ate nothing but corn and watermelon.' 'Starting around that time, I was plagued by a recurring nightmare about penguins.' Deadpan details like these have no point to make, and that's their point. When she's pursuing her formidable gift for the charmingly inconsequential – to the point where it sometimes feels as if she's got a slightly bored-looking guy with a bass drum and hi-hat permanently stationed behind her, ready to go *ba-boom-tish!* every few sentences – she's also making an argument.

As she puts it in the opening chapter, 'Events and places succeed one another like items on a shopping list. There may be interesting and moving experiences, but one thing is guaranteed: they won't naturally assume the shape of a wonderful book.' Among other things, *The Possessed* is a record of her decision to become a reading kind of writer rather than a novelist herself. She could have closed the life–art gap the traditional way, by shaping life in art's image. (The book includes a spectacularly unappealing comic summary of the contemporary American short story.) Instead, she says, she chooses to live out the art, 'by study instead of imitation, and metonymy instead of metaphor'. She'll go to the places and see the things and be true to what *that* feels like. It's a kind of manifesto, comical-scholarly-documentary. 'What if you wrote a book and it was all true?'

Well, there's true and there's true. It's a rare piece of even conventional non-fiction that doesn't steal from the coherence of fiction to glue its narrative secretly together, and this is no exception. The emotional strand we're following out here is the by-no-means-unheard-of autobiographical one in which a smart aleck with charm – in this case maybe a smart alexei – gets some wisdom. Moreover, though it seems churlish to point this out of something so beautifully made, paragraph by paragraph: where *The Possessed* doesn't work, it tends to be because, very conventionally, it isn't structured enough, it hasn't borrowed *enough* on the sly from the coherence of the novel. Beneath its eloquent skin, *The Possessed* is palpably a fix-up, rather than something devised from the start as a whole book-shaped book. It's a brilliant piece of opportunism, retrospectively sutured together from (I'd say) three existing Russia-related magazine pieces, with the Samarkand material serving as a spine, and the genuine commitment to the comedy of desultoriness serving as a warrant for incorporating desultory stuff she happened to have by her. Friends who serve one function in one context of reading turn up later in another one and are reintroduced as if for the first time. So it isn't, quite, the promised book in which everything is true. But the faint disappointment here attaches to 'book', not to 'true', where her irony is in astonishingly perfect working order; and you should read *The Possessed*, preferably while having unruly adventures of your own, in order to take your reader's share in the first outing of a major voice.

(2010)

IN MEMORIAM, IAIN M. BANKS

Iain Banks wrote literary novels and science fiction turn by turn for nearly thirty years. He banged out a piece of well-reviewed lit fic – this is not a derogatory way of putting it, just a reference to the smoking speed with which he always seemed to work – and then hoisted the M in the middle of his name to signal to the world that 'Iain M. Banks', the world's most penetrable pseudonym, was next about to embark on some SF. His readerships and his reputations overlapped a bit; nevertheless, he really did have two careers. Just before he died of liver cancer, he took to his blog to quash the idea someone had mooted, that he'd been writing SF all this time to cross-subsidise the proper literachewer. It was the other way round, he pointed out. His straight novels outsold the SF fourfold or five-fold. It was the science fiction that was the subsidised labour of love, the impractical art pursued as a vocation.

Reading this as someone who's principally a fan of Banks-with-an-M made immediate sense to me. (And made me even sadder at the cruelty with which his time had been cut short by the cancer.) Because, while he was a good novelist, he was a *great* SF writer: an iconoclast, a changer of the landscape of imagination, a once-in-a-generation talent. Let me try and explain why, for those of you who happen not to have read him, who maybe haven't seen reason to dip much into SF at all. In particular, let me try to explain why this part of his work ought to be cherished by British atheists, in whose company he was proud to number himself. (Unlike me, but let's not talk about that today.) Some of this will be a bit of a reach. Thanks to the specific choices he made, it is possible for a new reader to bounce back, baffled. Nick Hornby, for instance, famously threw his hands up in comic despair when he tried *Excession*, one of the very best of the books. But it is worth persisting.

Back in the mid-1980s, when Banks had made his (literary) name with *The Wasp Factory*, and was contemplating his perverse swallow-dive into genre, there were, roughly speaking, two available ways of doing SF. (I exaggerate and simplify.) With immense difficulty, over the course of the 1960s and 1970s, the better writers within the field had dragged it away from its pulp roots; they had brought in good prose and ambitious characterisation; they had opened it to politics, to feminism, to formal experimentation; they had redirected it away from the traditional subject-matter of adventure in space and Things With Tentacles, and pointed it instead at plausibly rendered near-futures, at psychological exploration of the alien within. 'Cyberpunk' was the movement of the moment, with William Gibson's glittering neo-noir Sprawl trilogy as its defining success. Serious SF was expected to be in this tempered literary mould: if not Gibsonian explorations of the Reaganised or Thatcherised street, and the uses it found for digital technology, then anthropological seriousness *à la* Ursula Le Guin, or dystopic seriousness to befit the threat of nuclear war. Because the only other way of doing it was the tacky, vestigial tradition of writing about rayguns and starships and galactic empires: still going, thanks to *Star Wars*, but tending to be practised only by the naive, the nostalgic, the conservative, or the featherbrained. 'Space opera', so-called, was an embarrassing low-status leftover.

So which would an ambitious, high-minded, young Scottish socialist choose, as he bounced on the end of the springboard over the genre lagoon? Why, Option B. Naturally, Option B. *Of course,* Option B. Banks's first SF novel, *Consider Phlebas,* featured interstellar space battles, settings measurable in parsecs, and characters called things like Juboal-Rabaroansa Perosteck Alseyn Balveda dam T'seif. I can remember reading it and feeling as if an electric fan supercharged to hurricane speed were blowing at me out of the pages every time I opened it. Also, feeling mightily puzzled, for from the T.S. Eliot allusion in the title onwards, this spectacularly un-serious-seeming story seemed to want to carry me to some serious and even melancholy places.

Banks was not alone. He was joined in the turn back towards space opera by a whole suddenly assembling group of British writers, Colin Greenland and Alistair Reynolds, Stephen Baxter and Paul McAuley, plus the 1970s SF grandee M. John Harrison, who had never quite given up on it in the first place. Among other things, it was for all of them a move towards narrative vigour, a kind of counterpart in writing to the punk/new wave return to rock's danceable 1950s roots after the wafty complexities of the prog scene. It worked as a kind of heavily ironic declaration of independence from American SF – taking over what had been the old heartland of the American future, with very different aims and (often) politics.

But Banks had noticed something else besides, it became clear as book followed book, each one a firework display of the disgraceful. He had seen that the bigness of pulp – the apparently naive splendour you get when you pop the scale of the expected by envisioning a whole planet pierced through like a Chinese puzzle, or a cosmos bursting with intelligent life, tentacled and otherwise – also prised open a kind of philosophical space, a domain in which a popular art could give serious elbow room to ideas, could let them unfurl experimentally on the grandest of stages. 'In widescreen baroque', as he put himself. Especially ideas which had been seen as being just as disreputable as rayguns 'n' starships.

Banks's SF series twirled the narrative focus around with virtuoso ease, but the books almost all shared a background: the Culture, a post-scarcity utopia populated by trillions, where humans and machine intelligences shared a plenty that made money irrelevant and could flick away any challenge. 'Basically, hippies with enormous guns', Banks joked cheerfully in interview. But the Culture was more than wish-fulfilment for leftists. Insouciant though it was, superbly casual though it always insisted on being in its outflanking of tyrants, it was a serious attempt (with the finest pulp tools) to imagine a state of existence beyond necessity, where stories would all be driven by conflicts of character rather than the pinching of environments, and, unnecessary tragedies dispensed with, some kind of irreducible bedrock of genuine sorrow would come into view. Like all serious utopians, Banks maintained a tender eye for mortality and heartbreak. The Culture was not a place for happy ever after. Often (*Look to Windward* and *Matter*) it was a place for farewells, for entropy unflinchingly acknowledged.

Much of the time of course, with an irony Banks entirely registered and relished, it had to fade to the literal background of the narrative, so that he could go on telling distinctly pre-utopian stories, as dark as might be expected from the author of *The Wasp Factory*. Then we tended to get the Culture represented by 'Special Circumstances', the Culture's far-from-stainless corps of meddlers. Then, the off-stage loom of utopia became a critical device, throwing into lurid question the cruelties we might have shrugged at if the Culture weren't available as contrast. A bright background darkened the foreground. He made his boldest experiment on these lines in *The State of the Art*, when a Culture contact team slips quietly into orbit around our very own Earth, circa 1978. The ordinary defects of our actual history shock these impressionable Chekists rigid, and having decided against intervention on moral grounds, the best they can do is take symbolic revenge by culturing stray cells of our nastiest dictators for a dinner party. 'Most of you over there will be eating either Stewed Idi Amin or General Pinochet Chili Con Carne; here in the centre we have a combination of General Stroessner Meatballs and Richard Nixon Burgers ... there are in addition scattered bowls of Fricasséed Kim Il Sung, Boiled General Videla and Ian Smith in Black Bean Sauce ...'

Now, as this dandy cannibal satire on the Last Supper suggests – blasphemy of a grade you just don't see much, nowadays – Banks is also engaging, with the creation of the Culture, in a piece of sly, prolonged and magnificent anti-theism. I don't so much mean because, here and there, he's used his wide screen for explicit attack on elements of religion, as in *Surface Detail*'s Hieronymus Bosch-worthy demonstration of the repulsiveness of the idea of hell. I mean that the Culture *itself* represents an elegant absorption of, and therefore displacement of, one whole department of religious yearning. It offers, in effect, a completely secular version of heaven. With its sentient ships as omniscient as any pantheon of gods, and a lot more obliging and benign, and its vision of human nature uncramped from disease and hunger and oppression, and its rationalised equivalent of transcendence, it gives its inhabitants (and you as you read the books) all the pie in the sky they could possibly want; but transformed by being made wholly material, by being brought within the reach of human aspiration. Where religion, on the Marxist reading of it, is a kind of comprehensible counsel of despair, the heart of the heartless world, Banks supplies a counsel of optimism. The handwaving physics and the cheerful vagueness of the economics don't matter. The Culture is a declaration of imagination's power. It wants to demonstrate that a materialist imagination can reach just as far as a religious one; further, even, since it can encompass within the order of nature everything that religion must reach outside nature to dream up. Give us enough real sky, says the Culture, and the pie will follow. Plus rayguns!

Iain Banks's medical bad news was the kind of catastrophe that even utopia cannot exclude, as his own utopia had been showing for decades with stoic melancholy. For him, we need to imagine a properly science-fictional counterpart to the honour guard of books that Proust had standing watch over the death of a novelist, silent in respect in every bookshop window. Explode the bookshop, for Iain Banks. Stretch its space out into immensity. And through the huge dark, set gliding in respectful procession the Culture's Ships, kilometres across, each as vast in proportion to mortal human bodies as our imagination is; but not silent, no, never that; all talking, all chattering in negligent grandeur, threading laughter, menace, wit, hope, wrath, through the vacuum, vaster still, where we must find our meaning for ourselves.

(2013)

THE DYER'S ELBOW

It's always struck me as unfair that writing has so little sensation when it's going well.

When it's going badly, then you feel it: there's the gluey fumbling of the attempts to gain traction on the empty screen, there's the misshapen awkwardness of each try at a sentence (as if you'd been equipped with a random set of pieces from different jigsaws). After a time, there's the tetchy pacing about, the increasingly bilious nibbling, the simultaneous antsiness and flatness as the failure of the day sinks in. After a longer time – two or three or four or five days of failure – there's the deepening sense of being a fraud. Not only can you not write bearably now; you probably never could. Trips to bookshops become orgies of self-reproach and humiliation. Look at everybody else's fluency. Look at the rivers of adequate prose that flow out of them. It's obvious that you don't belong in the company of these real writers, who write so many books, and oh such long ones. Last, there's the depressive inertia that flows out of sustained failure at the keyboard, and infects the rest of life with grey minimalism, making it harder to answer letters, return library books, bother to cook meals not composed of pasta. All vivid, particularised sensations, familiar from revisiting though somehow no less convincing each time around.

But there's no symmetrical set of good feelings when the work goes well. I find that hours pass without my being aware of myself enough to be in the business of having sensations; at least, of having any marked, distinct ones. It isn't just that the dyer's hand is stained the colour of what it works on. The dyer's elbow follows it in, the dyer's arm, the dyer's whole body plop into the vat, to disperse into my attention to the thing being made. When things are going right, almost all I notice is the fiddly half-created structure of the writing, with all the mutual dependences of the pieces of it upon each other, including the delicate dependence of written parts upon parts not yet written, and vice versa; and the whole thing in motion, or at least in a kind of state of responsiveness, ready to flow into new positions and new configurations as the possibilities alter. To try to attend to my own state of mind while this is happening would be to throw myself abruptly out of it, back to a place where there's nothing to feel but that I'm cold from sitting still so long, and wouldn't mind visiting the cottage cheese pot in the fridge with a teaspoon. So far as I can look at my own mind at all, it is in a state of flow, mirroring the responsive flux I feel in the writing. What I know, from a thousand books read and conversations had, works itself together as if by itself; what I need next comes to my hand without being forced, ready to be turned, examined, compared, remoulded, adjusted, smoothed until it aligns itself in parallel with the other pieces of what seems at this moment to be the design.

Why do I write? From selfishness. Because this state of liquefied, complex concentration, however faintly and dimly I'm able to perceive it, is the greatest pleasure I know.

(2007)

SOURCES AND ACKNOWLEDGEMENTS

The author and Yale University Press gratefully acknowledge the original publishers of the pieces included here for permission to reprint them. Every effort has been made to obtain permission from copyright holders for the use of copyright material; the author and publisher apologise for any errors or omissions.

COLD

'Winter Night' was first broadcast on BBC Radio 3, 1996.

'Ice' was first published in a slightly different version in *Patterned Ground: Entanglements of Nature and Culture*, edited by Stephan Harrison, Steve Pile and Nigel Thrift (Reaktion Books, 2004), pp. 279–81. Copyright Reaktion Books 2004.

'Worst Journey' was first published as the introduction to the Folio Society edition of Apsley Cherry-Garrard's *The Worst Journey in the World, 2012*.

'Shackleton' was first published in slightly different form in *Waterstone's Books Quarterly*, 2001.

'Read My Toes' first appeared as a review of Tom Lowenstein's *Ancient Land, Sacred Whale* and *The Things That Were Said of Them* in the *London Review of Books*, August 1993.

'Borealism' was first published as a review of S. Allen Counter's *North Pole Legacy* in the *Times Literary Supplement*, May 1992.

'Huntford's Nansen, Huntford's Scott' was first published as a review of Roland Huntford's *Nansen: The Explorer as Hero* in the *Times Literary Supplement*, April 1998.

'The Uses of Antarctica' was first given as a lecture at the 'Imagining Antarctica' conference in Christchurch, New Zealand, September 2008, and then published in the essay collection *Imagining Antarctica*, edited by Ralph Crane and Elizabeth Leane and Mark Williams (Quintus, 2011). The author and Yale University Press gratefully acknowledge the permission of Faber & Faber Ltd to quote from 'Malcolm Mooney's Land' in the book *Malcolm Mooney's Land* by W.S. Graham (Faber & Faber Ltd, 1970).

RED

'The Soviet Moment' was first published in the *Guardian*, August 2010.

'Plenty' was first broadcast on BBC Radio 3 as 'Plenty: The Land of Cockaigne', April 2005.

'Responsible Fiction, Irresponsible Fact' was first given as a talk, in different form, to the Open University Historians' Group, December 2011.

'Idols of the Marketplace' was first broadcast on BBC Radio 3, September 2007.

'Unicorn Husbandry' was first posted in different form at www.crooked timber.org, June 2012, as a response to the Crooked Timber seminar on *Red Plenty*.

SACRED

'Dear Atheists' was first published in the *New Humanist*, August 2012.

'Contra Dawkins' was first delivered as a speech at the Faclan Book Festival, An Lanntair Arts Centre, Isle of Lewis, November 2012.

'Puritans' was first published as 'The World Cannot Be Disenchanted' in the *New Statesman*, 27 March 2013.

'Who is God? An Answer for Children' was first published in *Big Questions from Little People ... Answered by Some Very Big People* (Faber & Faber Ltd, 2012).

'C.S. Lewis as Apologist' was first published in a shorter form as 'When an Apology Was Called For' in *Church Times*, 22 November 2013, as part of the paper's anniversary coverage of C.S. Lewis, which remains available online at www.church times.co.uk.

'What Can Science Fiction Tell Us About God?' was first published on the *Guardian*'s Comment is Free website, July 2011.

'Uneasy in Iran' was first published in shorter form as 'Inside the Shrines of Iran' in the *Tablet*, June 2000.

'Wild Theism' was first published as 'Spiritual Literature for Atheists', a review of Barbara Ehrenreich's *Living with a Wild God* and Sam Harris's *Waking Up*, in *First Things*, November 2015.

'The Past as Zombie Hazard, and Consolation' first appeared as part of the 'Common Creed' series of essays at the Theos website, www.theosthinktank.co.uk.

'Three Ways of Writing Faith' was first given as a talk at an event for Marilynne Robinson at King's College London, November 2013.

TECHNICAL

'Difference Engine' was first published as 'The Difference Engine and *The Difference Engine*' as a chapter in *Cultural Babbage*, edited by Jenny Uglow and Francis Spufford (Faber & Faber Ltd, 1996).

'Boffins' was first given as The George Hay Memorial Lecture, entitled 'The Fall and Rise of the British Boffin', at Eastercon, Blackpool, 2004.

PRINTED

'Half in Praise' was first published as 'Half in Praise of Reading' in the *Independent on Sunday Magazine*, 2004.

'Kipling's Jungle' was first published as the introduction to the Everyman paperback edition of *The Jungle Book*, 1993.

'Robinson's Mars' was first published in much, much shorter form as a book review in the *Guardian*, 1994.

'The Amazing Terence', updated for this edition, was first published as a book review of Terry Pratchett's *The Amazing Maurice and His Educated Rodents* in the *Guardian*, 2001.

'You Could Read Forever' was first published as a review of Robert Irwin's *The Arabian Nights: A Companion* in the *Guardian*, 1994.

'This Grand Cause of Terror' first appeared as a blog post, 'But When This Grand Cause of Terror Makes Its Appearance, What Is It?' as part of the Crooked Timber seminar on Felix Gilman's *The Rise of Ransom City*, September 2013.

'Bats of Some Kind' was first published as a review of Elif Batuman's *The Possessed* in the *Guardian*, 2010.

'In Memoriam, Iain M. Banks' was first published in the *New Humanist*, June 2013.

'The Dyer's Elbow' was first published in *The Arvon Book of Literary Non-Fiction*, edited by Midge Gillies and Sally Cline (Bloomsbury, 2012).

NOTES

1. *The Things That Were Said of Them: Shaman Stories and Oral Histories of the Tikigaq People*, told by Asatchaq; translated from the Inupiaq by Tukummiq and Tom Lowenstein (University of California Press, 1992).
2. Tom Lowenstein, *Ancient Land, Sacred Whale: The Inuit Hunt and Its Rituals* (Bloomsbury, 1993).
3. S. Allen Counter, *North Pole Legacy: Black, White and Eskimo* (University of Massachusetts Press, 1991).
4. Well, Colonel Bluford still looks pretty good.
5. Review of Roland Huntford's *Nansen: The Explorer as Hero* (Duckworth, 1997).
6. Jason Anthony, 'Vostok, or A Brief and Awkward Tour of the End of the Earth' (2006), available at: www.albedoimages.com/vostok.html
7. Stephen J. Pyne, *The Ice: A Journey to Antarctica* (University of Washington Press, 1998), p. 291.
8. Richard Byrd, *Alone* (G.P. Putnam's Sons, 1938), p. 7.
9. Byrd, *Alone*, p. 85.
10. Henry D. Thoreau, *The Maine Woods* (James R. Osgood & Co., 1873), pp. 70–1.
11. The crash of 2007–8 was just around the corner when I wrote this.
12. http://louisproyect.wordpress.com/2012/04/22/red-plenty/
13. Henri Bergson, *Le Rire* (1900); translated by Cloudesley Brereton and Fred Rothwell as *Laughter: An Essay on the Meaning of the Comic* (Macmillan, 1914).
14. http://crookedtimber.org/2012/05/30/in-soviet-union-optimization-problem-solves-you/
15. Alan Jacobs, *The Narnian: The Life and Imagination of C. S. Lewis* (HarperCollins, 2005).
16. Sam Harris, *Waking Up: A Guide to Spirituality without Religion* (Simon & Schuster, 2014).
17. Barbara Ehrenreich, *Living with a Wild God: A Nonbeliever's Search for the Truth About Everything* (Grand Central Publishing, 2014).
18. Harris, *Waking Up*, p. 81.
19. Ehrenreich, *Living with a Wild God*, pp. 47–8.
20. Harris, *Waking Up*, p. 21.

21. Barbara Ehrenreich, 'A Rationalist's Mystical Moment', *New York Times*, 6 April 2014.

22. Since I wrote this, Catherine Fox's three Lindchester novels have appeared, scabrous, soapily plotted, theologically serious comedies of cathedral life, proving that the village-life of religion *can* still be narrated in England, so long as you adopt a teasing omniscience that lets you explain everything as you go along, and offer the metaphysic on visibly take-it-or-leave-it terms.

23. Yes, I really said in 1996 that the internet was becoming less and less important. I preserve this as an example of technological prediction at its most breathtakingly clueless.

24. David Lewis, *Counterfactuals* (Basil Blackwell, 1973), pp. 85–6.

25. Geoffrey Hawthorn, *Plausible Worlds: Possibility and Understanding in History and the Social Sciences* (Cambridge University Press, 1991).

26. John Crowley, *Great Work of Time*, in *Novelty* (Doubleday, 1989), p. 113.

27. The American edition. There *was* only an American edition, at this time.

28. Sven Birkerts, *The Gutenberg Elegies: The Fate of Reading in an Electronic Age* (Fawcett Columbine, 1994), pp. 100–1.

29. 'Coriolanus', in William Hazlitt, *Characters of Shakespeare's Plays* (1817).

30. Angus Wilson, *The Strange Ride of Rudyard Kipling* (Secker & Warburg, 1977).

31. Rudyard Kipling, *The Jungle Book* (Everyman, 1993), p. 27.

32. Kim Stanley Robinson, *Red Mars* (Bantam Spectra, 1993), *Green Mars* (Bantam Spectra, 1994), *Blue Mars* (Bantam Spectra, 1996).

33. Robert Irwin, *The Arabian Nights: A Companion* (Allen Lane, 1994).

34. Felix Gilman, *The Half-Made World* (Tor Books, 2010), pp. 127–8.

35. Elif Batuman, *The Possessed: Adventures with Russian Books and the People Who Read Them* (Granta/Macmillan, 2010).

INDEX